EUROPEAN DRAM/
EARLY MIDDLE

P9-EDU-290

English and European Literature

———

Editor
JOHN LAWLOR
Professor of English
in the University of Keele

6

EUROPEAN DRAMA OF THE EARLY MIDDLE AGES

Richard Axton
Fellow of Christ's College, Cambridge

HUTCHINSON UNIVERSITY LIBRARY
LONDON

HUTCHINSON & CO (*Publishers*) LTD
3 Fitzroy Square, London W1

London Melbourne Sydney Auckland
Wellington Johannesburg Cape Town
and agencies throughout the world

First published 1974

© Richard Axton 1974

This book has been set in Bembo,
printed in Great Britain by
William Clowes & Sons, Limited,
London, Beccles and Colchester, and bound
by Wm. Brendon, Tiptree, Essex

ISBN 0 09 119250 1 (cased)
0 09 119251 X (paper)

In memory of my father
H. E. D. AXTON

CONTENTS

ACKNOWLEDGEMENTS

Over the past few years I have shown versions of the text to friends and have gained from them much scholarly information and constructive criticism, as well as encouragement. To my wife, Marie, I owe most. To Leslie Topsfield, Glynne Wickham, J. A. W. Bennett, J. M. Cohen, Stanley Kahrl, Robert Wright, David Miller, Richard Beadle, Margaret and Ian Bent, Elizabeth Salter and Michael J. Smith, I am indebted for generous advice and suggestions on specific points. The help of two friends in particular has been long-standing and continuous: Peter Dronke first gave me the courage to attempt a comparative treatment of the drama and then guided me in many unfamiliar areas; John Stevens has helped me at every stage in understanding something about liturgy and medieval music and in shaping, reshaping and improving the text. I offer them my warmest thanks.

My pervasive material debt to E. K. Chambers' *Medieval Stage* and Karl Young's *Drama of the Medieval Church* will be readily apparent to students of the field. My numerous specific debts to the editors of the play texts and to other writers are acknowledged in the Notes (pp. 205–16). Texts are quoted verbatim from the manuscripts or printed sources cited in the Notes, except that I have made the modern distinction between *u* and *v*, and have altered some capricious or nonexistent medieval punctuation. The translations are all my own, except where specifically noted; I hope that they, together with the glosses, will resolve any occasional difficulties the reader may have with medieval orthography.

Much of the material of the book appeared in different form as a doctoral dissertation (Cambridge, 1967). Some short sections appeared in an article called 'Popular modes in the earliest plays' in *Medieval Drama*, Ed. Neville Denny (Stratford-upon-Avon Studies 16, Edward Arnold 1973).

INTRODUCTION

The diversity of the earliest drama in medieval Europe forms the ground of my argument. The importance of traditions of profane drama, independent of the sacred drama of the Church and constantly enriching it, has not often been recognized. If the theme is unfamiliar, it may be because so many of the dramatic texts surviving from the early Middle Ages are scripts for church plays. It is understandable that most accounts of the beginnings of European drama have dealt exclusively with the ecclesiastical tradition, for the Church's virtual monopoly of written records and its concern with conserving the Word, led to rather full documentation of its own traditional Latin drama. On the other hand, the plays of feudal courts and village festivals, of taverns and guildhalls, lacked scribes and historians in their own day and as a result are relatively neglected in ours. Like most drama, these plays were ephemeral, occasional entertainments, often unscripted or dependent upon oral tradition for their 'text' and upon a particular audience for their life and meaning.

The problem of giving a balanced critical view of medieval drama is complicated by the clerical bias of almost *all* records of the period. Paradoxically, we only know that mimic actors in Anglo-Saxon England satirized monastic life, or that an eminent German bishop took the part of Attila the Hun in battle-plays of the eleventh century, or that a thirteenth-century Scots village priest performed in a priapic dancing-play, because clerical Latin writers were intrigued or offended by these examples of profane drama. The bias of the 'clerical perspective' can only be redressed by examination of scattered and fragmentary sources and by comparative study of plays in different languages, so as to bring out the elements of the common traditions upon which drama depends. This is the task I undertake briefly in the first part of the book.

The first three chapters attempt to reconstruct three separate traditions of secular drama: mimicry—the art of the professional entertainers; combat—the predominant pagan form of drama among the 'folk' of northern Europe; and the dancing-game—the dramatic self-entertainment which courtly society refined from popular models. In each of these traditions there was, I argue, a distinct 'idea of drama', as well as a body of forms and motifs and conventions for play-acting, which are entirely different from those of the better known and more literary ecclesiastical drama. This ecclesiastical drama, sung and in Latin, is the subject of the fourth chapter, completing the discussion of 'Origins and Traditions'. By approaching the church drama via three profane traditions, I hope that the uniqueness of its conventions will be better appreciated. This uniqueness is, to me, so striking as to make any easy assumptions about the 'evolution' of all medieval and Renaissance drama from one ecclesiastical 'seed' quite untenable.

In the second part, I discuss in detail some of the best plays of the eleventh, twelfth and thirteenth centuries. By treating them in relation to common traditions rather than (as is often the case) seeing them as a prelude to the more familiar drama of the fifteenth and sixteenth centuries, I try to show both their individual artistry and something of the social 'meaning'. I illustrate, first, the range of achievement in the Latin music-drama; then, the variety of popular religious plays in the spoken vernaculars; and, finally, the purely secular drama which survives, almost uniquely, from Arras in northern France. My treatment of two plays is unusually full, because I have found them the most rewarding to study. Both Le Mystère d'Adam and Le Jeu de la Feuillée are rich in the themes and conventions of earlier drama and offer almost inexhaustible opportunities for 'interpretation'. But, more important than this, in these two plays, it seems to me, the sacred and profane aspects of human experience in a whole age are polarized and brilliantly focused. The first shows man in his place in a universe fashioned and watched over by God the Redeemer; the second shows man as judge of himself, mocker of his own beliefs and absurdities.

To extend the detailed discussion of play texts into the later Middle Ages would clearly have been impossible. The sheer bulk—chiefly Passion and cycle plays of the late fourteenth, fifteenth and sixteenth centuries, in French, English and German—ruled out any but ruthlessly selective procedure. Attention in the third part of the book is therefore confined almost entirely to the English drama of this later period. The number of excellent studies of the Middle English drama now available seemed to justify my leaving aside many important aspects of this area and pursuing my main theme: the unrecognized importance of the *secular* traditions. A brief survey of the earliest

English drama during the 'dark' centuries before Chaucer's Absolon played Herod upon a scaffold high, is followed by discussion of some aspects of the cycle plays, miracles and moralities. I suggest by example how the clerically composed religious drama was dependent upon older secular forms and conventions.

The relationships that I trace between the clerical and popular drama do not usually involve questions of literary debt, but something more purely histrionic. Drama is the most collaborative of the arts, shaped by actor and audience, as well as by scriptwriter. Throughout the book I have emphasized the active and social nature of this collaboration, in the hope that the life that is lost when a scribe reduces a play to written 'text' may be in part regained.

PART I
Origins and Traditions

I

MIMICRY

At its simplest, the art of drama is mere mimicry. The performer, lacking a story to tell his audience, makes the audience itself his subject. The ancient art of the *mimus* is wittily described in some elegiac lines which were probably composed in Carolingian times and which purport to be the epitaph of the mime Vitalis:[1]

> Fingebam vultus, habitus ac verba loquentum,
> Ut plures uno crederes ore loqui.
> Ipse etiam, quem nostra oculis geminabat imago,
> Horruit in vultus se magis isse meos.
> O quotiens imitata meo se femina gestu
> Vidit et erubuit totaque mata fuit.
> Ergo quot in nostro videbantur corpore formae,
> Tot mecum raptas abstulit atra dies.

> (I used to mimic the face, manner and words of those talking,
> so that you would think many people spoke from one mouth.
> The subject, presented with a twin image of himself before his eyes,
> would tremble to see a more real self existing in my faces.
> Oh, how often a lady saw herself in my performance,
> and blushed for shame, horribly embarrassed.
> Thus, as many human forms as were seen in my body
> were snatched away with me by the dismal day of death.)

The mime's audience are also his subject, his fictional repertory of characters; when he dies, so must they. The poem's playful sophistry supposes that the performer's skill is illusionist in intention and consists in accurate mimicry of 'real people'. This is, quite simply, Vitalis' idea

---

[1] Superior figures refer to Notes, pp. 205–16.

of acting. The idea is a common and fundamental one, discovered instinctively by children and practised—as the Middle Ages were fond of observing—by apes. Mimicry is an end in itself since it is a source of amusement. It is worth labouring the commonplace because so much of the drama of the Middle Ages is not obviously mimic, still less illusionist or amusing in the sense of Vitalis' performance.

The various activities of the *mimi* form one bridge between the dramatic entertainments of the late Roman empire and the medieval world. Within the large and undefined group of entertainers referred to by writers in the period between the sixth and fourteenth centuries it is often impossible to distinguish between *mimi* (originally popular entertainers of the Roman 'burlesque' theatre), *histriones* (professional actors), *lusores* (players) and *scurri(æ)* (jesters ?).[2] *Joculator* (rare in classical Latin but a common medieval term) and its vernacular equivalents *joglar, jongleur*, etc. is often used for a performer with mimic skills, but he is usually a musician (voice and stringed instrument) and teller of tales, akin to the Germanic *scôp* and Anglo-Saxon *gleoman*. Although, no doubt, some were specialists, the medieval *mimus* or *histrio* was normally much more than 'a mime': his skills might include dancing, juggling and acrobatics, singing, manipulating puppets. Vitalis makes clear that his was not a silent art, nor was it always improvised, though the performance he describes is lacking in 'story'. Vitalis' knowing jibe about the ladies in his audience suggests that his show had elements of parody and impropriety which prove as embarrassing to the subject as they are delightful to the rest of the company. To judge from historical references to mimic performances (e.g. an admiring eleventh-century account of a *ludus histrionum* concerning a tame bear, an actor's naked *membra*, and honey), it seems that obscenity was normal.[3] The same implication may be drawn from the frequent medieval association of acting with exhibitionism and actors with prostitutes, and the understanding of the word *theatrum* to mean a tavern-cum-brothel with a floorshow.[4]

Ecclesiastical writers complain of indecent performances by actors representing old men, young women, and clergy. The fragmentary mime texts from late antiquity confirm the general impression of knockabout, sexual bouts, and the lampooning of official religion.[5] The medieval church often condemned professional playing but, on occasion and informally, became patron to the *mimi* and, by Vitalis' logic, the subject of mimic performances. Visits of *mimi* and *histriones* to monastic houses are the subject of episcopal stricture from the time of

Charlemagne onwards. In A.D. 967 (at the same time as the famous *Regularis Concordia* of Winchester promulgated the first ecclesiastical play for use in the Easter liturgy at English Benedictine monasteries) King Edgar was concerned over the secular entertainment which some English monks had been enjoying. In a speech of 969, 'published for those of monastic status', the king complained that 'a house of clergy is known . . . as a meeting place for actors . . . where mimes sing and dance'. That a monastic visit might easily provide the professionals with fresh satirical material for use in the lay world is implied by another letter in which Edgar complains that the scandals of monastic life are the subject of mimic shows in the market places.[6] Indeed, much earlier than this, an episcopal capitulum of 789 prescribes corporal punishment or exile for any *histriones* who ape priestly garb or the habit of a monk or nun.[7] Whether the monastic patrons gained more than temporary amusement from these visits is a question to which I shall return.

The recurrent motifs, stock figures and situations of mimic performance left their mark not only on offended clerical sensibilities but on the themes and conventions of medieval narrative. The eleventh-century Latin romance *Ruodlieb* describes feats of juggling and ventriloquism, tricks and dances performed by men and animals, a crude farce, in which an old man watches from the privy while a youth makes love to his wife.[8] French vernacular *contes* and *fabliaux* of the twelfth and thirteenth centuries refer to such 'turns' as *l'ivre*, *le cat* and *le sot*. The *histrio*'s use of 'horrible masks' to impersonate dogs, birds, asses and monkeys, is observed by the Bishop of Salisbury *c.* 1300 and is illustrated in the Jehans de Grise miniatures of the Bodleian *Romans d'Alexandre*.[9]

These widespread records give fascinating glimpses of the range of professional 'acting' in the early Middle Ages. It is not surprising that literary texts of secular plays are scanty; no doubt unscripted improvisation upon routine outlines was common; but it is obvious that a performer's acting role in constant use would have little chance of survival into the post-medieval world. Three vernacular texts of the thirteenth century can be connected with the tradition of professional mimic performance: the Middle English *Interludium de Clerico et Puella* and the related fabliau of *Dame Sirith*, and the Flemish farce, *Le Garçon et l'Aveugle*. Together, they allow reconstruction of an ephemeral drama that is largely lost.

The fragmentary text of the *Interludium* survives in a small parchment roll and is a playlet in three parts. Like the later Tudor interludes it may have been performed between the courses of a banquet.[10] The *Interludium* shares a plot with the contemporary *Dame Sirith*: a clerk's wooing of a reluctant girl (or wife) succeeds through the cunning sleight of hand practised by a female bawd. Beneath the lively verse dialogue with its exclamations of greeting and farewell, its salty colloquialisms, the roles of the three 'characters' are patently conventional —they are variations on stock types.

The clerk's love-sickness, with its extravagant declarations and pious asseverations, echoed in contemporary love-lyric, is a transparent pose:[11]

Clericus
> Nu, nu! By Crist and by Sant Ihon,
> In al þis land ne (wot) Hi none,
> Mayden, þat Hi luf mor þan þe,
> Hif me micht ever þe bether be!
> For þe Hy sorw nicht and day—
> Y may say 'Hay, wayleuay!'
> Y luf þe mar þan mi lif;
> Þu hates me mar þan gayt dos chnief!
> Þat es nouct for mysgilt—
> Certhes, for þi luf ham Hi spilt.
> A! suythe mayden, reu of me
> Þat es ty luf hand ay sal be!
> For þe luf of þe moder of efne,
> Þu mend þi mode and her my stevene.   (13–26)

The girl recognizes the convention of the 'clerc fayllard' (drop-out) and scolds him in general and satirical terms:

Puella
> By Crist of hevene and Sant Ione,
> Clerc of scole ne kep I non,
> For many god wymman half þai don scam,
> By Crist, þu michtis haf ben at hame!   (27–30)

Mome Elwis's pretence that she is not a bawd but a 'holy woman' is presented satirically, by a string of pious formulae:

---

gayt goat   *chnief* knife   *mysgilt* my misbehaviour
reu of me pity me   *mend þi mode* change your mind   *stevene* voice
kep care for   *michtis haf ben at hame* should have stayed at home

Mome Elwis
> A, son! vat saystu? Benedicite!
> Lift hyp þi hand and blis þe ...
> Can I do non oþir dede
> Bot my pater noster and me crede
> To say Crist for missedede,
> And myn Avy Mary
> (For my scynnes Hic am sory),
> And my *De profundis* ...   (63–75)

Performance of this spirited dialogue requires the speakers to imitate stock characters who are themselves feigning, adopting conventional postures. The stock poses are undercut by the satirical mimicry of the performers, who must register both vocal and facial transformations— the very skills on which Vitalis prides himself. It is possible that a skilled mimic might play all the parts, but in the case of the *Interludium* there is no evidence for this: the text consists entirely of dialogue rubricated with the speakers' names. Proof that such wooing plays were acted by several performers is found in a Cornish text (*c.* 1340) of the bawd's part in a play concerning a similar trio.[12]

Dame Sirith, however, has a first person narrator. He rapidly disappears, leaving the characters to speak for themselves, and solo mimic performance may have been the case here. Of course, many medieval dialogue poems may have received a partially dramatic performance by a ventriloquist mime. But a solo performer of *Dame Sirith*, however skilful, could not have worked quite alone. In order to show the trick by which the bawd wins round the reluctant Margeri he needs the collaboration of a dog. Dame Sirith's 'wicchecrafft' consists in feeding mustard to her bitch to make its eyes 'weep'. Nine lines of the scene pass before the dialogue reveals that the Dame is addressing her dog and the sequence would thus be meaningless unless accompanied by impersonated action:[13]

(*Dame Sirith*)
> So Ich evere brouke hous oþer flet,
> Neren never pones beter biset
>   Þen þes shulen ben!
> For I shal don a juperti
> And a ferli maistri,
>   Þat þou shalt ful wel sen.

So Ich evere brouke hous oþer flet as I hope to keep house and hearth
Neren never pones beter biset pence were never better spent
juperti stratagem   *ferli maistri* remarkable feat

> Pepir nou shalt þou eten;
> Þis mustart shal ben þi mete,
> And gar þin eien to rene.
> I shal make a lesing
> Of þin heie renning—
> Ich wot wel wer and wenne.

(*Wilekin*)

> Wat! nou const þou no god!
> Me þinkeþ þat þou art wod—
> ʒevest þou þe welpe mustard?

(*Dame Sirith*)

> Be stille, boinard!
> I shal mit þis ilke gin
> Gar hir love to ben al þin.   (273–90)

Performing dogs scarcely figure in modern notions of legitimate theatre but they were a standard feature of professional medieval entertainments (a 'gleeman's bitch' was a proverbial phrase for Langland). The eleventh-century *Ruodlieb* already mentioned for its stock of set-pieces from minstrel repertory, contains an improvised diversion occasioned at a feast by a weeping dog.[14] Much later, Shakespeare played upon the tradition in his *Two Gentlemen of Verona*. Lance (his name suggests his bawdy function as go-between) goes a-wooing for his master Proteus, equipped with an 'understanding staff' and a dog that will not weep.

The indecency of the 'dame' (played, one may suppose as in modern pantomime, by a man) provides much of the humour in the conclusion of *Dame Sirith*. If her encouragement to the lovers to set-to was accompanied by appropriate mimic action, then the result might easily have offended clerical sensibilities; no wonder popular *ludi* and *spectacula* at feasts and weddings in thirteenth-century England were so often condemned for their 'filthiness'. In conclusion, the dame turns to the audience, offering her services to any who need them—for a price:

---

gar þin eien to rene make your eyes run   *lesing* deception
heie renning eyes running
nou const þou no god have you no sense   *wod* mad   *boinard* fool
mit þis ilke gin with this very device   *Gar* make thine

And wose is onwis
And for non pris
   Ne con geten his levemon,
I shal, for mi mede,
Garen him to spede,
   For ful wel I con.   (445–50)

The stamp of professionalism shows there in the ingenious incorporation of a collection (like the *quête* of the traditional mummers' drama)
into the performance. A different but comparable device for collecting
money from the audience is used in the Tournai farce, *Le Garçon et
l'Aveugle* (*c*. 1270).[15] This savage knock-about has all the marks of
popular drama performed by professionals. There are two performers,
the blind man and his boy; no properties are needed and performance
could be improvised anywhere. The play is virtually plotless, consisting as it does of a series of cruel deceptions practised by the boy on
his master. Begging constitutes the chief activity of the two rogues and
their prayers, patriotic songs and blessings are directed at the 'passers-
by' who form the play's audience.

   Dialogue and action are realistically crude. The boy pretends to
guide the man safely past a cellar shaft and flights of steps. Having
reached his home, the man describes to his new helper how the key is
hidden under a leaf of periwinkle growing above the lintel. Of course,
the 'stage effects' need not have existed in performance. The simple
device of the play depends on the blindness of the one performer to the
other's actions and true nature. If the visual objects described by the
boy have no reality for the audience, and if the blind man avoids nonexistent obstacles, this merely adds to the comedy. The boy functions
here as both tempter and moralist: he excites the old man to an obscene
reverie by offering to fetch him a 'bele garce', then retires to relieve
himself (a basic form of humour used also in *Courtois d'Arras*, *c*. 1220,
and in the fifteenth-century English *Mankind*, see below pp. 137, 202);
returning, the boy assumes a false voice and rebukes the man for his
foul language. After beating his master, the boy resumes his previous
role, comforting him and administering a healing ointment whose
chief ingredient is dung. Finally, stimulating the old man's imagination once again with a speech of double meanings, the boy persuades
him to hand over his coat and breeches belt and, on the pretext of

---

And wose is onwis whoever is inexperienced   *levemon* lover   *mede* reward
Garen him to spede make him succeed

fetching a girl, new clothes, food and wine, leaves him for good. In a final address to the audience, the boy boasts of his trickery:

> Seignor, ai je bien mis a point
> cel aweule la qui n'a point? (232–3)

> (Gentlemen, haven't I fixed him up well,
> that blind man there—he's nothing left.)

In this popular and frankly professional tradition (if one may generalize on the basis of these three plays) the basis of performance is a conception of drama as a mimic show. The mode is 'low-mimetic', partly obscene, physically vigorous. It makes use of pretence and disguise, impersonation-within-impersonation, comic tricks and deceptions practised by one actor on another for the amusement of a 'knowing' audience.

The mimic concept of drama as exemplified in these popular vernacular entertainments is similar in essence to that of the Roman comedies known in the medieval world. The plays of Terence in particular (and, to a lesser extent, Plautus) were widely studied as models of style from the ninth century onwards. During the twelfth century Roman 'theatre' became a fashionable matter of interest among the new humanists. How far medieval scholars and grammarians understood the nature of Roman stage presentation is disputed. But that they did on occasion 'stage' a Terence play is indicated by a fragmentary text of Latin dialogue between the figures of Terence and his Mocker from about the ninth or tenth century. The text has rubrics for performance and seems to have served as a prologue to performance of a Terence play or Terentian imitation. The argument is about the worthiness of ancient poetry. Terence's Mocker begins by haranguing the old poet:[16]

> Mitte recordari monimenta vetusta, Terenti;
> cesses ulterius; vade, poeta vetus.
> vade, poeta vetus, quia non tua carmina curo.

> (Put away your old relics, Terence;
> don't go on; go away, old poet,
> I have no taste for your compositions.)

According to the Mocker, the old poetry is good for nothing but teaching small boys grammar, its verse and prose are indistinguishable and send him to sleep. At this point a rubric indicates Terence's appearance to answer the challenge: 'Now Terence shall go forth, hearing this, and shall say' (*Nunc Terentius exit foras audiens haec et ait*). Terence looks about for his accuser, perhaps among the audience, demanding by Hercules who has insulted him. A further direction says, 'Here the person of his Detractor shall be shown; hearing this, he replies' (*Ecce persona Delusoris praesentatur et hoc audiens inquit*). The young man's admission, 'I am the man you ask for' begins the conflict. The Mocker reveals in an 'aside' that he has no better work to offer the audience, but he continues to rail, youth against age.

This curious dialogue conveys the sense of a cultured society for whom Terence is both an entertainer and a schoolmaster. For there would be no point to the dispute unless modern imitations were known to the audience. The most curious thing about the staging is that the dramatized figure of Roman Terence presides, prepared, apparently, to 'perform' his own work. This feature accords with the medieval Lives of Terence, which state that the Roman poet or a friend read his text aloud while other performers mimed the action. Whilst the earlier manuscripts of Terence's plays follow closely the scenic groupings of masked actors in late antique manuscripts, the famous fifteenth-century *Terence des Ducs* illustrates the idea, showing performance in an amphitheatre before the *populus Romanus*.[17] At the centre of the arena is a raised platform on which stands a curtained booth, its open top revealing the poet's friend holding Terence's playbook. In the arena before him masked figures labelled *joculatores* cavort and gesticulate in accompaniment to the recitation. The artist's conception (or, rather, misconception) of the Roman *theatrum* corresponds to the definitions of twelfth-century glosses. The grammarian Hugutio interprets the *scena* (stage) as 'a shaded place (*umbraculum*) enclosed by curtains, similar to a merchant's stall, in which are hidden masked figures (*personae larvatae*) who express by gestures the substance narrated by the poet'.[18] The English poet Lydgate (himself author of dramatic 'mummings' at the court of Henry VI) gives in his *Troybook* a description of Priam's theatre in Troy. Again, the scene is set with the 'awncien poete' standing in a pulpet, 'singinge his ditës' while,[19]

> Amydde the theatre, showdid in a tent,
> Ther cam out men gastful of her cheris,
> Disfigurid her facis with viseris.
> Pleying by signes in the peoples sight,
> That the poete songon hath on hight.

---

showdid shrouded   *gastful of her cheris* with frightening expressions

Is it possible that this curious performance is entirely a fiction of medieval minds? Some think so. Yet, even supposing that no one in the Middle Ages ever tried the method out (which seems implausible), one might fairly expect medieval imitations of Roman comedy to be influenced by it. Before asking if these medieval 'comedies' are suitable to this way of playing, it is worth considering briefly the social advantages it offers.

We have seen that visits of troupes of *mimi* and *histriones* to monastic communities are well documented in the ninth and tenth centuries, although what they did there is largely conjectural. It is also a fact that Roman comedies were imitated in the tenth century by Roswitha, the famous Saxon canoness, and in the twelfth by contemporaries of John of Salisbury, Joseph of Exeter and Walter Map in England and northern France. These compositions are learned pieces for learned readers, but must have been 'performed' in public somehow. The advantages of a humanist author engaging professional mimic actors are several. First, the actors required for the plays need not learn lines of often teasingly difficult Latin, for the author–reciter could explain his plot in half an hour before performance (as Hamlet explains the basis for an *ex tempore* dumbshow) to actors skilled at improvisation. A further advantage of separating author and actor is that it allows the scholar to engage in the laudable exercise of imitating profane models of writing and showing off his accomplishment, while protecting him from the censure and severe penalties pronounced against actors by the higher and stricter clergy. If medieval playwrights ever animated the pseudo-Roman theatre whose image they cherished, there were distinct social advantages in preserving the dichotomy between recited word and mimed action which it embodied.

But the strongest case for considering the learned medieval Latin comedies within the tradition of mimic drama lies in the plays themselves. Terence's most famous imitator, Roswitha of Gandersheim (*fl. c.* 960) composed six *comediae* in praise of the virgin life, 'adopting the same form', she says in a preface, 'in which the shameless acts of licentious women have been related'.[20] It is important to note here, at the risk of digression, that the modern sense of incongruity in Roswitha's undertaking would not have struck her contemporaries. She was not a cloistered nun but a canoness, a member of an intelligentsia of nobly-born and well-educated Saxon women in a house of royal foundation. She would have been free to leave the convent and to entertain guests of both sexes. Her abbess and friend Gerberga was

niece of the Emperor Otto I and it was she who apparently persuaded
Roswitha to compose a biography of him. The Archbishop of Mainz
who visited the cloister and encouraged Roswitha's literary efforts was
bastard son of the same Emperor. So in this context, the imitator of
Terence is no Victorian prude, and performance of Roswitha's plays
is not inconceivable.[21]

Roswitha's plays, as her most recent editor has shown, have no
'stage directions'; they have no narrative lines either. The plot of each
is related in a brief preface, but the ensuing action is conveyed entirely
by means of a dialogue, using scenic alternations of place, as in Terence.
Action is imagined to take place either at a 'house' (a throne, a cell, a
brothel) or in a neutral space to which characters who are 'off' come.
Entrances and exits, references to facial expressions and costumes,
to actions performed by other characters, or to unscripted words which
have been improperly heard, as well as the frequent use of disguise,
have all been seen as showing Roswitha's familiarity with a living
tradition of performance. Certainly, it is more natural to suppose so
than otherwise. It has been suggested that she knew some liturgical
drama (although only one or two plays are dateable within her lifetime). But Roswitha's dialogue is for speaking, not singing, and her
stagecraft has nothing in common with that of the liturgical plays, as
we shall see later.

In reading aloud Roswitha's dialogue some gesture and movement
is required for comprehension; comic hallucination, disguise and self-
revelation are recurrent techniques. The central farcical situation of
Dulcitius relies on comic hallucination. The eponymous governor,
thinking he will enjoy the Christian virgins whom he has imprisoned
in an inner room, mistakenly enters the scullery. The three girls peep
through a crack in the dividing door and exclaim in ridicule at his
fondling of the pots and pans. When Dulcitius emerges, his face is
black and the guard take him for the devil and flee. There follows a
series of comic confrontations in which Dulcitius tries to assert his
dignity, unaware of his facial transformation. In this sacred buffoonery,
the essence of humour lies in the pantomimic absurdity of 'the detest-
able *dementia* of illicit love'.

Abraham revolves about disguise, turning the stock figure of the
monk-as-lover from satirical mime to good account. The old hermit,
learning that his niece has fallen to a brothel, disguises himself as a
soldier and, borrowing a hat to cover his tonsure, visits the house as a
client. The humorous potential of the disguise is gently revealed in

the exchanges between the old hermit and the innkeeper before Mary is brought in to display her charms. In the rapid dialogue which ensues, a double drama is played out: both 'client' and his amiable hostess reveal their inner feelings in asides, Abraham cloaking the distress of a father confessor with 'the lascivious jests of youth' (*Nunc, nunc est simulandum* . . .), whilst Mary recalls plangently the abstinence of her former life which the touch of the old man's lips has brought back. Once they are alone and Abraham is seated on a bed, Mary kneels to remove his shoes; the ambiguous gesture from the scriptures prepares the way for Abraham's revelation of himself (by showing his tonsure) and for the remonstrations and repentance which follow.

The martyrdom of Fides, Spes and Karitas, in *Sapientia*, presents problems which might be thought to preclude performance in the tenth century. Flogging, boiling in oil and beheading the girls, seem on the face of it impractical and, possibly, improper. But one must remember that aesthetic toleration of suffering then was much higher than it is now. Tenth-century canonesses were used to public executions and flogging of servants was considered a desirable accomplishment in noble ladies. The torments of saints were the objects of sacred veneration in iconography, so why not in sacred plays? In England, at least, plays of the martyrdoms of saints are recorded (outside church auspices) from about 1100 onwards (see below p. 161). Besides, the nature of Roswitha's drama does not require realistic presentation of the tortures of the women. The keynote is comic, and the lighthearted gaiety of the little girls is set against the increasing frustration of the Emperor's torturers. Faith jumps laughingly into the boiling oil. She is thrust on a gridiron and mockingly calls it 'a little boat becalmed'. When a cauldron of pitch and wax is brought, she pretends to swim about in it. The horrors of torture are turned to child's play and, as in *Dulcitius*, the efforts of evil are shown to be ludicrous. The more grotesque the torments, the more triumphant the delight of the little virgins:[22]

Fides
Ubi sunt minae tuae? Ecce, illaesa inter ferventem liquorem ludens nato!

(Where are your threats? Look, I am swimming unhurt, playing in the hot liquid.)

By imaginative study of Terence's plays Roswitha could have been able to develop the main principles of her own dramatic method—a story told by dialogue and the use of multiple locations. But it seems very unlikely that she could have invented the techniques revealed by even this cursory examination of the plays if she had worked in a merely bookish way.

In suggesting Roswitha's knowledge of a living tradition of secular mimic drama I have hardly done justice to her great achievement, or to the delicacy of feelings generated in the distinctive undulating prose of her dramatic dialogue. The tenderness of the hermit in *Paphnutius* for the reclaimed courtesan Thais, his self-questioning at the severity of her mortification of the flesh, are perhaps Roswitha's greatest achievement. In *Paphnutius* and elsewhere her characteristic genius is for modulating secular feelings into sacred ones, and this process is supported by a dramatic method which transforms pagan models. She is alone among the imitators of Roman drama in having completely reformed her models to a new Christian civilization. The artistic method to which she refers with elegant humility in her Prefaces is restated in her play *Gallicanus*: in a small allegorical scene, the Roman Emperor's servant, significantly named Terentius, is converted to Christianity.

It is not until the twelfth century that we find fresh attempts to recreate Roman drama, in the elegiac Latin 'comedies' of the northern French and English schools.[23] Six observations about the construction of *Babio*, possibly the best of these farces, have recently been adduced to show the play's dependence on a living tradition of performance.[24] Action must often be imagined where none is described in the dialogue; 'asides' are freely used; two characters are often simultaneously 'present' to the audience but unaware of each other; exits and entrances must be imagined to take place; non-speaking characters are 'present'; finally, references in the dialogue establish a set, a courtyard flanked by a house and a hedge which allows for eavesdropping and for simultaneous action in different parts of the acting space. Again, it is hard to see why the author of *Babio* should have gone to the trouble of reconstructing the conventions of live performance so minutely as to make the text difficult for private reading, if public performance had not been his intention.

Babio is notable for its indecency and its grammar—twin marks, perhaps, of the youthful 'schools' milieu to which it belongs. The plot is composed of typical farce situations: the old farmer Babio lusts after Viola but is deceived by her and she is won by Babio's young overlord Croceus. Meanwhile, Babio's 'faithful' wife Petula is seduced by his servant Fodius. The characters' names indicate stock types (e.g. *Fodius* >

fodio: dig or prick). The motifs and visual comic routines of mimic tradition are recognizable beneath the ornate Latinity. Thus Babio's opening account of his sorrows, addressed to the audience, is interrupted by the appearance of a dog; he mistakes it first for a man, then complains of the dog's indifference to his grief. The conclusion of the play is both indecent and mildly anti-clerical: Fodius and Petula castrate Babio (a giant 'phallus' was a routine property of both antique mime and medieval folk-play), suggesting that he becomes a monk. Babio then takes farewell of the audience, warning them against his fate.

The play differs from its literary Roman models principally in the obscenity of the performed action and in the studied rhetoric of the dialogue. Puns and grammatical games complicate the dialogue (Babio's suspicions about Croceus' behaviour with Viola are expressed in terms of the 'conjunctive participle': *Non procul est etiam quod que sit inter eos*—'it is not long before a conjunctive [*que*: Fr. *queue*] will be between them'). Babio's foolishness and hypocrisy are displayed in his attempt to *grammatizere*; he gets tangled in sophistical knots—the metaphor Fodius uses to boast of his own skill in trickery. In Babio's speeches mythological parallels are adduced for the comically sordid situation.

The effect of this deliberately incongruous rhetoric is to emphasize the discrepancy between word and deed. In its striking alliance of verbal pretentiousness and crude action *Babio* is precisely suited to performance by recitation and mime—the manner its author would have been taught was authentically Roman.

It seems then that the ancient notion of drama as mimicry was firmly embedded in the tradition of secular entertainment. If the early vernacular farces may be thought of as representing a relatively pure development of a mimic theatre, then the learned Latin *comediae* of Roswitha and the twelfth-century schools inherited a Roman form in which a mimic base was embroidered in accordance with a medieval concern for fine literary language. The attitude of Christian writers towards this secular drama in both its vulgar and learned forms was, as we have seen, necessarily ambiguous. It may be that a Platonic or dualistic element in early Christian thought encouraged suspicion of any *ludi* or *spectacula* which directly mimicked real life. But it is also clear that a weight of offensive matter was carried along in the muddy stream of profane medieval entertainment. Both the ideological and moral objections to profane drama were established in Christian tradi-

tion through the writings of Tertullian, Jerome and the early church
fathers in response to the scurrilous pantomime theatre of the late
Roman Empire. The moral attitudes and the precise vocabulary of
condemnation used by the early fathers were adopted wholesale by
later medieval writers and retailed for new social contexts.

Some of the objections medieval churchmen make to *spectacula* and
ludi concern professional entertainments of the mimic sort. Others
relate to folk pastimes, 'disguisings', dramatic dances, contests and
games of all sorts; others refer to clerical unruliness and revels like the
'Feast of Fools'.[25] Occasionally, from the second half of the twelfth
century onwards, the weight of traditional disapproval is brought down
on the ecclesiastical drama. That such condemnations are not more
frequent suggests that early medieval writers did not at first think of
church drama as a species of secular 'play' at all. The Church's hostility
to 'theatrical' gesture and impersonation showed itself in criticism of
the celebration of Mass. In the twelfth century, Ailred of Rievaulx
condemned English priests for using histrionic gestures and emotive
pauses, for pulling faces and singing expressively, a style he thought
more fit for the *theatrum* than the church.[26] The German reformer
Gerhoh of Reichersberg, writing in about 1160, railed indiscrimin-
ately against ecclesiastical plays, applying to them a spate of terms
usually reserved for pagan drama. He accuses priests of 'turning their
churches into theatres, filling them with the mimed shows of plays'
(*in theatra commutent ac mimicis ludorum spectaculis impleant*).[27] Those who
play Herod or Antichrist think that they represent only a feigned like-
ness of evil, says Gerhoh, whereas in truth 'they participate in the very
mystery of iniquity'. How can one know, he asks, that the effigies of
Antichrist, the masks of devils, the rages of Herod, are not real? The
infant Saviour, the Virgin Mother, the slaughtered Innocents, all are
turned by representation into deceitful madness; men are transformed
into women, clergy into soldiers, humans into the forms of devils.
Beneath the bluster, Gerhoh voices a deep-seated suspicion of the illus-
ionary power of drama. His language is conventional, but the tirade
itself is unique in being directed against the ecclesiastical rather than the
secular drama. It suggests strongly that Gerhoh has been forced to this
position by the contamination of church drama by secular tradition.
His concern at the violence of German church plays is shared by his
much more moderate contemporary, Herrad of Landsberg (Abbess of
Hohenberg, 1167-95), who objects to priests wearing soldiers' garb and
plays which include 'the clashing of weapons' (see below p. 44). What

is objected to here is something quite different from the knockabout violence of mimic performance; it is, rather, the representation of armed combat. Other medieval writers, both earlier and later, associate drama with physical conflict and in doing so point us towards a second vital tradition of secular drama in the early Middle Ages.

2

COMBAT

If the pagan people of northern Europe ever thought of their own traditional drama in any generic sense, it may well have been as a kind of contest or physical combat. This sense is within the Roman meanings of *ludus*, which include sports and physical exercise as well as spectacles and 'shows'. The double implications of *ludere* to mean both practise and perform is nicely caught in the chronicle accounts of the battle of Hastings. According to chronicle tradition, the Norman invaders were urged into battle by the example of a *joglere* or *histrio*, named Taillefer, who 'played' with his sword before the English (*ludens coram gente Anglorum*) as he performed part of an epic chanson of Roland.[1] On a more parochial scale the constant association of popular plays (*ludi*) with wrestling contests (*luctae*) suggests the vigour of this popular concept of drama. In about 1300 King Edward I wrote to the Abbess of Clerkenwell that he had received her complaint that 'crowds *attendentes luctas et alios ludos* have caused damage to crops'.[2]

Battle-plays, often danced with swords or staves, were noted among the Germanic tribes by Tacitus in his *Germania* and among the Swedes by Olaus Magnus in 1555.[3] A splendid and little-known example is recorded in the *Book of Ceremonies* of the Byzantine court of Constantine VII Porphyrogenitus (A.D. 905–959).[4] The book describes how, one Twelfth Night, c. 953, Gothic tribesmen dressed in skins, bearing shields and staves, performed a battle-play after dinner to keep a drowsy Emperor awake. A 'director of the theatrical games' rode (or pretended to ride) horseback in a circle about the Emperor's dining table and hall. He then called two teams of warriors into this prescribed playing circle. Each team had a leader and was accompanied by

musicians playing stringed instruments. The warriors were clothed in
reindeer skin cloaks and wore various kinds of mask, carried shields in
their left hands and staves in their right. At a command from the
master of ceremonies, the leaders signalled their men to combat; the
teams danced, rushing together in perfect symmetry, striking their
shields and staves together and crying in one voice the battle chant,
'Tul, tul'. One party surrounded the other and circled three times in
stylized battle. Falling back into facing ranks they began an antiphonal
chant, telling of Gothic heroes. The book records only the concluding
fragments of these Gothic verses; they were followed by Greek verses
in which the warriors commemorated the battles of the Old Testament,
won by the heroes of the Christian God. Finally, the Goths sang
in praise of the Emperor, hailing him as inheritor of the fief of
Rome, sun-like in his virtue, and invoking Christ's blessing on his
empire.

    The language of the Gothic text may be as old as the sixth century,
but what we have here is not an 'original', 'folk' drama; it is, rather, a
traditional performance firmly enclosed by a courtly and Christian
framework. A highly formal traditional action, relating in some way
to historical hero–victories, has been re-formed by a Christian society.
The Gothic tribesmen are set to imperial flattery and made to realign
their traditional heroes with Old Testament figures, as forerunners of
the Christian Emperor.

    This earliest example of medieval battle-play shows some of the re-
current features of 'folk' combat drama: it is the offering of a servant
class ('folk') to a class of overlords (court); its *form* is traditional, but
its content and allusions are altered to suit the occasion of performance. It is only through a study of formal and structural elements
that the tradition of non–literary 'folk-drama' can be reconstructed at
all.

    Medieval sources give only a little help in identifying specific forms
of combat-play, or in suggesting meanings attached to them, and must
be complemented with relatively modern evidence. An ancient
Scandinavian drama has reasonably been hypothesized from medieval
pictorial evidence and from the poetic speeches inset in the prose sagas;
this drama concerned the combat of a hero and another contestant
masked as a beast-god.[5] Some form of beheading 'play' belonging to
village New Year festivals may lie behind the Middle English poem
Sir Gawain and the Green Knight, hinted at in King Arthur's jocular
reference to Christmas 'enterludez'. A contest between impersonated

representatives of the seasons seems implied by Bishop Grosseteste's pronouncements (*c.* 1244) against clergy taking part in 'plays called Inductions of May or of Autumn', and may have formed the occasion for learned poems (known since the ninth century) of the kind 'a contest of Summer and Winter'.[6] But, for the most part, the 'folk' element in medieval drama can only be recognized by comparison of medieval texts with folk forms surviving in the relatively modern world in so-called primitive cultures.

A number of 'primitive' plays and ceremonies observed by anthropologists at the beginning of this century have served since then as archetypal models for interpreting folk drama. Whatever the shortcomings of this methodology (I shall return to this point briefly, p. 37) it provides a useful way of classifying the material and one way of understanding what folk-drama is 'about'. According to this tradition of scholarship, folk plays are magical rituals, concerned with celebrating and inducing fertility.

Among the performances noted by Jane Harrison in Thrace and northern Greece early in this century was one performed by perambulatory masqueraders in masks, goatskin caps and bells.[7] In the performance a bridegroom with a phallic club fought with, killed and skinned his opponent. The slain man was lamented by a bride and brought to life by a doctor. The combat action was preceded by dances, mimic copulation of a man and a boy-dressed-as-a-woman, and of an old 'woman' and a baby, and by the mimic forging of a ploughshare. After the mock funeral and revival, the show concluded with a procession dragging a real plough through the village, scattering grain and praying for harvest. This bizarre performance can only make sense to the sophisticated interpreter as 'sympathetic magic' of a primitive kind, in which the life of the year, and the fertility of the grain are assured through the mimetic human action, 'as if god's death were but a play'. Yet, however sacred its 'meaning', the performance is also entertaining—absurd, knockabout, bawdy fun.

The English equivalents of this strange Dionysia survive in the performances of modern village mummers and in demure Victorian chapbook texts, full of strange poeticalities and references to Lord Nelson, Old King Cole and the Recruiting Officer.[8] If one disregards the frequent incoherence of the surviving English texts (orally transmitted and, consequently, garbled) as well as the differences of historical 'style' between the Thracian performance and the English mummers' tradition, the similarities are nevertheless striking. Of primary importance is the fact that in virtually all the surviving versions of folk-play, the action includes the killing and resurrection of a protagonist. Secondly, the same play figures recur in similar configurations (two or more combatants, a 'lady', a 'dame' with a baby, a doctor, etc.). Thirdly, the performance itself has definite characteristics which constitute a strong sense of folk tradition. Performance is seasonal, it is by an all-male troupe, it belongs to rural communities. The actors are perambulatory and make a series of visits (in England to pubs or private houses) so that the audience must wait for the play to come to them. In England and France the exact auspices of the play are a matter of secrecy (as in the thirteenth-century *Jeu de la Feuillée*, see below, p. 148) and if revealed beforehand would 'break luck'. Performance begins with the preparation of an acting place. In England the presenter may cry, 'Room, room!' and clear a space among the audience by walking a circle or sweeping with a broom. In the Gothic play the presenter 'rides' about to describe the acting circle. Dress is, with odd exceptions, non-representational. Masks, disguise, or blackened faces provide the mummers with anonymity. Readers of *The Return of the Native* may remember how Eustacia Vye, having persuaded the mummers' boy Charley to let her stand in for him as the Turkish Knight, so as to gain a view of Clym Yeobright at the Christmas party, is hindered in the candlelight by her beribboned visor. The acting style is a mixture of formalism (most extreme in the movements of the sword-dance) and improvised antics. The characters rant or squeak or gibber; they never act or speak 'normally' as if impersonating real people. In some of the plays the words are spoken in an incantatory manner, broken up by periodic and apparently senseless banging of swords or sticks, and death is conveyed by simply hanging the head. Nowadays, in general, as Hardy observed, the affair is carried on 'with a stolidity and absence of stir which sets one wondering why a thing that is done so perfunctorily should be kept up at all'.[9] With the introduction of the doctor, however, following the death of the protagonist, some improvisation may be licensed and his stock patter may be larded with topical references and asides. The champions sometimes threaten and chase the audience with their swords. In this tradition of playing, then, there is much that suggests an affinity with medieval English religious drama—the peripatetic staging, the all-male cast, the audience-address of gladiator tyrants, the local orientation.

Three types of folk-play are traditionally distinguished: the English (particularly western) hero-combat, such as Eustacia took part in; the northern British sword-dance; and the wooing ceremony (associated with agricultural communities of the East Midlands). The hero-combat has a presentation of the actors, followed by the vaunting and fight of the champions, the death of one (or more, successively) and a lamentation for him, his revival by the doctor (by administering of medicine or the pulling of a giant tooth, etc.); it concludes with a *quête* or collection, taken by a motley pageant of traditional figures who beg from the audience. Good examples are the Netley Abbey play and the Leicestershire St George play.[10]

The sword-dance uses five or more actors. There may be many individual danced combats, but the significant action is a communal one: the dancers form a circle about one man, raise their swords and 'weave' them about his neck to form a 'knot' or 'lock'. Olaus Magnus, describing this intricate figure in 1555, called it a *rosa*.[11] In British plays the dancers' 'lock' about the neck of the 'fool' causes his 'death'. He is resurrected by the doctor and a collection follows. A fine example is the sword-dance play from Greatham in Durham.[12]

The third type, the wooing ceremony of ploughing communities, is most like the Thracian Dionysian play. A 'lady' is wooed and won by a gladiator-fool. An older 'dame' with a bastard doll sometimes lays claim to the fool and an old man to the lady, but both of these are rejected before the fool's marriage is celebrated. The men's and boys' plays from Bassingham in Lincolnshire are famous early nineteenth-century examples of this type.[13]

These three types of folk play are almost invariably treated as the survivals of fertility rituals whose 'original' shape and magical purpose have become confused. Most recently, Alan Brody, building on the tradition of Cambridge anthropology followed by Chambers and more recent folklorists, has argued that the three forms represent the crystallization of rituals at three stages of religious development: the sword-play, as most 'primitive', is a communal action, a totemistic ceremony; the wooing play embodies a 'mythic interpretation' of the forces of fertility into representatives of young and old; finally, in the hero-combat, the contestants are individualized in a quasi-historical manner. Illuminating as this framework is, the 'original' and cogent forms of ritual (always located in the 'distant past') are somewhat hypothetical. It therefore seems worthwhile asking, quite simply, why the plays continue to be performed. What is there in them for the audience?

Birth, copulation and death are their subject. Each of these three is

celebrated by mockery or inversion of normal assumptions. The child
is an unwanted rag-doll, wedding with the old dame is rejected and the
young 'lady' is gained, death is not real and can be remedied by any
number of farcical devices. Man is shown as a gladiatorial phallus-
waving show-off, a yokel who is king for half-an-hour; woman
(always played by a man) is either a disdainful unwed 'lady' or a
lecherous hag with a baby, trying to tie down her man. The patent
absurdity of the means keeps the fantasy firmly within the realm of
licensed buffoonery. Possibly, the juggling between styles, already
noted, reflects the ambivalence of the players towards the performance:
a quasi-religious reverence for precedent (the traditional forms and
figures must be used, together with the traditional verbal formulae,
however meaningless) combined with a sense of the absurdity of the
whole play which finds release from embarrassment in foolery.

The plays may also serve to release social tensions. For it is notable
that the communities where folk drama survives are mostly small and
rural; the actors are known to the audience and under these conditions
disguise may give licence to mutual name-calling, which can be done
without offence.[14] In England the plays are usually identified with a
sense of tradition hallowed by both church and pub. By mocking
birth, marriage and death, the plays liberate these basic human
events from the traditional precinct of the church as well as from the
constraints of 'normal' social life and behaviour. If their purpose is the
release of energy cramped by authority and convention, then their
mode is distortion and aggression. The aggression which is stylized in
the conflicts between heroes also forms the basis of the actors' attitude
towards the audience. The vaunting champions, the fool, the quack-
doctor, and the freaks of the grotesque tail-piece, all clamour for the
audience's attention. The audience is expected to acknowledge the
traditional authority of these fantastic play characters by contributing
to the collection. It is only when hard cash has been exacted that the
social catharsis is complete and the actors give their blessing, wishing
the audience 'good health' or 'Merry Christmas', and the normal
respect of the villagers for the 'ladies and gentlemen' is reestablished
before the troupe moves on.

Whether the early Middle Ages knew a drama recognizably like
that of the nineteenth-century mummers' tradition remains partly conjectural. Nevertheless, motifs of action, gestures and even formulae
which are common in surviving versions can be found in a scattering
of medieval play texts. The common features may not be specific

borrowings by the clerical drama from the folk drama (though sometimes this is the case); rather, they may derive from a common tradition of popular acting. A number of these elements may be mentioned here. A presenter who uses traditional formulae ('A rome, a rome, a rome I cry. Let good King Gaarge step this way!') introduces several Old Testament plays in the Chester cycle (see below, p. 185). His promise to the audience that the approaching champion will 'pierce your skin' is paralleled in numerous boasts by the messengers of potentates in miracle plays from the thirteenth century onwards. The exordium of the peripatetic ploughboys, 'Remember us poor plough-lads that runs through muck and mire' (Bassingham, 1823 text), is used in the Towneley play by Cain's ploughlad to present his master (see p. 77). The vaunting of champions appears in the mid-fourteenth-century morality *Pride of Life* and in the Chester *Slaughter of Innocents* (see pp. 167, 180–1). The quack-doctor boasts his skill in Rutebeuf's thirteenth-century *Dit de l'herberie* (a solo piece of 'patter'); the same figure is given a realistic turn in Adam de la Halle's *Jeu de la Feuillée* (*c.* 1276) and is parodied in the exchange of Isaiah and the Jew in the twelfth-century play of *Adam*. Complete with cures for 'the itch, the stitch, the pip, the palsy and the gout' he pops up again as a diversion in the fifteenth-century Croxton *Play of the Sacrament* (see p. 197). A 'dame' like the one in the Bassingham play ('Here comes old dame jane, been dabbling about the meadows, jumping about to show such sport'), who comes with her doll-bastard to lay claim to its reluctant father, causes a good deal of fun in the *Jeu de la Feuillée*; so does an obscene bovine fool (see p. 149). Nonsensical elements of 'beheading' and the 'showing' of a devil-monster as well as a collection from the audience are used in the fifteenth-century *Mankind* (see p. 200).

From these examples it is clear that folk drama has its best chance of survival when it is caught and transformed within the framework of more 'literary' drama. C. R. Baskervill, whose work some fifty years ago on the social origins of English folk plays remains classic, proposed three stages in a cultural process whereby folk rituals became social pastimes ('game'), which in turn were refashioned by semi-professional troupes into 'plays'.[15] According to Baskervill, the forms of folk play familiar to us now received their typical structure in the period 1200–1400. Baskervill argued that folk games and entertainments belonging to particular seasonal festivals became the plays performed by groups of 'ploughlads' or shearmen at the obligatory feasts (*gesta*) held for them by their overlords.

Baskervill's theory is largely upheld by examination of the earliest
known (and unique medieval) text of a plough play. This has received
little attention from historians of the drama since it was first identified
in the text of a Scots 'pleugh song' of about 1500.[16] The song itself, in
three parts, may have been in the repertory of the Chapel Royal at the
time of James IV. It presents a rustic practice as the object of aesthetic
pleasure in a courtly society.

The background to the curious dramatic action informing the song
text is the celebration of a new agricultural year, beginning, after the
Christmas holidays, on Plough Monday. Among his manorial duties a
medieval tenant might count ploughing for his lord on fixed days, an
obligation which was ceremonially expressed in Plough Monday practices. Ploughs are still blessed in English village churches, though
nowadays they are rarely drawn about the village as the medieval
'fool plough' was, by a team of ploughlads dressed in white and wearing harness. These 'plough bullocks' may have been accompanied by
a fool wearing horns and a bull's tail, carrying a bladder on a phallic
stick, and by a 'bessy' (man-woman). This team sometimes performed
plays like the wooing ceremony. The ploughlads collected money and
spread blessing, or, receiving nothing, ploughed up the street in revenge. Plough silver often went to church funds.

Returning to the Scots 'pleugh song', something of its social purpose becomes clear. The words describe a ceremony of renewal concerning the plough and plough ox. Each of the three verses concludes
with a cadence calling for an action which must then be mimed. The
killing of the old plough ox is enacted, a new ox is found and the
plough lads are summoned and harnessed to the plough; finally, a general blessing is invoked. The startling primitiveness of the action is
belied by the sophistication of the song and its music.

The tenor voice, leader of the sport, addresses his 'lord', owner of the
land upon which the 'hyndis' who offer him their services wish to re-
new their annual 'pastorie' or grazing rights. He announces the immi-
nent death of the lord's plough ox: 'he is weak and wonder sweer';
he invites the standers-by to hasten its death with strokes (do they perhaps have staves?): 'suppose ye brod him whill he die'. In the second
verse, the ox is referred to as still alive, and some remedy is proposed
'or he be dead'. Rather than leave the plough idle, another ox must
be yoked up and the labourers called to service.

---

sweer recalcitrant

> And I am wo your pleugh suld lie
> and I might come and be near-by
> to yoke another in his steid
> to drug and draw whill he be dead.
> Out of ane uncouth fair laysour
> to do your Lordship more plesour
> and if it be your proper will
> gar call your hyndis all you till.

The lord is invited to take part by calling the names. There follows the
setting of forty-odd typically 'rustic' worthies, including Arthur,
Hector, Dounie, Mackay Miller, Fergus Falselips. Each presumably
dances up to offer his service.

In the third section the leader asks the lord and all the men to sur-
round him in a complicated figure as he plays the death of the old ox:

> and mak me als so fast and sicker
> as I wer bound ev'n with ane wicker
> for to deliver me be the heid
> the old ox Trip-free he be dead.
> Then sall I come be robles cocks
> and bring with me my fair fresh ox
> with all that belongs to the pleugh.

The action is not entirely clear, but the 'delivering' of the leader 'by
the head' accomplishes the death of the old ox. Perhaps the man uses
an ox head which is taken off and then restored. In the binding of the
men together around the central victim one may perhaps see a symbolic action comparable with the 'lock' of sword dance around the
neck of the fool, leading to his execution and immediate resurrection.

The parts of the plough are now enumerated. There is one ox (or
ox-man) and yet it is composed of the whole team of men. Nine traditional names are used to hail the ox, who, to shouts of 'wind about',
is praised as the finest in Scotland and is offered for hire contract to the
lord. With the blessing of the Trinity upon the lord and company the
performance apparently ends.

How one interprets this play, song and dance, will depend on one's
point of view. Anthropologists of the Cambridge school will see in it
the form of the Buophonia festival of Thrace described by Jane
Harrison: an ox is killed, the guilt shared by all participants; the beast

---

and if   *whill* when   *or* before
Out of ane uncouth fair laysour for very good sport   *you till* to you
sicker sure   *robles cocks* rood-blest God

is then flayed, its skin stuffed with straw and the 'new ox' yoked to the plough. The act is one of sympathetic magic and the ox's resurrection is the 'mimetic representation of the new life of the year and this resurrection is meant to act magically'.[17] More explicitly, the ceremony is a 'ritual of social relationships', in which the ploughlads act out their allegiance and are literally bound together in the service of their lord, the ox and plough representing an undying obligation to work. The mutual social advantages are affirmed. Beyond the structural and explicitly social meanings, the play is also a festive entertainment, an 'uncouth fair laysour'. The festive spirit of the underlying action, the merry-making at death, which brings 'luck', are rendered in the courtly song by the intricate gaiety of the vocal parts.

In this, anthropologically speaking, most primitive of folk plays, the participants are invited to take part in the slaying of the victim in order that they can affirm the victory of life over death in the community of the new plough-ox. The world of the 'folk' glimpsed here seems far from that of the fifteenth-century mystery plays. Yet, as I shall argue later, the patterning of the action and manner of playing in certain plays can be seen to betray the shaping power of a subliterary tradition of folk drama.

Because the formal elements of traditional drama are all important, and the historical elements secondary and changeable, St George will rub shoulders with King George, and the Turkish Knight with 'Bonapurt'. The same process is apparent in the 'ancient storiall show' performed by the men of Coventry for Queen Elizabeth I on her visit to Kenilworth in 1575.[18] This spectacular display showed the massacre of the Danes by English Knights upon St Brice's Night, 1002. But two 'unhistorical' things about the 'show' are noticeable: its name Hox Tuesday seems to connect it with some ox festival; secondly, women are shown leading captive the defeated Danes. The Coventry Annals date the invention of Hox Tuesday 1416–17. It seems that at that time the historical episode (surviving perhaps in ballad form) was recast in terms of a folk custom known as 'hoxing' or 'hocking'. This was concerned with a battle of the sexes and seems to have lost any connection it ever had with an ox (except perhaps in the ceremony of *binding* a man). Chambers tells how,[19]

On Hock-Monday, the women 'hocked' the men; that is to say they went abroad with ropes, caught and bound any man they came across, and exacted a forfeit. On Hock Tuesday, the men retaliated in similar fashion upon the women.

In other words, the popular game form accommodated and reinterpreted the historical event.

The Coventry battle-play was introduced by Captain Cox and another fence master. First came 'the Danish launsknights on horsbak and then the English, each with their alder poll marcially in their hand . . . Even at the first entree the meeting waxt somewhat warm'. The footsoldiers march in intricate formation:

both the hostez, ton after toother, first marching in ranks: then warlik turning, then from ranks to squadrons, then in too triangles; from that into rings and so winding out again.

The combat here is in no way realistic, but ballet-like. It is reminiscent of the Gothic play described earlier in the formation of circles and geometric patterns of rhythmic movement, in the use of wooden staves rather than real weapons, and in the triply repeated pattern of action: the English are overcome twice, but in the end their women participate:

Twise the Danes had the better; but at the last conflict, beaten down, overcom, and many led captive for triumph by our English women.

In a fifteenth-century Low German play from Lübeck a simple form of the sword-dance combat has absorbed the figure of the Holy Roman Emperor and 'history' is stylized according to the demands of the dance for a locking circle.[20] Kaiser Karl (Charlemagne) summons in turn each of five 'kings' (Joshua, Hector, David, Alexander, Judas Maccabaeus; in another version they are the kings of England, Saxony, Poland, Denmark and 'Moorland') to 'fecht' with him. They introduce themselves in turn, each dancing forward to engage in combat with the Kaiser, each in turn conceding victory. Finally there comes in a curious fool-figure called Sterkader (Stark-athr: 'the strengthened one', the Odinic fool-hero of Viking legend), who fights them all. The rubric says, 'At last he comes to stand in the middle and they all thrust at him with their swords' (endlich kümt he in de mirr to stân, un all' steken up em in). This comic figure, powerful in diabolical associations, calls for a horse to ride away on and then 'collapses' (he verswimelt: possibly, 'he disappears'), presumably falling to the ground within the circle of dancers. The presenter, Santa Klaus, asks the audience:

Het em de duvel halt? ut is dat spil;
nu lat uns dansen . . .

(Has the devil taken him? The play is over,
now let us dance . . .)

Secular combat plays did not go unremarked by medieval church-men, who may on occasion even have taken part. The scandalous be-haviour of Gunther, Bishop of Bamberg, is the subject of a letter (dated 1057-64) by Meinhard of Bamberg:[21]

You ask what our master does? What battles does he wage with his army of helmeted hares? What victories do they celebrate? Great gods, that is a collection of mice, not men! What an empty din is esteemed there—no gravity, no discipline . . . wretched and to be pitied life of a bishop: O *mores*! He never studies Augustine or Gregory, not he! He must always be playing the part of Attila the Hun, Amalric, and such-like heroes. He is ignorant of the sweetness of books, admiring instead the harsh clashing of spears.

The point of Meinhard's wit is that the bishop neither studies nor undertakes real military campaigns, preferring to revel and celebrate battle in plays in which he can play the lead.

The existence of a tradition of battle-play in Germany may have been decisive in determining the course of ecclesiastical drama there, by predisposing clerical German dramatists to choose biblical subjects which would enable them to present armed combat. Gerhoh of Reichersberg complains that when he was schoolmaster at Augsberg (*c.* 1122-3) the monks occupied the dormitory or used the refectory only when some *ludus* or other was provided for their entertainment; his example is Herod and the Slaughter of Innocents.[22] The more moderate Abbess of Hohenberg approves of ecclesiastical plays in general but, as we have seen, abhors their license to represent violence:[23]

The clerical habit is changed and confused with military garb, no difference between priests and soldiers; the house of God is disordered with a confusion of clergy and laity, eating together, with drinking, buffoonery, disgusting jests and self-indulgent plays of the clashing of weapons . . .

Such spectacles could be stirring occasions. A chronicle from Riga describes a Christian battle-play performed to instruct 'pagans and neophytes' in the summer of 1204 (Riga, on the Baltic, was at that time a frontier town):[24]

That summer there was given a very elaborate prophet play such as the Latins call a *comedia*, in the centre of Riga, in order that the heathen might learn the rudiments of the Christian faith by visible demonstration. The substance of this play or comedy was diligently explained to the neophytes and pagans who had been brought there by means of an interpreter. When, however, the army of Gideon fought with the Philistines, the pagans, fearing that they were about to be killed, started to run away and had to be called gently back.

The invective hurled against ecclesiastical drama by Gerhoh of Reichersberg in his *De Investigatione Antichristi* (*c.* 1161) was probably occasioned by the great Tegernsee play of Antichrist. This extraordinary combination of eschatological legend with militaristic wish-fulfilment will be discussed in detail later (p. 88). The reasons for Gerhoh's polemic are pertinent to the present discussion. As a supporter of the papacy Gerhoh objected to the play's imperial theme, epitomized for him in the theatrical presentation which demanded that clergy be transformed into soldiers (*clerici in milites . . . transfigurant*).[25] Directions for staging the *Antichristus* are full, suggesting in their lack of specific detail of the many battles, that the director would know how such spectacles were to be managed. Each national group consists of a king and his army, who, as they march in are allowed to sing 'whatever seems suitable'.[26] Decorum and vigour are suggested by the directions that the Emperor should fight the King of Franks 'in battle lines' and that the French king, 'rushing to meet with him', is overcome and made captive, forced to kneel before the imperial throne. The imperial polemic (in a play probably performed before the Holy Roman Emperor, Frederick I) connects it back to the ceremonial flattery of the Gothic Christmas play at the imperial Byzantine court.

Other, structural, elements suggest a debt to popular tradition. A pattern of boast, challenge, counter-challenge, battle and submission, is repeated three times in the first half of the play and then, after the imperial relief of Jerusalem, three more times. In the second half, Antichrist (shown through his words and deeds as an exact parody of the Holy Roman Emperor) defeats the Christian kings and wins the female figure of Synagoga. His triumphs complete, Antichrist calls together the five kings of Jerusalem, Franks, Teutons, Greeks and Babylonians, into a circle. The kings 'gather from all sides with their armies', summoned by Antichrist's messenger into the circle (*ad coronam*). The *corona* of champions, like the 'knot' of the sword play, is the prelude to a sort-of-death. Thunder strikes suddenly above Antichrist's head, he falls and his followers flee.

The formal parallel with the Lübeck folk-play will be apparent: not merely is the warrior king in each case the Holy Roman Emperor; each play has the same curious double structure, involving parodic repetition of the king's victories by his demonic shadow. In Antichrist's sudden collapse in the ring of warrior kings, the demise of the fool-hero Sterkader and the death of the sword-play fool are recalled.

The influence of the pagan combat-drama on Christian drama of the

Middle Ages is impossible to gauge. It may extend beyond the prompting of German dramatists to choose militaristic subjects, to include the
figure of the spice-merchant-cum-quack-doctor who sells life-restoring
ointment to the Marys in some liturgical Easter plays, and also some
forms of the *planctus* (lament for the dead) in the Passion plays.[27]
Among liturgical subjects at the periphery of the canon, the Harrowing
of Hell (told in the apocryphal Gospel of Nicodemus) offered an action
readily conceived as combat. Indeed, in allegorizing the Mass as a
tragedy of Christ's Passion, Honorius of Autun (in the twelfth century) described its plot as a conflict (*duellum*) between Christ and his
adversary the devil, including the hero's death and resurrection.[28] Yet
it is notable that this great subject is scantily treated in liturgical Latin
drama. There is no confrontation, let alone conflict, between Christ
and Satan in the earliest (eighth-century) play of the Harrowing, nor
is there in the fourteenth-century play from Barking (see below p. 63).
In contrast to this liturgical restraint, the popular vernacular drama
presents fully- and even comically-realized conflicts of Christ and
Satan, in the thirteenth-century Swiss fragments of a Passion play from
Kloster Muri and in the contemporary Middle English 'Strif of Jesu
and of Satan'.[29]

As one might expect, the vernacular religious drama was altogether
more receptive to folk traditions. Its authors, writing for popular
audiences, expected the actors to greet the audience, to vaunt and wave
their swords in intimidatory rantings, to engage in 'flyting' and to
physically assault one another. Their drama, like the folk drama, is
often a physical game, a strenuous affair in which there are 'goodies'
and 'baddies' and life is played as a combat between them.

3

DANCING-GAME

Many of the social pastimes referred to by medieval writers as *ludus* or 'game' or 'pleye' would probably be thought of in modern English as 'games'.[1] Calling them 'games' would imply, perhaps, that they were non-real, 'pretend' activity, involving the participation of a whole social group. In that sense they would be distinct from 'plays', where we might see a formal distinction of 'actors' and 'audience'. Of course games may be watched; but that seems accidental, not essential. The important thing is to enter the game and take part.

Dancing is the characteristically medieval form of rejoicing and self-entertainment, appropriate to secular revels, seasonal festivals and Church feasts. Many of the dances contained song-dialogue and mimetic action, thus verging on drama. Twelfth-century villagers were observed by Gerald of Wales (in his *Itinerarium Cambriae*) to dance, singing *cantilenae* (popular songs) in both church and churchyard; men and girls performed imitations of the workday occupations forbidden on feast days, 'the hands of one laid to the plough, another driving oxen as if with a goad'. Others made the motions of shearing sheep, washing and carding wool, spinning and weaving, all performed 'in time'.[2] Although impersonation as well as plot was apparently lacking in such dancing games, they may have made an important contribution to the more literary drama of the Middle Ages by establishing a repertory of motifs and a style of acting.

Other dances, for which song texts or scenarios survive, have recognizable story elements and demand the impersonation of human roles by soloists. Some are fairly sophisticated sung ballet-dramas and were performed as plays, to be watched by an audience. They form a

well-defined genre, first recognized by Joseph Bédier in 1906.[3] But, to
my knowledge, the importance of this tradition to the development
both of secular and of ecclesiastical drama has not been much explored.

Bédier's texts were Old French and Provençal songs for the thirteenth century or later. By identifying traditional refrains he showed
which parts of the songs were choral and which solo. He showed that
the texts, often incoherent when read in the study, made perfect sense
as the accompaniment to actions of the soloists in the dance. The context of these earliest dancing songs is almost invariably aristocratic;
they are described in romances or accounts of courtly entertainments
as being performed by knights and ladies; or they are envisaged as the
picturesque 'rustic' entertainment of *bergers* and *pastoriaus* in the idyllic
landscape evoked by a writer of *pastourelle*. It is a typically pastoral
device to idealize a rustic culture as an object for courtly imitation. But
in the case of the dancing-songs, as Peter Dronke has recently written,
'there is no evidence whatever that they were originally restricted to an
exclusive milieu'. Many of the songs are popular in the sense 'that they
perpetuate beliefs and fantasies of the people which are older than, and
essentially independent of, clerical and aristocratic traditions'.[4]

Whether popular or courtly, the majority of dances are amorous. A
refrain preserved among the German and Latin songs of the *Carmina
Burana* shows the girls taking the lead in provoking the men to dance:[5]

> Swaz hie gât umbe,
> daz sint alle megede,
> die wellent ân man
> allen disen sumer gan!

> (Dancing in circle here
> are all maidens;
> they want to be without a man
> all this summer long!)

The solo part for a more intricate and aristocratic dance is described in
detail by Jehan Bretel as one of the delights of the tournament of
Chauvency in 1285.[6] The account, in his long poem *Le Tournois de
Chauvency*, tells how the Countess of Luxembourg led a dance called
the *chapelet* for the solace of the wounded knights. The structure is
simple: the girl provokes the advances of a young man, 'leading him a
dance' before granting him a kiss. Delicacy of performance was all,
and required, it seems, some improvisation on a known pattern. The
heroine plays with a garland of flowers (her *chapelet*), putting it on

and off her head, as she dances alone, singing softly, as if to herself: *Si n'a plus joliete de me* (There's no one more joyful here than I). The minstrel, a viol-player, asks why she stands all alone, without a lover; she replies in song:

> Sire, qu'en afiert il a vos?   Ne vos voi pas bien sage.
> j'ai fait mon chapelet jolif,   la jus en cel boschage.

> (What business is it of yours? I see you are not wise.
> I have made my pretty garland down there in the wood.)

He asks, *Douce dame, volez baron?* Does she wish for a husband? She replies that she would rather a maiden's garland than a bad marriage:

> Naie; se ne l'ai tres bon,   j'averoie damage.
> J'aim mieux mon chapelet de flors   que mauvais mariage.

The minstrel promises to find her a good one; she dances provocatively towards an imaginary wood, possibly a ring of dancers, a 'grove of love', to await the man. A knight is chosen by the minstrel, at first denying his own worthiness, but then allowing himself to be led to the girl, as she sings:

> Dieus! Trop demeure; quant vendra?   Sa demouree m'ocira.

> (Lord! He delays too long; when will he come? His delay will kill me.)

She takes him by the hand and gives thanks to God for her great delight.

The play lacks both narrative element and true impersonation. The roles are clearly defined by the pattern of the action, but their basis in 'story' is vague, so that there is little for the actors to do. But the slenderness of the action as a performed spectacle is compensated for by its nature as an inviting 'game'. Any one of the men in the escort may be chosen for the next turn. This light-hearted *ballerie* expresses the aspiration of a leisured, courtly society to aesthetic and erotic refinement through 'game'.

Most commonly the songs accompanied a ring-dance (this is true of the *carole*, a widespread form of undoubtedly popular origins). The chorus circles to the left about a soloist. (As one clerical definition expressed it, 'a *ring-dance* is a circle at whose centre is the devil, and everyone is turning perversely'—*chorea: enim circulus est cuius centrum est diabolus, et omnes vergunt ad sinistrum.*[7] The Latin pun here points out the anti-Christian implications of the 'widdershins' movement.) When the soloist has sung one or two verses, with the appropriate steps and mimed gestures, the chorus marks time, singing a refrain in which lines from the solo verses may be repeated.

The ring itself is a sacred figure, signifying the harmony of the linked dancers about the central one, and also their exclusiveness. In a Provençal song, 'all those who are in love' are invited to 'come and dance, the others not at all'. Another refrain from northern France, *Voist en la qui n'aime mie* ('Let him flee who does not love') expresses the same sense of initiation. The function of the chorus is to protect the lovers from hostile forces. In the Provençal song *A l'entrada del tens clar* they are the attendants of a Spring queen, whose amorousness within the charmed circle induces the joy of the season. She must be protected from the clutches of an old 'jelos' king, her husband.

> A l'entrada del tens clar, eya,
> per joja recommençar, eya,
> e per jelos irritar, eya,
> vol la regina mostrar
>   qu'el est si amoroza.
>
> *Alavi! alavia, jelos!*
> *Laissatz nos, laissatz nos,*
> *Ballar entre nos, entre nos!*
>
> (At the coming of fine weather,
> so as to begin joy again
> and to annoy the jealous one
> the Queen wishes to show
> how amorous she is.
>
> *Away, away, jealous one[s]!*
> *Leave us,*
> *to dance among ourselves!*)

According to Bédier's reconstruction of this play (which he calls the *regina avrillosa*) the April queen dances within the circle, choosing from among her attendants a young man. Outside the ring a dancer representing the old king tries to break the circle (*la dansa destorbar*) and claim her back. In some versions he may have been successful, to judge from a Middle English fragment:[8]

> Alas hou shold Y synge?
> Yloren is my playnge.
> Hou shold Y with that olde man
> To leven, and let my lemman,
>   Swettist of all thinge.

Yloren lost

When there is more than one *jelos* the actions of the chorus can become a vigorous combat, as indicated in another southern French song:

Li jalous sont partout fustat
Et portent corne en mi la front.
Partout doivent estre huat:
La regine le commendat
Que d'un baston soient frapat
Et chacie hors comme larron.
S'en dançade vuellent entrar,
Fier les du pié comme garçon!

Tuit cil qui sont enamourat
Viegnent dançar, li autre non!
La regina le commendat . . .

(The jealous ones are everywhere beaten
and [made to] wear horns upon their foreheads.
They must be hooted away on every side,
The Queen commands
that they be beaten with a stick
and chased out like thieves.
If they try to enter the dancing-ring,
Kick them with your feet like urchins.

All those who are in love
Come dance, the others not.
The Queen commands it . . .)

The use of staves as weapons and of 'horns' for the figures of the 'jalous' brings us close to the world of folk-play. (In the Abbots Bromley 'horn-dance' six of the performers wear sets of reindeer horns and are 'shot at' by an archer, whilst a wooing action involving a clown, a 'woman' and a hobby-horse, takes place.[9]) In yet another French version, the girl calls out to the dancers to make their circle so tight that the husband cannot spy on her; if the *vilain* touches her 'with even one finger' she will surely die.

The imitative action of this dance-play might be seen as a stylized cuckolding, and the three roles as the familiar triad of fabliau: May and her lusty lover, old 'blind' January and the pear-tree, the accommodating *bois d'amour*. Yet the dance expresses relationship rather than story. The narrative sequence in this dance is far from clear, and I think this is because action is continuous, with all the elements presented simultaneously: love-making within the charmed circle, while outside the *jelos* is forever thwarted by the circling dancers. In its primitive meaning it is an act of affirmation—of youth and love and Spring, an exorcism of age, and conventional marriage and Winter. But it is not a primitive ritual, despite the elements of inductive magic, for who could not be on the side of Spring? Someone must play Winter and the more the merrier. It is a game, inviting participation.

Although there is great variety in the dancing-song plays, certain patterns of action are recurrent: there is usually a sacred place, *le bois d'amour*, or *l'olive*, or *la tor*, which protects the lovers: in performance it may have been symbolized by the choral ring, or properties may have been used. Then there are hostile forces who wish to steal away the girl, queen or bride from her guard. In the dance of *Le bois d'amour*, where the trappings are both pastoral and courtly, reference is to a paradise garden with a fountain guarded by a knight who prevents the stealing of a *chapel de flor*. He sings in explanation that 'My love sleeps there and I shall wake her'. In the course of the dance all the dancers visit the garden, *deux à deux*. In *La belle enlevée* (the stolen bride) the girl is stolen away by an *anemi*, and the lover-guard sings:

> Or ai ge trop dormi:
> On m'a m'amie amblée.
> C'out fait mi anemi;
> Or ai ge trop dormi.
> Mielz amasse estre ocis
> Au tranchant de m'espée.
> Or ai ge trop dormi:
> On m'a m'amie amblée.

(Now I have slept too long and my sweetheart has been stolen from me. That was my enemy's [rival's?] doing. . . . He deserves rather to be slain upon the point of my sword. Now I have slept too long and my sweetheart has been stolen from me.)

In *La balerie du jaloux* the shepherdess heroine hides among dancing shepherds. In *la danse robardoise*, described in detail in *Le tournois de Chauvency*, two shepherds dance to protect the heroine from the advances of a *garçonet* (in this instance played by a female *jongleureuse*) who finally steals a kiss from her. The pipe-and-*flajot*-playing shepherds of *pastourelle* narrative sometimes play at *gaite la tor*. The chorus urges the horn-playing watchman (*guetteur*) to look out for the thief and to blow his *trompe*, crying, 'Hu et hu et hu et hu!'. The watcher and the lover's friend sing in alternation, reassuring each other of the lovers' safety, calling to them to lie softly in their chamber. The lover then appears

from the tower and leaves his mistress to their care, describing in song
how he lay 'in the chamber of joy' and lamenting the coming of dawn.
The lyrics here suggest a circular action, in which the sleep of the
watchers allows the lady to be either visited by a new lover or stolen
away so that a new pair of lovers can take their turn in the *tor* or
maydenes-Kastel, as it was called in English.[10]

The most widely known of the songs, *La bele Aelis*, provides
merely a framework within which the soloist must improvise her own
story. The choral introduction tells how,

> Main se leva la bien faite Aelis
> Bel se para et plus bel se vesti . . .

(Lovely Aelis rose early, made herself up beautifully and dressed even more
so . . .)

Aelis acts out each line, pouring water, washing her face, combing her
hair, before going into a garden to meet her lover. In performance
each line sung by the chorus could be further expanded by interpolations in which Aelis and her lover sing of love, and of nightingales, or
are instructed by the chorus in the doctrines of courtly love:

> Ki bien aime joie atent,
> Et ki d'amer se repent
> Ne poet joie recouvrer.

(Whoever loves whole-heartedly attains joy, and whoever regrets loving cannot
recover its joy.)

As we have seen, many of the dancing-songs assume a pastoral
setting and performance by 'shepherds and shepherdesses'. The pheno-
menon of pastoral idealism in the courts of northern France and
Burgundy has been characterized by Huizinga as 'courtly love trans-
posed into another key'.[11] Performance of the dancing-songs may well
have formed part of larger aristocratic festivities known as *bergeries*; in
these, courtly people masqueraded (as they did in the court of Marie
Antoinette) as shepherds and shepherdesses, dancing and playing country
games. The *bergerie* tradition provided both a style of acting (using
dance, mime and song) and a repertory of plot motifs which might
readily be worked into a fairly ambitious musical drama. The earliest
for which a complete text survives is Adam de la Halle's well-known
Jeu de Robin et Marion (c. 1283).[12] The plot, in which the knight woos
and is rejected by the shepherdess faithful to her rustic swain, is provided by traditional narrative lyric. But, following the departure of the

knight, the second half of the play is plotless and consists of a pastoral picnic and a series of games and dances performed by *bergerie* characters. Beneath the apparently effortless 'realism' of this jolly and youthful party, the 'game' elements are entirely traditional. The shepherds and shepherdesses choose and crown (with a straw hat) a 'summer king' who then has the right to ask embarrassing questions of the company. Possibly this was one of those *ludi de Rege et Regina* which the Synod of Worcester in 1240 order clergy not to tolerate.[13] In another game, still known in France, one of the company plays 'Saint Coisne' and receives absurd 'offerings' from his kneeling devotees, who try not to laugh. The songs which accompany the 'rustic' dances are also traditional, having as Jacques Chailley puts it, 'la caractère d'une citation musicale'.[14] They are meant to be recognized as 'epigrams in song' expressing a common experience of love in a pastoral vein.

The play begins, significantly, not in realistic scene-setting dialogue, but in song: Marion sits all alone, singing *Robins m'aime*. The love of Robin and Marion is 'proved' to be true in a dance-song which belongs directly in the tradition we have been following: Robin begs for the garland of flowers that Marion wears, and offers her, in return, his belt, purse and buckle. When she has granted him her *chapelet*, he performs for her each of the dances she names:

Robin

>   Marote, et jou esprouverai
>   Se tu m'ies loiaus amiete,
>   Car tu m'as trouvé amiet.
>   (*he sings*)
>   'Bergeronnete, douche baisselete,
>   Donnés-le-moi vostre chapelet,
>   Donnés-le-moi vostre chapelet.'   (170–75)

>   (Marion, I am going to test
>   whether you are my sweetheart true,
>   for I have been proved your own true love.
>   'My shepherdess, my little pretty darling,
>   give me your garland, your garland, do.')

Other elements in the play betray a dependence on the dramatic conventions of the dancing-songs: Marion's abduction, the introduction of the horn players, the practical use of a central bush (*bosket*) for hiding in. *Robin et Marion* is very far from being a direct imitation of rustic life; there is much incidental and satirical realism, but the basis of the drama is not mimicry but the aristocratic game of an innocently erotic pastoral make-believe.

Turning now from the courtly developments of the dance-play tradition, what use could ecclesiastical writers make of this wide-spread form? Stricter clergy often condemned the performance of *choreae*, but a flood of pronouncements, reaching from the Council of Rome in A.D. 826 down through the thirteenth century to fourteenth-century Wells, show how often ring-dances in fact took place in church or churchyard.[15] That these dances were often in themselves dramatic is suggested by the frequent mention of masks (as in a prohibition *c.* 1250 against Oxford students performing *choreas cum larvis*); along with 'wrestling and other dishonest plays in cemeteries, theatrical plays and filthy spectacles', *choreae* were prohibited by a Synod of Exeter in 1287.[16]

Sometimes the diabolical *choreae* were performed as relics of an old pagan religion whose calendar had been usurped by the Christian feasts. The Chronicle of Lanercost tells (1282) how a parish priest of Inverkeithing was responsible for the observance of profane rites of Priapus during Easter Week. He compelled the girls of the village to engage in *choreae* in honour of Father Bacchus, while he himself bore aloft on a pole before the dancers a representation of the human organs of reproduction. The Chronicle tells how he danced himself and 'stirred the spectators to wantonness by mimic actions and shameless speech'.[17] The vigils of church feasts were notorious occasions for dancing and licensed revelry, keeping clerical composers of hymns and sequences constantly in touch with the forms and melodies of popular song.[18] A miniature in a thirteenth-century manuscript of the *Cantigas de Santa Maria* shows a typical Spanish scene inside church on the eve of a feast of the Virgin.[19] Some figures kneel before the altar holding lighted candles, while others gaze at the antics of *juglares*, some flirt, and a group of women perform a round dance. That such a dance could be in a general sense devotional is implied by the author of the eleventh-century *Chanson de Sainte Foy* telling his reader that the song is 'good to dance to', and by the refrain (probably twelfth-century) of a Provençal dancing-song performed at the abbey of Saint-Martial of Limoges on the feast of the saint:[20]

> Saint Marçau, prega per nos,
> Et nos espringaram per vos!

(Saint-Martial, pray for us and we will dance for you!)

A manuscript from Saint-Martial, dated between 1096 and 1099, and containing four of the earliest liturgical Latin plays, has also some lyrics in the Limousin dialect. *Mei amic e mei fiel* is a song of the Annunciation, composed to the melody of a dancing-song with refrain; musically simple, with the balanced phrases typical of popular song.[21] The same melody is assigned to a Christmas hymn, *In hoc anni circulo*, but unlike this Latin hymn *Mei amic* is composed for a soloist and chorus. Like many of the dancing-songs which provided its metrical and musical models, it contains a dramatic dialogue of the protagonists. Beginning with the familiar audience address of an oral performer, the soloist asks his 'friends' to leave off their frivolity and to learn a 'new song':

> Mei amic e mei fiel,
> Laisat estar lo gazel!
> Aprendet un so noel
> *De virgine Maria.*

(My friends and faithful ones, leave aside frivolity and learn a new song *about the Virgin Mary.*)

The call to leave aside 'lo gazel' has particular point in the context of the popular revelry at a vigil. If Aurelio Roncaglia is right, then *gazel* relates to the Arab word *ghazal*, meaning a love-song. The clerical poet makes a deliberate contrast (a traditional one in patristic writing) between the *cantica diabolica amatoria et turpia* of popular usage, the 'old song' of profane love, and the *so noel* of Christianity, the *novum canticum* of salvation sung by the elect in the New Jerusalem. The poet's transposition of a secular song into a sacred one typifies the approach of medieval Christianity to pagan practices. The feast of the Annunciation, celebrated just before Christmas in many parts of Europe in the eleventh century, was just such a reconsecration of a pagan festival known as *Modranacht*; Mothernight, a feast of dancing women, became the night of the divine mother.[22] The Church fathers explained to simple congregations that the Virgin Mary redeemed an ancient curse upon women since Eve. In the words of Saint Bernard, in twelfth-century French translation, 'Om ostet l'ancienne maldeçon des femmes'. Gabriel's song of A–V–E reverses the fateful name E–V–A, in whose ear the serpent whispered the *canticum diaboli*. Instead of Eve, the archetype of 'l'amistié qui vient par delit' (sensual love), Christians are offered Mary, the archetype of heavenly love.[23]

Mei amic reenacts Gabriel's song of grace and in doing so recasts the Gospel story of the Annunciation in terms of the dancing-song tradition. After three instructional verses, action begins suddenly with Mary's voice, unheralded:

> Non perdrai virginitat,
> tostemps aurai chastitat,
> si cum es prophetizat,
>   Pois er virgo Maria.

(I shall not lose my virginity, but always keep my chastity as it is prophesied, *I shall still be Virgin Mary*.)

The singer may change his voice here, but it seems to me as likely that another soloist with an unbroken voice is used. The audience forms the chorus to a wooing dialogue in which Gabriel plays the part of heavenly minstrel-go-between:

> Eu soi l'angels Gabriels.
> Apor vos salut, fiels:
> Deus descen de sus deu cel
>   In te, virgo Maria.

(I am the angel Gabriel. I bring you greetings truly: God descends out of heaven *into you, Virgin Mary*.)

Hearing his song, she rejoices. The poet urges his audience to 'sing out loud each new verse to our song of the Virgin Mary'. By adopting the mask of the *joglar* of popular poetry he turns an ancient tradition to ecclesiastical use and produces the earliest extant song-play of the Annunciation.

Popular songs often formed melodic models for pious compositions. The practice was encouraged in his diocese of Ossory by Bishop Ledrede in the early fourteenth century. Among the *cantilenae teatrales turpes* (profane 'show-songs') used as models in the *Red Book* of Ossory was the lament of the spring queen, 'Alas hou shold Y synge' already quoted (p. 50). Many preachers, however, took a firmer attitude to the dancing songs. Jacques de Vitry, exasperated by the popularity of the *bele Aelis* game in the early thirteenth century, told his congregation:[24]

> Quant Aeliz fu levee
> Et quant el fu lavee,
> Quant ele su fu miree,
> Bel vestie et mieus paree . . .
> Ja la messe fu chantee:
> Diable l'en ont portee.

(When Aelis had risen, and when she had washed herself, and preened herself, dressed beautifully and adorned herself more beautifully . . . Mass had already been sung and devils carried her away.)

A sermon attributed to Stephen Langton allegorizes the same dance in an opposite sense: the *carole* symbolizes man's dance with God; Christ is the soloist, man the chorus; Aelis is the Virgin Mary, plucking the flowers of chastity and charity in the sacred garden.[25] It is doubtful whether the sermon was ever directly linked to a performance of the dancing-song in so moralized a version. On the other hand, the many Franciscan and Dominican exemplary tales of the thirteenth century of how the devil appeared among a ring of dancers to claim his own may have more relevance to the course of religious drama. In *La bele enlevée* the ravisher of the bride is known as *l'anemi*, a common term in Old French for the devil. It needs only for this sinister figure to be replaced in the dancing-game by an impersonation of the devil or of death for the *danse-macabre* to be born. The origins of the Dance of Death have been traced in poetry, painting and sermon, but none of these 'sources' helps explain why it should have been a *dance*.[26]

The most astonishing use of the dancing-song play is in the Passion play of the *Carmina Burana* manuscript (*c.* 1230), which has already been mentioned as an important source of Latin and German dancing songs. Although the *Passio* is composed largely in Latin, using the liturgy of Passion week and the narrative of the Gospels, one scene is chiefly in German and is highly original. This is the scene which shows the sinful life of Mary Magdalene before her repentance. When Magdalene is introduced into the play she brings with her an attendant chorus of dancing girls. Mary sings of the delights of the world, then goes, accompanied by her girls, to buy cosmetics from a merchant. She sings:[27]

Magdalena
>Chramer, gip die varwe mier
>>div min wengel roete,
>da mit ich di iungen man
>>an dir danch der minnenliebe noete.

>(Merchant, give me colouring
>>to redden my cheeks,
>with which I may compel the young men—
>>even against their will—to love.)

The chorus of girls joins in the refrain, a lilting melody with these provocative words:

> *Seht mich an,*
> *iungen man,*
>> *lat mich eu gevallen.*

> (*Look at me,*
> *you young men,*
>> *let me give you delight.*)

Mary Magdalene now sings a verse to instruct the audience in the doctrines of *amour courtois*:

> Minnet, tugentliche man,
>> minnekliche vrauwen.
> Minne tuot eu hoech gemuet
>> unde lat euch in hochen eren schauwen.

> (Love, you worthy men,
>> love women capable of love.
> Love makes you full of the highest joy
>> and lets you appear in high honour.)

Later, she takes up the theme a second time:

> Wol dan, minneklicheu chint,
>> schauwe wier chrame.
> Chaufe wier di varwe da,
>> di uns machen schoene unde wolgetane.
> Er muez sein sorgen vri,
>> der da minnet mier den leip.

> (Come then, lovely girls,
>> let us see these wares.
> Let us buy these colours
>> that give us grace and beauty.
> That man must be free from cares
>> who is to enjoy my love.)

The merchant assures her that his rouge will make the girls lovable (*wunnechliche*).

The wooing scene continues with Magdalene retiring to bed with a lover, whilst an angel sings, urging her to repent. After a while she calls her girls again and the visit to the merchant is repeated. Magdalene returns to her bed and the angel repeats his message. Mary, now repentant, takes off her worldly clothes and puts on a black gown of penitence. The lover and a devil (who has apparently supervised the bedroom, perhaps as keeper of the curtain) depart. Mary goes to the merchant a third time and, using the traditional words of Latin Easter plays, buys the precious ointment which she will later pour over Christ's feet. The triple pattern of the action thus reveals the earlier visits to the merchant as secular prefigurations of this moment of repentance and also of the final visit of the three Marys to buy spices with which to anoint the dead body of Christ.

The *Carmina Burana* playwright lacked scriptural details for the sinful life of the woman traditionally identified as Mary Magdalene and was luckily prompted by his knowledge of the ring-dance play to invent a scene. Here, in an old popular pastime, he found a ready-made dramatic form with solo actors and ring-dance chorus. The preexistent form (as in the case of the Lübeck and Hox Tuesday plays, discussed in the previous chapter) has reshaped 'history'. An audience of clerks and laity who, according to the testimony of other compositions among the *Carmina Burana*, may well have danced together, are thus shown Mary Magdalene set among a chorus of 'girls in love'. Mary acts out her self-adornment and love-making, while the choral refrains offer direct provocation to the men in the audience, inviting appreciation and, perhaps, their entry into the dance of profane love which will end in an act of repentance. Despite clerical hostility, indeed because of it, Bele Aelis finds a place in the drama of the church.[28]

From the vantage point of the later religious drama, the *Carmina Burana* Passion seems an excellent example of the 'secularization' of ecclesiastical drama in matter and spirit. But if we change the perspective and approach the play, as I have tried to do, via the traditions of the dancing-plays, the conclusion is rather different. For it seems that the drama that originated in the church—to which we must now turn— was a receiver as well as a generator of dramatic forms. Its own proper scope and means were expanded and vitalized by the deliberate incorporation of a secular drama of independent origin, which had its own motifs and conventions, its own distinctive idea of drama as a dancing-game of love.

4

CHURCH CEREMONY

Although Easter ceremonies of the Visitation of the Sepulchre are by far the most numerous of the ecclesiastical plays and have long been thought of as the *fons et origo* of medieval drama, the earliest of all liturgical plays deals with a non-biblical, apocryphal subject: the Harrowing of Hell. The text, edited recently from the Anglo-Saxon *Book of Cerne*, was almost certainly composed in the eighth century.[1] It consists of a fragmentary 'oratorio' for two soloists, Adam and Eve, and a chorus of 'the just' (*omnes antiqui iusti*) who, according to theology and to the *Gospel of Nicodemus*, were chained captive in hell since the fall of man. Short narrative sections, differentiated from three vocal parts, may have been sung by a 'narrator' or may (since some are in the present tense) be thought of as stage directions. There is no indication how, when or where this poetic drama was to be performed. However, its nature and structure (though probably incomplete) are plain enough.

The chorus of souls announces the advent of the redeemer and calls upon him for deliverance. The 'narration' describes their release and prostration at Christ's feet, praising him for bursting their bonds. The 'narration' then tells how Adam and Eve remained chained. Adam then prays for mercy, acknowledging his sin. His release and prostration are narrated. He praises the Lord in his own voice. The 'narration' tells how *Eva persistit in fletu*. Weeping, she begs Christ not to turn the face of his mercy from her. The text, cut short here, was probably intended to conclude with Abraham and, perhaps, all the souls in chorus.

A trefoil structure repeats itself for each new figure. In the chorus, and then in each solo voice, a prayer for release leads to an account of liberation, followed by a song of praise. The emotional pattern is a series of reversals, wave-movements from sorrow to joy.

The poetic dialogue explains the action but, without indications of actual movement or *mise-en-scène*, it is not possible to see how the performers are to enact the story which they celebrate. As acted drama the composition remains tantalizingly unrealized.

The Harrowing of Hell, as described in the *Gospel of Nicodemus* (*Descensus Christi ad Inferos*), is a myth of great power, embodying as it does the conflict of good and evil at the turning point of Christian history. The light shining before the imprisoned patriarchs in darkness precedes the advent of Christ as a warrior, a lord 'mighty and strong in battle', who hurls a triple challenge at the gates of hell:[2]

And again there was a cry without: Lift up, ye princes, your gates, and be ye lift up, ye everlasting doors, and the King of glory shall come in. And again at that clear voice Hell and Satan inquired, saying, Who is this King of glory? and it was said unto them by that marvellous voice: The Lord of hosts, he is the King of glory.

And lo, suddenly Hell did quake, and the gates of death and the locks were broken small, and the bars of iron broken, and fell to the ground, and all things were laid open. And Satan remained in the midst and stood put to confusion and cast down, and bound with a fetter about his feet. And behold, the Lord Jesus Christ coming in the glory of the light . . .

Then the Lord Jesus the Saviour of all men, pitiful and most gracious, greeted Adam with great kindness, saying unto him: Peace be unto thee, Adam . . .

Then all the saints adoring him cried out, saying: Blessed is he that cometh in the name of the Lord.

It may not seem surprising that this account indirectly inspired the earliest church drama. Nevertheless, its apocryphal status and exclusion, in this form, from use in the liturgy, may explain why liturgical Harrowing plays are so scarce and so disappointing in their conception. They lack clearly realized action. In this connection, the existence of a very ancient ceremony based upon the Harrowing is particularly important. This is the spectacular rite of cleansing and consecrating a church, which until the bishop's ceremonial entry, is regarded as a house of Satan. Karl Young prints a ninth-century *Order for Dedication of a Church* from Metz, and gives the following admirable summary:[3]

According to this *ordo* the bishop begins the purifying of the building by sprinkling the exterior of the walls. The procession of clerics marches round the exterior of the church three times, halting each time at the west door, and performing there a special ceremonial. The bishop strikes the door thrice with his staff, saying *Tollite portas*, and receives the response *Quis est iste rex gloriae?* from a cleric concealed within the church. After the third recital of this dialogue, the bishop declares himself in the words *Dominus virtutum, ipse est rex gloriae*, the doors are flung open, and the procession enters the building. Meanwhile the cleric who has been concealed behind the closed doors slips out and, resuming his vestments, joins the procession as the bishop proceeds with sprinkling the interior of the church.

This splendid ceremony for the expulsion of evil is very like drama, but differs from it in two chief respects: the roles of the contestants are incompletely realized, so that the actors *recall* without really *representing* the conflict of Christ and Satan; secondly, there is no proper 'audience', but rather a congregation of *participants* in a procession. The mimetic act is both functional (to cleanse the church) and commemorative of an 'historical' and transcendent event.

These two features are typical of much church ceremony and of 'primitive' ritual in general. Such quasi-dramatic forms are only 'primitive' if viewed teleologically, supposing that they are 'trying to become' representational drama. On the contrary, the two elements of *incomplete impersonation* and *communal participation* are essential to the religious life and purpose of these quasi-dramatic ceremonies. At the risk of labouring the point, I shall refer briefly to a much later treatment of the Harrowing of Hell action in an Easter ceremony from Barking, near London.[4] This office was composed by the abbess between 1363 and 1376, that is, about two centuries later than the greatest of the liturgical plays of the Middle Ages, and at a time when models of representational religious drama were readily available to the abbess—had she wanted them—in huge three- or five-day Passion cycles in the vernacular. But the Barking ceremony makes no concessions in this direction: it is intended as a corporate act of devotion and commemoration, to 'dispel completely the sluggish indifference of the faithful'. Before Easter Matins (i.e. still in the night), all members of the convent are 'imprisoned' behind the doors of the chapel of St Mary Magdalene. They are said to 'figure (*figurantes*) the souls of the holy Fathers before the advent of Christ descending into hell'. A priest outside represents Christ (*sacerdos repraesentabit personam Christi ad inferos descensuram*), dressed in white, and is accompanied by two deacons, bearing respectively a cross with emblems of the Passion and a thurible, and by candle bearers. He sings three times the antiphon *Tollite portas* and strikes the doors three times with the cross, 'figuring the breaking of hell gates'. The chapel door opens, the priest enters with attendants.

He leads forth all the palm-bearing souls from the chapel ('that is, from the Limbo of the Fathers') and they process, singing antiphons which conclude with *Cum rex gloriae*, towards the Easter sepulchre, where a ceremony of raising the host is performed.

In this Barking ceremony, both the marvellously 'dramatic' dialogue of Christ and Satan and the possibility of *representing* the devil are ignored in the interests of an action which the whole congregation can participate in and which does not distance the liturgical emotion of the Easter season by setting out to represent past 'history'. Here is a fourteenth-century drama which does not think of itself as drama.

It may not now seem surprising that the earliest manuscripts lack a specific generic term for the phenomena we have been discussing. Most commonly, the descriptions *officium*, *ordo* and *processus* are used—the same terms as refer to non-dramatic 'offices' and 'orders' for processions and ceremonies in the normal course of worship. The occasional use of the term *repraesentatio* and its cognates suggests an increased awareness of the genre, but this is rare; so is the 'secular' term *ludus*, applied to church plays. The twelfth-century use of *ludus* (and one usage of *comedia* in 1204) to connect the festive drama of the church with traditions of popular 'plays' may, it has been recently suggested, reflect the greatly increased awareness of the terms of Roman drama during this period.[5] Most plays, however, are referred to by their principal figures (*Mariae*, *Pastores*) or properties (*Sepulchrum*, *Stella*). The great majority are *Visitatio Sepulchri*, and this title applies equally to plays in which figures representing the three Marys visit the Easter sepulchre, and to visitations of the Sepulchre made by clergy or congregation, and which may have been a much older practice.

It is time now to examine the *Visitatio Sepulchri*, the most famous of all church plays, surviving in over four hundred texts. The sudden appearance of the *Visitatio* in monastic worship of the tenth century, its widespread adoption in Europe and its persistence over the next six hundred years, have stimulated an intense and unresolved dispute about its origins which can only be glanced at here. It may not be too controversial a simplification to say that, in all likelihood, the *dialogue* of the play (*Quam quaeritis in sepulchro, O Christicolae?*) with its particular *music*, and also the ceremonial *action* of the play existed independently in forms of worship before the play was composed.[6] The dialogue is that of an invented 'trope' (here meaning a verbal and musical interpolation, combining with the Gregorian introit of Easter Mass). Its action is that of a candlelit ecclesiastical *procession* to remove a host or crucifix (minus the figure of the Corpus Christi) from an Easter sepulchre in the body of the church. The creation of the drama may then be seen as a deliberate act, combining words and action by means of actors who actually represent and stand for historical person-ages.

This representation of 'story' by means of impersonation dis-tinguishes the church drama from most mere ceremonial practices and from the Mass. Some modern writers, taking a lead from medieval allegorists, would see the Mass itself as a drama of Christ's Passion, played by the celebrant in the theatre of the Church.[7] But, while it is clear that vocal colouring and gesture could encourage a congregation to take this view, neither the actual form of words and actions used, nor the nature of the Mass as a communal feast give much support to this view. Protestant reformers referred scornfully to the 'Mass play' and there is a danger that modern critics, holding a higher opinion of the drama and a lower one of religion, may simply invert the equa-tion.

To say that the liturgical plays are conceived in some sense (lacking in the Mass) as representations of 'story', does not imply that this is their primary purpose or that one should expect from them anything like realistic impersonation or 'dramatic illusion'. The earliest play text with rubrics for performance is the Winchester *Visitatio Sepulchri* (contained in St Ethelwold's *Regularis Concordia* for English Benedic-tine monasteries, *c.* 965–75). A brief examination of the play will make the points above quite plain.[8]

Referring to the movements of the three clerics who are directed to approach the sepulchre 'as if seeking something', the text says that 'these things are done in imitation (*ad imitationem*) of the angel seated in the monument and of the women coming with spices to anoint the body of Jesus'. The imitative means of 'strengthening faith' are explicit. But the use of imitation is, in fact, severely limited and the play's notion of acting is far from any mimic notion of impersonation. The four 'brethren' who are to perform this play are instructed to dress while the third lesson of Matins is being chanted. Their costumes are eccles-iastical vestments: the one who plays the angel wears an alb and apparently attracts no attention as 'he enters as if to take part in the service' but sits down quietly at the place of the sepulchre. The three Marys wear clerical copes and carry in their hands, not the spices men-tioned in the Gospels (*cum aromatibus*), but thuribles filled with incense. These garments and properties are not in the least 'realistic', rather they are symbolically suggestive in the manner of contemporary icons. Indeed the whole manner of the performance seems distinguished as little as possible from the 'office' in which it takes place. The historically imitative action (the three walk 'slowly . . casting about as if seeking something') accompanies the singing of a choral responsory in which the visit of the women is recalled. The seated figure addresses the others, singing 'in a dulcet voice of medium pitch':

> Quem queritis in sepulchro, o Christicole?

> (Whom seek ye in the sepulchre, O followers of Christ?)

They respond in unison, behaving here, as everywhere in the play, as if they were one person:

> Jesus of Nazareth, which was crucified, O heavenly one.

And the angel replies:

> He is not here; he is risen, as he foretold.
> Go and announce that he is risen from the dead.

Any sense of historical impersonation in the scene is now left aside, as the three turn themselves to the choir, announcing:

> Alleluia! The Lord is risen today!

The angel must now recall (*velut revocans*) the 'Marys' to show them proof of the resurrection, singing:

Come, and see the place where the Lord was laid. Alleluia! Alleluia!

If realism or representational cause and effect were the purpose here, the progression of events could scarcely be more ineptly handled. But they are not. The three figures have an office to fulfil that is more important than their role as historical Marys: they herald the joy of the resurrection and point to the visual tokens of that miracle.

The actors here are functional. They are less important than the symbolic and traditional tokens which they display. Just as the angel turns to the Marys, so the Marys turn to the clergy:

And saying this, let [the angel] rise, and let him lift the veil and show the place bare of the cross, but only the cloth laid there in which the cross had been wrapped. Seeing this, let them set down the censers they have carried to the sepulchre, and take up the cloth and spread it out before the eyes of the clergy; and, as if making known that the Lord had risen and was not now wrapped therein, let them sing this anthem:

> *Surrexit Dominus*, etc.

Between the historical scene of the gospels and this animated iconography lie centuries of formal ceremony attached to the Easter
sepulchre. The focus of the drama is not the human agents but the mysterious place where God has lain. The mystery is celebrated in a more
and more public manner: the winding cloth is placed upon the altar;
the prior then rejoices with (*congaudens*) the actors as both play and
office conclude in a single, communal, chant of rejoicing. The *Te Deum
laudamus* begins, the bells ring out, carrying the joy of the Easter
mystery beyond the monastery walls.

The sense of community is very strong throughout; all who witness
the play are assumed to anticipate the Easter miracle, to be intellect-
ually and emotionally prepared for the release of joy which the discovery brings. Indeed, they could make little sense of the stylized and
allusive action and dialogue unless they were so prepared. Even though
the play may be an innovation (in England at least) its story, its meaning and its 'style' are familiar to its congregation; without the sense of
shared belief it would be nothing. At every point the 'play' is attached
by fine threads to the customs of Easter worship.[9] It is precisely because
liturgical customs were shared so widely across Europe that the play
could be readily adopted and persist, in many places unchanged, for
centuries. As representational drama it may have been unsatisfactory,
but as the induction to a commemorative, communal experience, it
provided a profoundly satisfying emotional experience.

It is along these lines that I think one should look to understand
many of the meagre texts whose play action seems to have been conceived without any anachronistic notions of giving the 'audience' a
'show'. A *Visitatio* performed at an abbey of nuns at Origny Sainte-
Benoîte in about 1284 can scarcely have been seen or heard by the
original congregation (which included laity).[10] The performance takes
place within an Easter sepulchre of the basilica type. Two priests
representing angels remain within the sepulchre, expressly out of view
of the congregation, until the play and Matins are over. The 'Marys'
approach the sepulchre via a side altar where they collect reliquaries
('Magdelainne' apparently carries a lock of her own hair!). They are
accompanied by candlebearers and a cantor, who give them cues and
vocal pitch. The dialogue is sung across a closed door, the congregation hearing only the final loud 'He is not here; he is risen', from
within. The Marys and attendants enter the sepulchre and, behind the
closed door, deposit their relics on the altar there, taking up the grave
clothes instead. Returning to the body of the church, they show these

to the congregation, announcing the resurrection. The laity then file up to the door of the sepulchre and kiss the relics left there by the Marys and held by the sacristan. Here the play functions, as usual but more explicitly, as an induction to worship. The procession of clergy-actors serves as a model to be imitated by the congregation seeking for the same assurance.

The Origny play is performed, like many others, during Easter night; that is, *in anticipation of* the resurrection. Some writers have denied that these Easter night plays are ritual drama, possessing 'super-natural efficacy'.[11] In a play from Ripoll (c. 1100) the magical power of mimetic action is quite explicit.[12] It is performed during the Easter vigil and is connected through its language with the Blessing of New Fire. This ancient practice marks the turning point of the calendar with the symbolism of new light in darkness. The new fire kindled in five grains of incense (symbolic of Christ's wounds) lights a huge paschal candle which is borne in procession up the darkened church and hailed three times in a rising chant as the *lumen Christi*. The priests and deacons, and then the congregation, light candles from this source, until the whole church blazes with flames of faith witnessing the resurrection. In the Ripoll play, as the Marys walk towards the sepulchre, the leading figure explains the mystery of the Easter liturgy: the faithful shall see the Lord raised through the power of faith.

> Cordis, sorores, creduli
> simus et bene seduli,
> ut nostra cernant oculi
> corpus Christi, vim seculi.

(Let us be believing in our hearts, sisters, and fully eager in order that our eyes may see the body of Christ, the strength of the world.)

The Marys go to the tomb since they desire to rejoice (*ut poscimus gaudere / eamus tumbam videre*), and there they conjure the Lord to rise:

> Nostra, surge, surrexio!

(Rise for us, our resurrection!)

This remarkable incantation can best be understood as mimetic magic, intended to induce the yearly miracle.

The action itself is simple, though complex in its meaning. Past events are related lyrically to past, present and future. Thus the 'vision of splendour and brilliant ceremony' (*visio splendoris et lustracio*) that the first Mary promises her sisters refers beyond medieval celebration of the resurrection to an image of Christ's second coming. The one who has rolled away the stone is described as having 'the healing power of the celestial banquet' (*virtus celestis epuli*). Christ is the Bridegroom of his own parable of Judgment, awaited at midnight by the faithful, with burning lights. The symbolism of the Easter vigil links past and future in present action, and explains the wholly 'unnaturalistic' scene between the risen Christ and Mary Magdalene which follows.

The episode (*Hortulanus*) concerns Mary's grief at the missing body and her mistaking of Christ for the gardener. Yet her words are those of the bride of the *Song of Songs* lamenting for her princely lover who has vanished in the night, 'descended' into his garden-grave. Mary seeks him, going 'hither and thither', together with the watchmen (the Easter *vigiles*) so that she may anoint his precious body with perfumes and spices.

Maria

> Rex in acubitum iam se contulerat,
> Et me redolens nardus spiraverat;
> in hortum veneram in quem descenderat,
> at ille transiens iam declinaverat.
>
> Per noctem igitur hunc querens exeo;
> huc illuc transiens nusquam reperio.

Angelis

> Mulier, quid ploras? Quem queris?

Maria

> Occurrunt vigiles ardenti studio,
> Quos cum transierim, sponsum invenio.

Ortolanus

> Mulier, quid ploras? Quem queris?

Maria

> Tulerunt Dominum meum . . .etc.

(*Mary*

> The King had withdrawn himself to his couch
> and my nard had given forth its fragrance;
> in the garden I came, where he had gone down,
> but he had turned aside and gone.
>
> Through the night therefore I go seeking for him,
> seeking hither and thither I cannot find him.

Angels

> Woman, why weep you? Whom seek you?

Mary

    The watchers run forth with ardent longing.

    When I have overtaken these, I shall find my bridegroom.

Gardener

    Woman, why weep you? whom seek you?

Mary

    They have taken away my lord . . .)

The echoes of the *Song of Songs* (i, 11; vi, 12; v, 6–8) are unmistakable, and show this 'fragmentary and disordered text' as the work of an original poetic mind.[13] The mystic eroticism of the *Song*, traditionally allegorized as the relationship of Christ to his lover the Church (the female figure of Ecclesia), is delicately transformed in the Easter story. Old Testament 'history' is shown as a foreshadowing, a *figura* of events which are fulfilled in Christ's death and resurrection. Yet these events are also in themselves incomplete; and the drama, which celebrates so radiantly the joy of resurrection, points forward to the fulfilment of the divine plan in the second coming of the Bridegroom.

There is, of course, a narrative inconsistency, shared by almost all Easter plays, both Latin and vernacular, in showing Mary Magdalene as one of the three who proclaim the triumphant Easter message but immediately afterwards as the mourner in the garden. It derived from the conflation of two Gospel accounts of the resurrection, two testimonies to the same event. The inconsistency would matter only in a drama constructed upon principles of naturalistic time sequence. This is not. Like the liturgy, liturgical drama dissolves chronological time and celebrates events lyrically, in a simultaneous apprehension of them. The inconsistency in Mary Magdalene's role persists in later, more 'naturalistic' drama, such as the Chester and Cornish cycles (see below pp. 171–2) and illustrates the determining power of their liturgical model. The Easter play is the most interesting, because the most widespread and persistent of these 'original models' of dramatic form, but there were others and their importance can now be briefly considered.

Reduced to its simplest form the *Visitatio Sepulchri* play is an act of seeking, discovery and adoration. It was a model that could serve for a Christmas play too. The altar had long been associated in Christian worship with both sepulchre and manger, and the substitution of three shepherds for the three women and two apocryphal midwives for the angels guarding the holy place, completed the transposition.[14] The earliest Christmas dialogue, too, follows the Easter play, with the midwives asking *Quem queritis in presepe, pastores dicite?* ('Whom seek you in the manger shepherds, say?') and, receiving the reply *Salva-torem Christum Dominum*, indicating the place with *Adest hic parvulus* ('The little child is here.') The Shepherds' *Alleluia* completes the performance. Like the Easter play it serves as an induction to worship, and in the *Pastores* episode of the Christmas play in the so-called 'Fleury play-book', the shepherds rise from their knees to invite 'the people standing about' also to adore the infant, saying:[15]

> Venite, venite, venite, adoremus Deum.

The dramatic ceremonies in the Christmas liturgy are, according to Young, 'unexpectedly meagre'. The Latin Church made little use of the humble shepherds and preferred to give richness to the Christmas festivities by focusing on the story of the wise men and the star. Here again the essential action is a procession (the Magi coming together from different parts of the church and following a candelabrum-star drawn along a wire above them to the altar), a discovery and an adoration. The offerings that the Magi make are patterned upon those of the Mass, having the aura of 'office' rather than 'play'. For the sacerdotal offertory of the Epiphany Mass was accompanied in the tenth century by the antiphonal singing of verses telling of the offerings made by the Magi. The practice constituted, according to Young, 'a direct invitation to the clergy to transform their oblation into a scene representing the kings bringing their gifts to the manger at Bethlehem'.[16] This transformation is made in a twelfth-century play from Limoges which begins after the singing of the Epiphany offertory and before the actual oblation.[17] Three choristers standing for the three kings (*ad instar trium Regum*) enter the choir, each dressed in silken robes, wearing a gold crown and carrying a gilded *cyphum* (probably a communion vessel). They are both actors and chorus, singing a liturgical composition *O quam dignis celebranda* which narrates how 'Kings hasten from the East', to celebrate Christ's birth. Holding aloft their vessels, they indicate with an economy verging on the cryptic the symbolism of their gifts: gold for a king, incense for a divinity, myrrh denoting death.

> Primus dicit elevando Cyphum
>   I: Aurum primo
>   II: Thus secundo
>   III: Myrrham dante tertio
>   I: Aurum Regem
>   II: Thus caelestem
>   III: Mori notat unctio

In terms of the story action they have not yet noticed the star. As they reach the middle of the choir, one of them points to it and all sing, 'Lo, the sign of a great king . . . let us go search for him'. The words and music are selected from an antiphon in the Lauds of Epiphany. They make their offertory at the altar (apparently no attempt here at representing the crib scene). As they retire, a choirboy, 'standing for the angel', announces Christ's birth, at which they make gestures of wonder and withdraw to the sacristy, singing an antiphon.

The play and the Mass here modify and complement one another: the play relates the Mass to historical events, while the form and style of the offertory determine the form and style of the play's action. The Limoges pattern of highly formalized offering persists in much later and more popular drama, side by side with the rantings of Herod.

Among the early forms, one of the simplest and fewest in number but most influential is the *Ordo* or *Processio Prophetarum*. This differs from the forms discussed so far in having its source not in scriptural narrative and liturgical ceremony, but in sermon. Attributed to St Augustine, the *Sermon Against Jews, Pagans and Arians* consists of a string of witnesses to the Christian faith spoken by Old Testament and pagan figures, and introduced by the narrative formula 'Speak thou'. Whether the prophet-play originated via dramatic reading or representation of individual prophets or with the solo performance of the sibylline chant (the last of the prophecies in the *Sermo*) it embodies a very simple concept of drama: a mere procession of 'historical' figures.[18] The prophets have no relationship to one another; they are merely a row of icons pointing to Christ. A few iconographic features (a crown, a mitre, a flowering rod, a book) serve to identify them. Within the framework of the *Ordo* a few scenes were enlivened by providing the sole figures with antagonists: in the thirteenth-century Laon play, Balaam's contretemps with the ass is shown, using a boy as 'the voice beneath the ass'.[19] In the *Carmina Burana* Christmas play (*c.* 1200), the Jewish Archisynagogus disputes with St. Augustine, author of the *Sermo*.[20] In the *Mystère d'Adam* (*c.* 1160) Isaiah is challenged by an obstreperous Jew.[21] But the prophet-play in itself requires no action from its pageant of animated icons.

Similar in this respect is the eleventh-century *Ordo Rachelis* from Saint-Martial of Limoges.[22] As a celebration of the feast of Holy Innocents, this sung dialogue of Rachel and a consolatory angel might seem at first wholly unhistorical. The presence of this Old Testament mother, weeping and mourning for her children and who 'would not be comforted', is explained by St Matthew (ii, 18), who sees in Herod's massacre of Innocents the fulfilment of Jeremiah's prophecy. The slaughter itself is further distanced through the familiar words and chants of the liturgy. In the Matins of Innocents' Day, the lesson taken from the gospel was embellished by the singing of a responsory (a fairly elaborate chant, divided between soloist or solo group and the whole choir, and making use of repetition and recapitulation):

From beneath the altar of God I heard the voices of the slain: Wherefore didst thou not defend our blood? And they received the divine response: Remain here now for a little while, until you rejoin the company of your brethren. *Soloist:* I saw beneath the altar of God the souls of the blessed, for they had the word of God and cried out in a loud voice: Wherefore ... etc.

The singing of this purely liturgical piece begins the Limoges play. In its question and response are posed the complementary elements of human suffering and divine consolation later embodied in Rachel and the angel. Suffering is seen as ever-present in human history and this is why Rachel's lament from the Old Testament of the Jews contains gestures of grief associated with the Virgin at the Cross:

> Heu! michi misere!   cum possim vivere
> Cum natos coram me   video perdere?

> (Ah! Have pity on me! How can I live
> when I see my children perish before my eyes?)

The angel's consolation, 'Weep not, Rachel' is an assurance of ever-lasting life:

> Summi patris eterni filius,
> hic est ille quem querit perdere,
> qui vos facit eterne vivere.
>   Ergo gaudere!

> (The son of the everlasting father almighty,
> whom Herod seeks to destroy, is here
> and he makes you live for ever.
>   Therefore rejoice.)

In the turning of sorrow to joy the emotional pattern of the Easter reversal is imitated. The historical events in their human squalor and anguish scarcely enter this world, so utterly different from the grotesque pathos and savage knockabout of the Chester and Coventry plays, where the frantic mothers of the Innocents berate Herod's soldiers with obscenities—and kitchen implements (see below p. 181).

It is a world in which historical events are filtered through a prism of
liturgical practice, historical words patterned to chants 'associated with
the immemorial authority of the Church'.[23] Melodies, either borrowed
from the liturgy or modelled closely on Gregorian chant, impose an
atmosphere of restraint and calm, in which grosser human emotions
are purged and individual features fade, leaving types of eternity. The
actors in this liturgical drama are not required to mimic historical
persons, but to stand for them as icons, as aids to worship.

I have stressed the common elements in the simplest liturgical plays.
Although they lacked the generic self-consciousness and specifically
'theatrical' artistry of the more ambitious plays in the same tradition,
my examples all show how distinctive was the liturgical concept of
acting, how little indebted to any of the three secular traditions discussed earlier. The suggestion—made more than once by scholars
swimming against the mainstream—that the infiltration of *mimi* into
the monastic church was for the purpose of acting the *Visitatio Sepulchri*
is as absurd as it is groundless.[24]

My account of 'origins and traditions' is now at an end. The examples discussed have mostly been on a small scale, though this does
not imply that I think them insignificant as dramatic works. From
now on the plays themselves must take first place in the discussion,
while the historian of separate 'traditions' puts himself in the position
of an ideal audience to enjoy the sheer variety of the achievement of
early medieval plays.

PART II

The Achievement of Early Medieval Drama

PART II

The Achievement of
Early Medieval Drama

5

PLAYS IN LATIN

In looking for the best liturgical plays, chronology can be misleading. Many of the latest texts (from the fourteenth or fifteenth centuries) are briefest in scope and most 'primitive' in their means. Some, like the Passion week offices at Padua in the thirteenth, fourteenth and fifteenth centuries, seem to have remained without impersonated action during several centuries.[1] Others, complex and highly wrought as poetry and dramatic action, are among the earliest texts: two plays of *Daniel* (*c.* 1140), Hildegard of Bingen's *Ordo Virtutum* (*c.* 1155), the Tegernsee *Ludus de Antichristi* (*c.* 1160), the Montecassino *Passio* (*c.* 1160), the *Carmina Burana* Christmas and Easter plays (*c.* 1200). The macaronic *Sponsus*, which makes extensive use of Provençal vernacular, can be dated well within the eleventh century. By the early thirteenth century all the greatest of the extant liturgical dramas had been composed and the most creative period of medieval Latin poetry was over. Many factors contributed to the remarkable diversity: varying liturgical practice on different feast days in different communities, the availability of musical, literary and dramatic models, rivalry, and the encouragement of patronage or a known audience. In this chapter I have chosen to illustrate four kinds of achievement within the liturgical tradition. The *Herod* and *Rachel* plays from the 'Fleury playbook' are the product of a monastic and conservative skill. The two *Daniel* plays belong to a more experimental poetic world of wandering scholars and of cathedral schools in northern France. In the *Antichristus* liturgical traditions are expanded and modified in order to treat contemporary politics in the Imperial court. Finally, Hildegard's *Ordo Virtutum* takes us into the world of a cloistered nun, a poetess with an intensely original vision of the psychological struggle of Christian faith. This, the earliest of all known morality plays, has no apparent connection with the liturgy of a particular day, but in its manner of presenting dramatic action and in its musical style it depends upon the more orthodox liturgical tradition of drama.

Monastery: the 'Fleury playbook' 'Herod' and 'Rachel'

These two thirteenth-century plays are the most extensive treatments of their subjects anywhere in the Latin drama.[2] Textually and musically they are mosaics, combining liturgical elements with innovations made by dramatists in northern France and Germany over more than a century, into a wonderfully coherent whole. A musical idiom that is essentially Gregorian in its 'fundamental restraint and economy' and its tendency to melodic progression by step up or down and not by emotive leaps serves to hold even the most striking composition (such as the *planctus* of Rachel) within a known aesthetic.[3]

Amidst the liturgical antiphons, Vulgate narrative, occasional Virgilian quotations and frequent lyrical set-pieces which make up the text, the 'cores' of three simple dramatic roles already discussed are evident: the shepherds' visit to the manger; the procession and offertory of the Magi; Rachel's lament and consolation. The 'Fleury' *Herod* begins with the shepherds making their visit to a manger 'set up at the doors of the monastery'. The three men act and sing as one during their dialogue with the midwives. When they have made their own silent adorations, they turn 'to the people standing round about' and, as has already been mentioned, invite them, priest-like, to worship. The Magi are similarly a triad, whose individuality extends only to their entering from separate corners of the church. At their meeting they exchange a kiss of peace in ceremonial fashion ('the one in the middle to the left and the one on the left to his right') together with the monastic formula *Pax tibi, frater*. Each must show the star (*Ecce stella!*) to the others. When they have made their offerings, traditionally formal, they return to their places in the choir, urging their fellows: *Gaudete fratres, Christus nobis natus est*; then the cantor leads the *Te Deum*.

Within this framework of 'office', the action concerning Herod is considerably developed through the ceremonial use of an armiger (squire or arms bearer) and various interpreters. The armiger greets the kings in the words of Evander's son to Aeneas (*Aen.* VIII, 112):

Que rerum novitas, aut que causa subegit vos
Ignotas temptare vias? Quo tenditis ergo?
Quo genus? Unde domo? Pacemne huc fertis an arma?

(What strange events or what motive has compelled you
to try unknown paths? Where, then, are you going?
From what people? Where is your home? Do you bring here peace or
war?)

His master Herod speaks Virgilian language, too. The issuing of commands, accompanied by ceremonial entrances and exits to repeat them,
forms the basis of action at Herod's court. This pompous and unneces-
sary to-ing and fro-ing is evidently a dramatic end sought in itself, for
it complicates and slows down the plot (courtiers are sent, for instance,
to summon scribes to bring the books of prophecy, instead of Herod
calling for them himself). And there is little concern for dramatic consistency, for, once the books have been shown to Herod, the relevant
prophecy ('Thou Bethlehem art not the least among the princes of
Judah') never passes his lips, but is sung instead by the monastic choir.
Herod's unfitness to mouth the divine word is further emphasized by
his mimic hurling of the book to the floor in a fury which has no set
lines and may require *ex tempore* acting. Four centuries before Hamlet's
scorn for bombast which 'out-Herods Herod' a Catalan writer, familiar with such a spectacle, coined the Latin phrase *ne Herodidemus
Herodem*.

The most striking intrusion into the biblical sequence of events
comes at this point, with the offer of Herod's son, Archelaus, to fight
against this 'baby king'. This strophic composition, used in an earlier
play from Rouen, has a strongly accentual rhythm and is set to a vigorous masculine melody:

Salve, pater inclite,
Salve, Rex egregie,
qui ubique imperas,
sceptra tenens regia.

(Hail, renowned father.
Hail illustrious King,
who rulest everywhere,
bearing the royal sceptre.)

Herod replies, *Fili amantissime*, using the same form and melody. There
is no question of naturalism here; it is rather a musical icon of worldly
power and energy. The scene ends, as abruptly as it began, with

Herod's dismissal of the Magi, in which the recitative style of composition is resumed for lines which follow closely St Matthew's gospel. As the Magi process towards the crib to begin their antiphonal dialogue with the returning shepherds, Herod and his son lapse into mimic gestures, brandishing their swords threateningly. The directions specify that the star shall not appear in his sight. Sacred history simply passes him by, as a strong sense of communal worship is finally established in the traditional words and music of the offertory. The Magi return to their places in the choir and all join in the *Te Deum*.

The same manuscript continues with directions for a play about the Innocents. The two plays were probably not performed consecutively; in fact, the slaying was probably played earlier (on Innocents' Day, 28 December) than the Magi (Epiphany, 6 January). This 'illogicality' (in terms of story) is a useful warning against applying the wrong criteria of judgment to the drama which follows, for the action is presented without regard to the demands of causal relationships in time. The opening rubrics say:

For the slaying of the children, let the Innocents [they are apparently choristers of the church] be clothed in white garments and, going about rejoicing through the monastic church, let them pray to God.

Their song ('O, how glorious is the Kingdom') is an antiphon of Vespers for the vigil of All Saints. The company of little saints is joined suddenly (*ex inproviso*) by the Lamb, a figure *portans crucem* (a person bearing a cross, or an emblem of a lamb with a cross attached to it, borne by an officiant) who processes before them. They call upon God to 'send forth the Lamb' to the mount of the daughters of Sion.

This sequence, which begins the historical action, is from the end of time: the Innocents are figures of the Apocalypse, the 144,000 virgins who 'follow the Lamb whithersoever he goeth' (Rev. xiv, 4) singing a 'new song' of joy, the song of the undefiled. In the sight of heaven their martyrdom (which has yet to be acted out) is cause for rejoicing. Their historical suffering is also shown, but within a double perspective. In fact the person of Christ is doubly represented in this drama—as the doll or child carried by Mary into Egypt and as the processional Lamb. The historical action unfolds simultaneously or alternately with a representation of its eternal meaning. In the rubrics, the repeated use of *interim* (meanwhile) indicates a use of the church playing space as truly 'simultaneous'.

Herod's throne is central in the church, well below the choir. While the procession of the Lamb continues about the inside perimeter, the armiger salutes Herod, offering him his sword with the words, 'He shall sit upon the throne of David and reign over his kingdom for ever, alleluiah'. Jeremiah's prophecy places for us this false icon of kingship. Meanwhile, in a third part of the church, the holy family, warned by an angel 'above' leaves the manger, proceeding through the church so that they do not pass Herod's throne. Joseph's song, 'Egypt weep no more', is a responsory from the Advent season foretelling the coming of the Lord of Lords 'before whose countenance hell shall tremble'. This is juxtaposed at once with the armiger's formula of praise of King Herod, *Rex in aeternum vive!*, as he announces the return of the Magi. Herod seizes a sword, preparing to slay himself, but is restrained. Meanwhile the Innocents continue their processional singing. At the armiger's proposal Herod orders the slaughter, handing him his sword. The two separate groups of action now converge with the slayers giving chase about the church. As they approach, the Lamb is secretly withdrawn from the procession of Innocents who hail him (*Salve Agnus Dei*) as he departs.

The slaying now takes place below the entrance to the choir and is mimed to the accompaniment of the intercessions of the mothers, a single line sung to a haunting melody which moves in seconds and fourths in a distinctly unliturgical manner:

> Oremus, tenere natorum parcite vite.

> (We pray you spare the tender lives of our babies.)

But this is the extent of suffering, and death is not dwelt upon. Instead, the play conventions (which will shortly allow the fallen children to get to their feet) are exploited: an angel from above calls upon the victims to rouse themselves and lift up their voices. The boys reply with the verse 'Why didst thou not defend us?' from the Epiphany liturgy, and the angel completes the 'divine response', telling them to 'remain here a little while until you rejoin the company of your brethren'. This 'little while' is literally enacted before the Innocents rise and take their places as choristers in the choir.

Before they rise, Rachel is brought in with two consolers, to stand over the children and mourn them. The exquisite dialogue which follows is one of the wonders of medieval melodic art. Rachel's rhetorically patterned Leonine hexameters, with their intricate repetition and variation of melodic phrase, their melismatic 'arpeggio' settings of 'O' disturb the normal musical idiom of emotional calm. John

Stevens, while stressing the 'general atmosphere of musical order' in the play, writes of one phrase of the *planctus*:[4]

If this does not, in the context, make us catch our breath with its bold strides across the octave, then we are not properly attuned to the melodic norms of the play.

Rachel's voice is answered by those of her two consolers, singing first in the same Leonine hexameters, then lines from Notker's famous tenth-century sequence:

> Quid tu virgo,
> mater Rachel, ploras formosa,
> cuius vultus Iacob delectat?

(Why do you weep, Rachel, virgin mother, lovely in your sorrow, you in whose countenance Jacob delights?)

Binding the dialogue together is a haunting four-note refrain taken up from the last four notes (*parcite vite*) of the mother's intercession. While there may be more 'expressiveness' intended here than Stevens admits (the consolers 'support Rachel as she falls', and later 'she falls upon the children'), his argument is surely right: that the suffering is presented 'in as stylized and generalized a form as can be'. Rachel's final lament, 'My spirit is troubled within me' is from an antiphon of Lauds on Good Friday and identifies her sorrows iconographically with those of the *mater dolorosa*. As she is led away, Christ's own words, 'Suffer the little children to come unto me', are sung by the angel. The children rise and enter the choir singing joyfully.

Simultaneous with this joyous procession of the youthful army of the blessed, the death of Herod and his son's accession are mimed. Then Joseph and Mary are summoned to return, proceeding through the church before withdrawing to a place signifying Galilee. As they go, Joseph sings an antiphon from the feast of the Assumption, *Gaude, gaude, gaude, Maria virgo*. The play ends with the communal *Te Deum*.

Sacred history is here dissolved from its chronological ties and receives the shape of things to come, foreseen in the divine plan since the beginning of time. The Old Testament Rachel finds her true meaning as the *virgo mater*, mourning the Innocents; they in turn find theirs in the worship of the Lamb of the Apocalypse, whose sacrifice and resurrection they anticipate. In the last of a series of subtle and beautiful transitions, Joseph's consolation of the Virgin is shown to encompass the joy which follows the crucifixion. It is precisely because the playwright works with traditional materials, mindful of their associations and emotional power, that the drama can embody for its congregation an assurance of the total meaning of human life and death. What more could it do?

Cathedral school: the Beauvais 'Ludus Danielis'

The heading of the 'Fleury playbook' text, *Incipit ordo ad represent-andum Herodem*, epitomizes the double aspect of the conservative monastic drama: it is a liturgical *ordo* or ceremony, closely related in many matters of content and style to the liturgy itself; it is also a representation, making use of mime and, in the action surrounding Herod's court, of techniques to elaborate a sumptuous spectacle. In contrast, the two plays of the Christmas season based on the story of Daniel are described respectively as *historia* and *ludus*. These terms link the compositions with secular scholarship and revelry.

The shorter play, whose text has no musical notation, is attributed to Hilarius (a 'wandering scholar', probably an Englishman, who studied under Abelard before 1125), helped by three fellow poets: Jordanus, Simon and Hugo.[5] Whereas the monastic *ordines* are anonymous, the names of these authors are important enough to record. (Hilarius's other compositions include not only three more plays, 'student songs', verse-letters to women and boys, but a verse autobiography.) The sung dedication to the longer play of Daniel tells that it was composed in Christ's honour by the young men of Beauvais cathedral school.[6] In the Beauvais manuscript are also two thirteenth-century settings of the famous 'Prose of the Ass' associated with the clerical revels at the Feast of Circumcision (1 January). This parodic office, known as the 'Feast of Fools' or 'Feast of the Ass', involved the procession of an ass through the west door of Beauvais cathedral and up the nave, escorted by canons bearing wine bottles and glasses, while the censing for the service was done with black puddings and sausages.[7] Not all ass-processions were so bizarre as this and there are no signs of asininity in the Beauvais *Daniel*. Nevertheless, the auspices of the New Year revels give some richness to the term *ludus* which is used to describe the play.

At this point a plot summary may be helpful. Both the Hilarius and the Beauvais plays follow chs. v and vi of the Book of Daniel, giving roughly equal weight to the story of Belshazzar's feast (Daniel's de-ciphering of the mysterious handwriting) and of Darius's imprison-ment of Daniel in the lions' den. At the beginning of the Beauvais play the plot is narrated in outline by the chorus. After a ceremonial entrance, Belshazzar calls for the gold vessels plundered from the

temple in Jerusalem by his father Nebuchadnezzar. These are brought
by courtiers. A hand appears, writing upon the wall three words that
the court and Magi cannot decipher. The queen, entering in procession,
urges that Daniel be sent for. He too enters ceremoniously attended;
he prophesies the downfall of Belshazzar's hubristic and blasphemous
kingdom and is elevated to a place of honour. Darius, king of Medes
and Persians, enters with his army and, in a swift reversal, expels
Belshazzar from the throne, killing him and taking his place. Daniel is
honoured but, returning to his own house, worships the god of Israel.
At the urging of envious counsellors, Darius condemns Daniel to the
lions, where an angel defends him. An apocryphal scene inserted here
shows an angel leading Habakkuk from his fields to bring a reaper's
dinner to feed Daniel. After his release from the lions' den, Daniel
praises the god of Israel and the envious counsellors are consumed by
the lions. Daniel prophesies the coming of the Holy of Holies, and both
the plays end with the sudden appearance of an angel announcing
Christ's birth.

This story (unlike the stories of the Easter sepulchre, the offering of
the Magi, the crossing of the Red Sea, the expulsion from Paradise)
apparently formed no part of any liturgical ceremony; indeed, the use
of the terms *historia* and *ludus*, instead of *ordo*, corroborate this. In the
plays themselves the absence of precise liturgical models is felt both
textually and musically. Neither play uses a liturgical choir (the chor-
uses are costumed attendants); proses and antiphons are absent, and
there is almost no plainchant. The texts are almost entirely composed
in metrical and rhymed strophes. In the Beauvais play, more than fifty
melodies, distributed roughly according to the principle 'new speaker,
new tune', seem to require mensural interpretation. 'Dance-like
measures' and 'highly organized melodies of the troubadour type' are
evident in what William Smoldon has described as a 'treasure house
of secular music'.[8] A variety of instrumental accompaniment is
assumed for the songs. The sense of splendour and pomp which informs the literary style of the compositions is reflected in the staging
demands that each king must enter *cum pompa sua*. Costumes are lavish
(Daniel is dressed 'in the most elegant clothes') and rich vessels are
carried in procession for Belshazzar's feast. Although the two plays are
to be performed in church (at either Matins or Vespers) the church
space is not used symbolically, but according to representational con-
venience. A single centrally placed throne serves for both kings; there
is a *lacus* for the lions (presumably a cage-house as in manuscript

illuminations, rather than a pit) and in the Beauvais play a 'house' for Daniel, in which he prays to the god of Israel, and a temple to which the vessels are carried. Stage effects include the sudden appearance of a hand, writing on the wall. In Hilarius's play this is 'over the king's head', perhaps above the canopy of his throne. There is also a battle, in which two of Darius's soldiers expel Belshazzar from his throne 'as if to kill him'. The lions have mouths which open, closing at the intervention of the angel in Hilarius's play, and the actors who play them are required, presumably with the help of masks, to devour the envious counsellors.

All these features suggest an approach to the story as material for representation *in play*. But a closer study of the ambitious Beauvais play will suggest the limits of its representational method and its common purpose with the central conservative tradition of liturgical drama.

As is usual in the liturgical drama, the sense of the present suffuses 'history' and the Old Testament story of the overthrow of Babylonian kingdoms is moulded into celebration of the coming of Christ. Daniel himself is the key figure in this transformation. His importance for medieval Christianity was two-fold: as a prophet of the Messiah he had appeared in the eleventh-century Limoges *Ordo Prophetarum* to testify that 'the anointing of earthly kings shall cease' (*Cum venerit Sanctus Sanctorum, cessabit unctio*).[9] Secondly, his own experiences prefigured those of Christ and his delivery from the lions' den was seen as foreshadowing Christ's resurrection from the tomb and the pit of hell. In the play, Daniel's power of prophecy is praised to both kings; he is the *Vir propheta Dei*. His importance is celebrated in a splendid *conductus* (processional song) accompanying his approach to the throne of Darius. The piece, *Congaudentes celebramus* is not ascribed to any of the persons of the play and does not 'fit' any of them; it may have been sung by the whole company. It exalts Daniel's deeds as *figurae* of Christmas:

> Congaudentes celebramus   natalis sollempnia;
> Iam de morte nos redemit   Dei sapientia.
> Homo natus est in carne.   qui creavit omnia,
> Nasciturum quem predixit   prophete facundia.
> Danielis iam cessavit   unctionis copia;
> Cessat regni Judeorum   contumax potentia.
>   In hoc natalitio,
>   Daniel, cum gaudio
>   te laudat hec concio.

Tu Susannam liberasti   de mortali crimine,
Cum te Deus inspiravit   suo sancto flamine.
Testes falsos comprobasti   reos accusamine.
Bel draconem peremisti   coram plebis agmine.
Et te Deus observavit   leonum voragine.
Ergo sit laus Dei verbo   genito de virgine   (270–84)

(Rejoicing together, let us celebrate the solemnity of the Nativity;
for the wisdom of God redeems us from death.
He who created all things is born in flesh,
whose birth was foretold in the words of the prophet.
Through [according to ?] Daniel the plenteous anointing has now ceased,
the insolent power of the reign of Jews ceases.
On this Christmas Day,
with joy, Daniel,
this company praises you.
You freed Susanna from a mortal slander
when God breathed into you his sacred flame;
you proved her accusers false, guilty in their accusation.
You overcame the dragon Bel before a multitude of people
and God watched over you in the lions' den.
So praise be to the Word of God, who was born of a Virgin.)

At the end of the play, after his deliverance and reinstatement, Daniel
delivers his prophecy of the coming of the Holy of Holies. Then, suddenly (*ex inproviso*) an angel appears, announcing the birth of Christ in
the words of a hymn:

Nuntium vobis fero de supernis:
natus est Christus, Dominator, orbis,
in Bethleem Iude, sic enim Propheta
dixerat ante.   (389–92)

(I bring you word from on high:
Christ is born, Lord of the earth,
in Bethlehem of Judah, as the prophet
told before.)

Hearing this, the choirmen begin the *Te Deum*. These two pieces—the
conductus and the angelic announcement—explicitly frame the represented story.

This is a drama of Christ the King, as Glynne Wickham has noted.[10]
Babylonian and Persian rulers of the Old Testament serve as antitypes
in a prelude to Christmas. The Christmas theme of the *conductus* contrasts sharply with the words in which Daniel addresses King Darius

when he arrives at the throne: *Rex, in aeternum vive*! Within the Christmas context the joyous revelry of Belshazzar's feast and the sumptuous pride of Darius's kingdom are elaborated as the regalia of pagan kingdoms. The dancing, clapping of hands and plucking of stringed instruments of which the Satraps sing as they praise Belshazzar are the prelude to a fall:

> Ridens plaudit Babylon,
> Jerusalem plorat.

(Babylon rejoices laughing, Jerusalem weeps and will weep again.)

A glorious harmony of sound and dancing (*tripudio*) heralds the approach of Darius, too:

> Simul omnes gratulemur;   resonet et tympana,
> Cythariste tangant cordas;   musicorum organa
>   resonant ad eius preconia   (243–5)

> (Let us all give thanks together; let the tympany sound,
>   the harp players pluck their strings, and instruments of the musicians
>   resound in praise of him.)

and one can be fairly sure that instruments were used. This musical splendour is not merely the pagan reverie of humanist scholars, though; for familiarity with Psalm 150 would have allowed the congregation to see here a sound fitting to Christmas solemnity too.

The kingship of Belshazzar and Darius is insisted on by the reiterated use of the formula of salutation *Rex, in aeternum vive*! Unlike the other pieces in the play this is always sung, fanfare-like, to the same melody. It is repeated four times for each of the kings, accompanied, one may suppose, by ceremonial gestures of homage. This extreme stylization is deliberate, for Belshazzar and Darius are not individuals but types. They have no personal characteristics (though Belshazzar has a queen): they occupy the same throne, each surrounded by princes and musicians. When Belshazzar falls, he falls alone, and Darius inherits his court.

The formalism of the play is not confined to structure and processional movements. Brief directions to the actors show that a statuesque, monumental style of acting is required. Why else would the rubricator say that King Belshazzar should 'open his mouth' before singing for the first time or that, when the queen offers him counsel, 'he should turn his face towards her'? The norm against which such emotions as stupefaction are portrayed must be one of monumental immobility of body and facial expression. Some of the stage action, though, strikes a modern viewer as almost pantomimic—for instance, Habakkuk diverted to carry his dinner to Daniel in the lions' den by an angel who 'draws him by his hair'. The iconographic gesture, by which the apocryphal aerial spirit stoops to show his divinity, is repeated without the slightest hint of comedy by a play angel whose feet are planted firmly on the ground.

The analogy with visual art is a useful one on which to conclude this brief discussion of a play whose dramatic and musical merits have been amply recognized by critics and modern directors. Despite its ceremonial movements and the change of cast at half-time, the play is static. Two massive tableaux of kingship succeed one another, almost in diptych fashion, separated only by the brief mime of Belshazzar's deposition. Each tableau is a setting for the acts of Daniel which occupy the foreground: the interpretation of the handwriting on the wall is balanced by the episode of the lions' den. The key to the meaning of this great gilded double panel with its stiff romanesque figures is provided by a presiding angel who appears, as it were, through a little window opening onto the spectacle to announce the birth of Christ.

Imperial court: 'Ludus de Antichristo'

For its sheer physical scope if nothing else, the Tegernsee *Antichrist* merits attention. Its scene is the whole of the known world, and its apocalyptic action sets forth the realization of an ideal Christian kingdom under the protection of the Holy Roman Emperor, followed by the reign of Antichrist, preparatory to the end of the world. Karl Young described the play as 'the best literary product of German ecclesiastical life in the twelfth century'.[11] Its auspices are not exactly known, but its milieu is the court of the Emperor Frederick Barbarossa. It seems likely that the play was performed before Frederick himself in the year 1160 to urge him to realize his ambition of becoming emperor of the East and West and military defender of Christendom.[12] It suggests that any abdication from this destiny would leave the Church defenceless, an open prey to the forces of Antichrist. As we shall see, the meaning of the apocalyptic action only makes complete sense as the manifestation of imperial chauvinism and polemic at a particular historical moment.

In its theme and dramatic method the *Antichrist* occupies middle ground between Church and State. Since the ninth century the legends of Antichrist had been inextricably connected with the Germano-Frankish conflict over the power of the Holy Roman Emperor. They offered a means through which contemporary events and secular ideals could receive the sanction of a place within divine history.

The legend of Antichrist originates in the Book of Daniel (chs. vii–xii) with the dreams concerning the overthrow of kingdoms and the appearance of a king claiming to be God. In medieval legend two strands of the original were developed, the first relating to the 'personal' life and miracles of Antichrist, the second to the identity of the last emperor of East and West under whom the world would be united for Christ before the coming of Antichrist. These legends, kept alive by a general interest in 'the pursuit of the millennium', were used more specifically as propaganda in the intermittent conflict between emperor and pope which followed the reign of Charlemagne.[13] The last emperor was variously identified as Constantine (returned from the dead to avenge the murder of his son), Charlemagne or Henry IV. Frederick I thought of himself as last emperor and either the French king or the anti-imperial pope as Antichrist. (Much later, half the world thought of Frederick II as the Antichrist.) The legends of Antichrist were drawn together by Adso, writing his *Libellus de Antichristo* for Queen Gerberga of France towards the end of the tenth century, and this book provided the basic story matter for the great Germanic play.

Frederick I's attempt to recreate the imperial role first attributed to Augustus is well known. He received the imperial crown from the pope in Rome (as Charlemagne had done) in 1155. His encouragement of the study of Roman law (with its crucial emphasis on the legal power of the emperor's word) in Germany and northern Italy met with criticism, but he appeared at the famous diet of Roncagla in 1158 flanked by Roman lawyers who upheld his imperial prerogatives by reference to Justinian's corpus of Roman civil law. This paraphernalia was marshalled in support of military ambition, and its legalistic bias is reflected in the play.

When, following the death of Adrian IV, the cardinals could not decide on his successor and struggled (literally) in a tug-of-war with the papal *pallium*, imperial soldiers routed the convocation. Frederick summoned a council and declared his own pope Octavian (Victor IV). But in July 1160 Henry II of England and Louis VII met and decided to support Alexander III.

The play's version of this situation is coloured by a good deal of Teutonic wish-fulfilment. The emperor triumphs over the 'heretical' king of Franks, and the 'pope' sits meekly by the imperial throne, never opening his lips. The emperor gains sovereignty over the Greeks (Byzantium) and fulfils the intention of liberating Jerusalem from the heathen which had haunted the real Emperor Frederick since the dismal failure of the second crusade (1147–9). Having become the last great emperor of East and West, the play hero then surrenders his crown and imperial regalia to God at the Temple in Jerusalem, returning home as king of Teutons. Unprotected, the Church now falls to Antichrist. The second half of the play inverts the pattern of the first, showing until the very end the world apparently won for Antichrist. By means of this double structure the imperial ideal is contrasted with its parody: the emperor, who alone can protect Ecclesia from Antichrist, and the Antichrist himself, described by Ecclesia at the end of the play as 'the man who made not God his strength'.

In the shaping of the material from Adso one may perhaps see the influential historical thinking of Frederick's uncle, Otto, bishop of Freising. Otto himself died in 1158, leaving unfinished his idealizing biography of his nephew, *Gesta Frederici*. But the influence of his earlier *Chronica de Duabus Civitatibus* was considerable.[14] The chronicle shows all human history as continuous conflict between good and evil, with the cycles of civilization forming periods of stability between conflict. The seven cycles of earth's history culminate in a prophecy of the reign of Antichrist in Book 8. In the regular patterning of the action of the play, in the ceremonies of vassalage which reestablish peaceful order after battle, the same logical and exemplary habit of mind is at work. A disciplined formalism controls the structure and all aspects of staging and performance.

The symmetry already noted in the overall shape and the conflict of opposites that is the essence of the theme are reflected in the manuscript directions for staging. A very large area (not necessarily in church) is required for more than sixty actors and for seven 'thrones' (that of the emperor has room for the pope and clergy, Ecclesia, Justice, Mercy, and the imperial army) and the Temple of Jerusalem. To the East are the Temple, the throne of Jerusalem and a place for Synagoga. To the West the *imperium*, the throne of the Teutons (vacant until after the emperor resigns his greater dignity) and that of the Franks. To the South are the thrones of Babylon (with the doctrinal figure of Gentilitas) and of the Greeks.[15] The opposition of *imperium* and Temple (where Antichrist later sets up his throne) is built into the spatial arrangement.

In a processional prologue each of the kings enters with his army sing-ing 'whatever seems suitable' (it is not clear whether this means hymns in honour of national saints or military marching songs). Their rivalry is expressed in the doctrinal assertions of the three female figures symbolizing their faiths, Church, Synagogue and Paganism. When all are enthroned, the 'first act' begins with the emperor's demand of homage and an oath of fealty from the kings of Franks, Greeks and Jerusalem. One battle is fought (in which the Franks are defeated by the imperial army) and three ceremonies of homage performed by the vassal kings. As soon as peace and order have been established, 'when the whole church is subject to the Roman Emperor', strife breaks out again. The uprising of the king of Babylon begins the second 'act'. The king of Jerusalem, attacked by the Babylonian heathen, sends to the *imperium* for help. After defeating the Babylonians, the emperor abdicates, resigning his crown, sceptre and imperial dignities to God in the Temple at Jerusalem, and returning West as king of Teutons. Ecclesia is instated supreme but unprotected at Jerusalem.

This pattern is then repeated with Antichrist as the protagonist. A second choral altercation of the three doctrinal figures forms the pre-lude to the entry of Antichrist and his Hypocrites. They depose the king of Jerusalem, enthroning Antichrist in the Temple. Ecclesia flees to the pope at the *imperium*. The scene has now been reset for the major conflicts. In the third 'act', mirroring the first, there are three demands for homage and one battle. Antichrist sets his mark, a red A, on the foreheads of the French and Greek kings; he is resisted in battle by the Teutons, but convinces them with his miracles of resurrection. With the submission of the king of Teutons, the cycle is again complete.

Conflict is renewed, following the pattern of the second act. The king of Teutons, now bearing the sword of Antichrist, defeats the Babylonians in battle and smashes their idol, sending their king to do homage to Antichrist. The reception of Synagoga by Antichrist at Jerusalem completes his triumph. The final act provides the climax and reversal. The prophets Enoch and Elijah denounce Antichrist and unveil Synagoga, who confesses her error. She and the prophets are killed. As Antichrist calls together all his subjects, thunder strikes and he collapses in ruin, leaving them to be welcomed back by Ecclesia.

Formalism in the structure of episodes is enforced by the repetition of songs, restating principal themes and emphasizing key ideas: the world as a Roman fief (*fiscus Romanorum*), the obligations of tribute (*tributum*), doing homage and swearing fealty (*hominium cum fidelitate*), the supremacy of the emperor's law (*ius regale*), and so on. The literary text, mostly rhymed couplets, and a mosaic of quotation or paraphrase from biblical sources (chiefly Psalms, Proverbs, Revelations) is in general not distinguished. Depending on the extent of repetitions there are only about four hundred lines. Yet the play itself would probably take well over two hours to perform, for action is its essence. There are four battles of national armies, as well as Antichrist's casual slaughters, six ceremonies of feudal homage, an abdication, a coronation, a dethronement, and numerous embassies posting to and fro across the vast set.

As we saw earlier, battle was the principal model of action in the pagan dramatic tradition of the Germanic countries. The Gothic warriors' play performed at the Byzantine court anticipates the *Antichrist* by two centuries in combining a traditional form of entertainment with Christian celebration and imperial flattery. About the actual staging of the battles in the *Antichrist* the normally explicit stage directions are cryptic: the armies may 'rush together' or simply 'join battle' (*concurrunt et preliantur*). Vigour is implied, and the clashing of weapons is among the complaints made by Gerhoh of Reichersberg in his account of church plays in the *De Investigatione Antichristi*. But whether strenuous improvisation was required, or whether some traditional ballet-like manoeuvres were used, such as those of the Gothic Christmas play or of Captain Cox's play of the Massacre of Danes, remains speculation.

The 'ceremonies of peace' in the play are not explicit either, but depend upon the established feudal conventions of movement and gesture which were contemporary practice at the imperial court. When the seated emperor accepts the kings of Franks, Greeks and Jerusalem as his homagers, a strict form is implied. The usual form of ceremony was for the vassal to kneel, bare-headed and weaponless, and to place his clasped hands between the hands of his lord, who closed his own hands over them. In the play these ceremonies also involve the surrender and return of the vassal's crown, with the formula 'Live through my grace and receive honour' (*Vive per gratiam et suscipe honorem*). The feudal forms of ceremonial action are mingled with forms inherited from strict liturgical tradition. As the emperor prepares battle to relieve Jerusalem, an angel appears 'suddenly' and sings the words of responsory, 'Judea and Jerusalem, fear not', repeated at once by a choir. But the feudal ceremonies were themselves thoroughly 'liturgicized' in the twelfth century. Ernst Kantorowicz

describes in his *Laudes Regiae* how, in the coronation, the handling of
the royal insignia, ring, sword, sceptre, orb, the donning of almost
every coronation garment 'became subject to the rites of the Church'.[16]
The emperor of the play resigns his power by taking off his crown and
laying it together with his sceptre and imperial regalia before the altar
in the temple of Jerusalem. Acknowledging that God is the *solus
imperator*, the 'king of kings through whom all kings reign', he offers
up his tokens of kingship and places them upon the altar. The act
simultaneously qualifies and vindicates the hierarchy of feudal power
which the ideal set out in the play assumes.

As in the more conservative liturgical drama the figures as well as
their actions are ritualized, they have no 'personal' qualities. Their
essential functions are conveyed by iconographic means: a crown and
sceptre for a king, a sword and balance for Justitia, a bottle of oil for
Misericordia, a blindfold on the eyes of Synagoga, ignorant of the
truth of Christianity. The deception practised by Antichrist and his
followers is symbolized by their wearing robes over battle gear. Mime
is used almost exclusively by Antichrist's followers: 'the Hypocrites
enter, bowing their heads in every direction in a show of humility, and
capture the favour of the laity'. The miracles of Antichrist are also performed as dumbshows. In this respect, the Tegernsee *Antichristus* differs
radically from the later vernacular plays of Antichrist. The *laude* from
Perugia (*c.* 1260), *Le jour du jugement* (*c.* 1390) and the fifteenth-century
Chester play all show the miracles of Antichrist as the principal action.[17]
The German playwright's preference for public battles and ceremonies reflects both the interests of his courtly audience and, I suggest,
the bias of a Germanic tradition older than that of the drama of the
liturgy.

The two traditions can be seen most clearly to cooperate in the final
sequence of action, the death of Synagoga and the collapse of Antichrist. First, the dramatist shows the conversion of Synagoga. As the
prophets strip the veil from her eyes, she sings, 'We were seduced in
truth, by Antichrist' and gives praise to the 'King of glory and three-
personed God'. Whilst she and the prophets are put to death for their
faith, Ecclesia sings in mourning these strange words:

Fasciculus mirre dilectus meus mihi   (401)

The line is from the bride in the *Song of Songs*, 'A bundle of myrrh is
my well-beloved to me'. Medieval interpreters saw in the bundle of
myrrh a symbol of Christ's crucified body held against his mother's

breast, the dead body from which the Church is to be born. In the death of Synagoga and the prophets we are reminded of Christ's Passion, the sacrifice destroying the power of the princes of darkness. The fall of Antichrist follows immediately, as he summons all his people about him:

> Ad coronam vocat suos deus deorum   (407)
>
> (The God of gods calls his people into a ring.)

I have argued earlier that this final spectacular gesture may, for a German audience, have identified Antichrist with the bogey-man of folk combat play, the Sterkader of the Lübeck text, champion over Kaiser Karl, who at the end is encircled by the warrior kings and disappears magically from their midst. The *corona* has also a symbolic meaning, recalled through Antichrist's ultimate blasphemy. The crown of heaven into which Antichrist calls his worshippers is a human ring of the 'elect', such as Dante later saw, 'making themselves into a crown, reflecting the eternal beams from Him' (*e vidi lei che si facea corona, | riflettendo da se gli eterni rai*).[18] In conclusion, the rubrics say: 'all shall return to the faith and Ecclesia shall welcome them, saying, *Laudem dicite Deo nostro*'. Her words are from Revelation xix, 5.

The meaning of the play's action is thus projected far beyond the flattering imperial paradigm with which it compliments the Holy Roman Emperor. The ideals and ambitions, the language, gestures and ceremonial rituals of imperial power are examined with the eye of eternity, and are found to be good.

Nunnery: Hildegard of Bingen's 'Ordo Virtutum'

Hildegard's morality play is even more startlingly original and further from the mainstream of liturgical drama than the *Antichrist*. The two plays are poles of a tradition adapted by statesman and mystic. In the *Antichrist*, five doctrinal figures give a general framework to historical conflict. In the *Ordo*, all the protagonists are personified forces, reflecting the struggle within the Christian psyche. Nothing in the earlier ecclesiastical drama prepares us for this fully-fledged morality play, more than a century earlier than the form is generally supposed to have 'evolved'.

The text of the *Ordo*, unnoticed by Young and consequently almost totally neglected by students of the drama, has recently been reedited by Peter Dronke.[19] The following account is much indebted to Dronke's sensitive discussion of Hildegard's poetic themes and ima-

gery; it will concentrate on the idiosyncrasy of Hildegard's dramatic
method in relation to the liturgical and popular traditions examined so
far.

The conflict between sixteen (possibly seventeen) Virtues and a
Devil for possession of the Soul is both psychological and meta-
physical. The Soul's striving towards the perfection of divinity is
symbolized in a vertical plane: the Virtues and their queen, Humility,
are on a raised throne reached by steps. On the lower level is the Devil,
who never reaches beyond the foot of the steps in his struggle to con-
strain soul within the carnal world inhabited by the audience. After
his defeat by the Virtues, he is bound with his own chains while Anima
is led aloft, aided by the condescending Virtues. This use of space,
though possibly modelled on that of altar and steps, has more to do
with Hildegard's own distinctive imagery and cosmology than with
orthodox ecclesiastical symbolism. So it is with the costumes. Dronke
draws attention to contemporary illustrations of the Virtues in Hildegard's book of religious instruction (*Scivias: 'Know the ways'*):[20]

There, for instance, Caritas has a dress the colour of the heavens, with a golden
stole reaching down to her feet; Fides, a scarlet dress, a token of martyrdom.
Obedientia wears a hyacinth colour, and has silver fetters on her throat and
hands and feet; Timor Dei has a dark mauve dress (the text simply calls it
umbrosum indumentum) on which many closed eyes are painted in silver—as if all
her attempts at seeing God had been dazzled by the excess of his light.

The opposition of the forces of light and darkness is further sharpened
by the contrast of song (the monodic melodies of the Virtues and
Anima, modelled on Gregorian chants and using many notes for
setting one syllable) and speech: the Devil speaks, or rather shouts, his
prose lines from the lower level; they are either derision or challenge.

This is a philosophical and esoteric drama, projecting an inner,
visionary world. It relies chiefly on a daring visual imagery to convey
its meaning. The chorus of patriarchs who sing the processional prologue are roots (*radices*) of a great cosmic tree, growing in the shadow
(*umbra*) of the eternal eye (*oculi viventis*). As they ascend the steps, they
point in amazement to the Virtues, seeing them not as human figures,
but as numinous emanations of a radiance filtering through them down
to earth:

    Qui sunt hi, qui ut nubes?

    (Who are these, who are like clouds?)

and as branches (*rami*) of the same single cosmic tree, limbs of the Logos becoming flesh, limbs of virtue strengthening the body of the virtuous man.

In this neo-Platonic cosmos, the orthodox doctrines of redemption familiar in a liturgical context are transmuted into something philosophically rich and strange. As the action opens, a chorus of souls lament that they have fallen from the first light of the living sun into the shadow of sins (*in umbram peccatorum*) and pray to the King of Kings to raise them upon his shoulders. *Felix Anima*, the Fortunate Soul, who becomes the protagonist, laments that her love is impure, that she is too impatient to weave her robe of immortality, the garments which, according to Hildegard's gloss of Genesis, Adam and Eve lost when they found themselves naked. Contact between this abstract and sensitive probing of human motive and the world of biblical history is made by the most delicate of threads fastened here and there; as in the Virtues' rebuke to Anima, *Multum amas*, recalling Christ's words to the sinful woman (Luke vii, 47), traditionally identified with Mary Magdalene.

Anima's temptation depends not on any crude encouragement to sin but on the awareness prompted by the Devil that her longing for divine love must be contaminated by sensual desires. Overcome by the burden of her carnality, Anima succumbs to his taunts of foolishness:

> Respice mundum, et amplectetur te magno honore! (48–9)

> (Look to the world and it will embrace you with great honour.)

Abandoning her attempt to regain the 'paradise' inhabited by the Virtues, the Soul sinks back to the level of the audience, captured by the Devil. His taunts at the Virtues are now concentrated in the form of a refrain: *Nescitis quod sitis* ('You know not what you are'). Being merely part of God's existence, they have no separate identity.

A long lyrical scene follows in which the Virtues dance, demonstrating their harmonious mutual dependence. Beginning with Humilitas, each in turn is soloist, introducing herself and calling the others into a circle about her in token of their coronation (*ad coronandum in perseverentia felicem*):

> Ego Humilitas, regina Virtutum, dico:
> venite ad me, Virtutes, et enutriam vos ... (68–9)

> (I am Humanity, queen of Virtues, I say:
> Come to me, Virtues, and I will feed you ...)

They sing in chorus:

> O gloriosa regina, et o sauvissima mediatrix,
> libenter venimus. (72-3)

> (O renowned queen, and sweetest mediatrix,
> willingly we come.)

Karitas follows as soloist:

> Ego Karitas, flos amabilis—
> venite ad me, Virtutes, et perducam vos
> in candidam lucem floris virge. (76-8)

> (I am Charity, a lovely flower—
> come to me, Virtues, and I will lead you
> into the radiant light of the flower upon the [virgin] branch.)

Meanwhile the Devil continues his mocking interruptions, demanding 'Where is your champion (*pugnator*), where is your rewarder?'.

The Virtues sing of the serene joy of the heavenly kingdom and of the embraces of the royal Bridegroom. Chastity sings in praise of a virtue greater than herself:

> O Virginitas, in regali thalamo stas.
> O quam dulciter ardes in amplexibus regis,
> cum te sol perfulget
> ita quod nobilis flos tuus numquam cadet.
> O virgo nobilis, te numquam inveniet umbra in cadente flore! (104-8)

> (O, Virginity, you stand firm in the royal bedchamber.
> O, how sweetly you shine in the embraces of the King,
> when the sun penetrates you
> so that your treasured flower shall never fall.
> O royal virgin, may the shadow never come upon your fallen flower!)

Beyond the circle of virgin initiates is the Devil, seeking wolf-like to steal the sheep from this pastoral paradise. Innocentia warns them:

> Fugite, oves, spurcicias Diaboli (112)

> (Flee, sheep, from the defilements of the Devil!)

and they answer, 'Let us flee them running to your aid'.

The action performed in this scene depends directly on the living tradition of dance-play. This dance of the daughters of God is the sacred counterpart to the dance of love, in which the chorus of maidens sing of love's mystery, excluding from their intimate circle the *vieux ielos*, the *anemi* who seeks to abduct one of their number. Hildegard's scene also recreates an ancient gnostic figure of the sacred Christian dance. The apocryphal *Acts of John* (chs. xciv–xcvii) tells how Christ danced in a ring of his disciples; his verses and their refrains voicing the oneness of those initiated into the Christian mysteries.[21] The thirteenth-century sermon which allegorized *La Bele Aelis* as a dance of Jesus and his disciples, with Aelis representing the Virgin Mary plucking the flowers of charity and chastity, may not, after all, have been a purely academic exercise (see above p. 58).

As the dance concludes with Humility's triumphant words, *Gaudete ergo, filie Syon*, the lost sheep returns to the foot of the steps to invoke pity of the Virtues. At first they urge the fugitive to come running to them, but, finding her too weak, they are ordered down to help her by their queen. As they descend, singing of the living fountain of love and the triumph of Christ over the serpent, Diabolus is roused and clutches at his prey. He claims that Anima has embraced him, allowing him to lead her into the world; in revenge for her reversion, he will hurl her down in battle. But Victoria leads the militant Virtues against him. He is defeated and bound in his own chains. His overthrow is made the occasion of a tableau in which Chastity (iconographically identified with the Virgin Mary) places her heel on his head, singing:

> In mente altissimi, o Satana, caput tuum conculcavi,
> et in virginea forma dulce miraculum colui...
> et nunc gaudeant omnes qui habitant in celis
> quia venter tuus confusus est   (229–34)

> (In the mind of the Highest, Satan, I trod down your head
> and in virgin form I nurtured a sweet miracle...
> now let all who dwell in heaven rejoice
> that the fruit of your womb has been confounded.)

The thought of the creator, uttered in the curse on the serpent of Genesis and fulfilled historically in the virgin birth, is reenacted in the triumph of the individual soul.

Satan is chained prostrate but not finally defeated. He adapts his refrain once more, claiming that it is Castitas whose womb is confounded, 'barren of the lovely shape received from man'. Her chastity is a transgression of God's command to nature, and therefore she is nothing. Chastity's reply argues that the incarnation of Christ reshaped nature, 'drawing all human kind to himself' in his birth. After the Virtues sing *Laus sit tibi*, there is a brief finale, sung by Virtues and the chorus of Souls from among whom the Felix Anima came. It celebrates the communal meaning of the redemption as the attainment of the fulness of creation, the incorporation of all souls into the body of the warrior king, the jewelled, sparkling Bridegroom. The song ends with an address to the congregation:

> Ergo nunc, omnes homines,
> genua vestra ad patrem vestrum flectite,
> ut vobis manum suam porrigat. (267–9)

> (So now, all people,
> bend your knee to your Father,
> that he may reach out his hand to you.)

Omnes homines has here a figurative and a didactic sense, for one cannot pretend that this drama reaches out to 'the people'. Nevertheless, the final address draws the shape of the play firmly within the context of church worship and gives explicit personal meaning to its action. The symbolic staging and iconographic costume, the use of monodic music in the Gregorian style, have throughout served to locate the action in the sphere of communal worship. But the uniqueness of Hildegard's poetic vision demanded richer means of expression than the liturgical tradition provided. In transmuting the dance-play of popular tradition and presenting the central action as a physical combat, she sanctified secular forms. This artistic process, akin to Roswitha's use of Terence, parallels the preoccupation of the play itself—the relation between earthly and heavenly love and the transmutation of the one into the other. The differences between the two women dramatists are great, the most obvious, perhaps, being that in Hildegard's drama the actors are not required to imitate or impersonate anything that exists in the material world. They are functional, figures in a cosmic pattern, explainers of a sacred mystery into which all can be initiated as into the dance of everlasting life.

6

PLAYS IN THE VERNACULARS

It is not always recognized that the first flowering of the vernacular drama was contemporary with, rather than consequent on, the Latin achievement; nor that the earliest vernacular plays are strikingly independent of any known liturgical models, both in their plot materials and in their dramatic methods. Four twelfth-century plays form the bulk of this achievement: the Old Castilian *Auto de los Reyes Magos* (c. 1155), the Norman or Anglo-Norman *Adam* (c. 1160), the Anglo-Norman *La Seinte Resureccion* (c. 1175) and Jean Bodel's *Jeu de Saint-Nicolas* (c. 1200). These plays, in the spoken vernacular, rather than being seen as developments from *within* the liturgical tradition, may be viewed as products of parallel traditions of religious drama.

The use of liturgical Latin removed the persons and events of sacred history both from their actual context and from the everyday life of the medieval laity, insisting on the irrelevance of 'personal' motives and dissolving the chronological links between events. Gregorian chant, ecclesiastical costume, setting and ceremonial action carried the process of abstraction still further. When homilists, poets and playwrights adopted the vernaculars for the purposes of explaining sacred history to lay audiences, the nature of the everyday language as well as the purpose in hand encouraged a different focus on the divine events as human happenings in the contemporary world. The contrast of the Provençal dialogue *Mei amic* (discussed above p. 56) with the Latin hymn *In hoc anni circulo* sung to the same melody is a good example. The one is 'story', personal and direct; the other has an impersonal, communal voice and alludes to rather than recreates the biblical events.

The sung Latin plays make occasional use of the vernacular for special effects and some of these may be quickly reviewed before discussing the spoken drama in more detail.

Provençal-Latin: the 'Sponsus'

In the same eleventh-century Saint-Martial manuscript as contains the *Mei amic* is found the Latin-Provençal play of the *Sponsus*.[1] Here verses in Latin and in the Limousin dialect of *langue d'oc* are subtly alternated and integrated into a unified musical structure through the repetition of motifs and use of refrains. The use of vernacular language and of silent *demones* who cast the damned souls into 'hell' both suggest the adaptation of the liturgical traditions to meet the interest of laity among the audience. But the composition entirely in strophic forms and the fact that the subject is a parable, rather than sacred history, distinguish the play from the bulk of liturgical drama which is modelled verbally and musically on the offices of the liturgy.

The parable of the Bridegroom (St Matthew xxv, 1–13) awaited at midnight by wise and foolish virgins alludes to the coming of Christ in judgment. The choice of it for a play depends, in my view, on the relationship between eschatology and the Easter vigil. The relevant link is supplied in the prayers for Blessing of New Fire in the baptismal Mass of the Easter vigil used in northern Spain. In St Isidore's Missal, the deacon tells the congregation of vigilants:[2]

It is fitting that the congregation of the faithful should wait up for the advent of the radiant bridegroom with lights ready kindled; lest at the wedding feast he refuse the company of those he finds sleeping beneath the shadow of old sins ... let us therefore be like the wise virgins and not like those foolish ones.

They are waiting for the Easter Bridegroom, as are the *vigiles* of the Easter play from Ripoll in Catalonia (discussed above p. 68). A fine romanesque fresco from Pedret in Catalonia, showing, as the *Sponsus* does, Gabriel at the Bridegroom's feast, suggests that a play on this theme was known there in the mid-eleventh century.[3] Links between Ripoll and Saint-Martial of Limoges were strengthened during the tenth and eleventh centuries by the exchange of liturgical and musical manuscripts.[4] The Pedret fresco and the deacon's prayer from the Catalan Missal show that the Easter night vigil was viewed as pre-figuring the Last Judgment and the Easter vigilants were epitomized in the ten representative virgin souls of the parable. The Easter rising carries with it the sense of a yearly judgment.

Five Latin strophes sung to a hymnic melody begin the play. In the

manuscript they are not assigned to any singer and the lack of agree-
ment among scholars as to who should sing them reflects the impersonal, unlocalized nature of the verses. They are 'choral' sentiments,
whether sung by a choir, by a figure representing the Church, or by
the angel of doom.

> Adest Sponsus,   qui est Christus.   Vigilate, virgines!
> pro adventu   cuius gaudent   et gaudebunt homines   (1–2)

> (The Bridegroom who is Christ approaches. Virgins, keep watch!
> For his advent men rejoice and shall rejoice.)

This is the language of liturgy, dissolving time, superimposing past,
present and future. The apocalyptic meaning of the coming is stressed;
Judgment and Harrowing of Hell are imagined in the same instant:

> Venit enim   liberare   gentium origines,
> quas per primam   sibi matrem   subiugarent demones   (3–4)

> (He comes to liberate the fathers of the nations,
> whom, through the first mother Eve, devils have held captive.)

The Bridegroom is hailed as the second Adam, through whom the
crime of the first Adam is washed away; his death on the cross was 'to
lead us free from the ranks of the enemy'. The theological language here
proclaims liberation through washing; the baptismal metaphor is
twice repeated, linking the mood of the celebration with its archetype
in the triumphant *Exsultet* of the Easter vigil, during which the 'new
fire' was held above, then plunged into, the baptismal font.[5]

   In sharp contrast to the impersonal, communal nature of this opening
hymn, the angel Gabriel now addresses the waiting virgins in Provençal.
He uses the self-important declamatory formula of the *joglar:*

> Oiet, virgines,   aiso quo vos dirum.   (12)

> (Hear, virgins, what we shall tell you.)

and later he introduces himself as God's messenger, sent by him:

> Gabriels soi   eu m'a trames aici.   (25)

> (I am Gabriel, he has sent me here.)

The melody of his song, with its vivacity and intricately balanced
phrases, its curious refrain starting on the lowest note of the register,
rising a minor third and falling in an even pattern, seems straight from
the world of troubadour music. Gabriel's message is cast in the form of

an *alba* (dawn-song for lovers), whose refrain embodies an urgent call
to awake:

> Atendet un espos, Ihesu Salvaire a nom,
> > *Gaire noi dormet!* (13-14)

> (Await the Bridegroom, Jesus the Saviour by name—
> > *Sleep no longer here!*)

Gabriel's song is not a translation of the Latin verses, but takes a
different course. In simple, direct terms he tells the story of Christ's life
from birth, through baptism, to focus on the Passion. It is human
suffering that is stressed in the vernacular language:

> Eu fo batut, gablet e laideniet,
> sus e la crot, pendut e claufiget,
> eu monumen desoentre pauset
> > *Gaire noi dormet!* (20-3)

> (He was beaten, mocked and maimed,
> high on the cross hanged and pierced with nails,
> in the tomb afterwards placed—
> > *Sleep no longer here!*)

Similarly, as the action of the parable is unfolded in the Latin and
Provençal exchanges between the wise and foolish virgins, and
between the foolish virgins and the merchants selling oil, the theme of
'Watch!' is reiterated in the haunting refrain to each stanza:

> Dolentas, chaitivas, trop i avem dormit!

> (Wretches, unhappy ones, we have slept too long.)

The contrast between the remote, allusive nature of the Latin lines and
the complementary immediacy and human concern of the vernacular
is most striking in the final address of Christ as he excludes the flame-
less foolish virgins from the heavenly feast:

> Amen dico, vos ignosco, nam caretis lumine,
> Quod qui perdunt procul pergunt huius aule limine.

> Alet, chaitivas, alet, malaüreas!
> A tot iors mais vos so penas livreas;
> En efern ora seret meneias! (83-6)

> (Verily I say, I know you not, for you are without light;
> Those who lose that shall stray far from the threshold of this palace.

> Go, you wretches! Go, cursed ones!
> All your days hereafter you shall be yielded up to tortures.
> And now you shall be taken to hell.)

The rubric says, 'Here the Demons shall take them and cast them into hell'. The final Latin words of Christ, sung to the melody of the opening hymn, keep strictly to the terms of the parable. His vernacular 'gloss' which makes use of Gabriel's troubadour-like melody, makes explicit a human situation, lifting the veil from the allegory to reveal the harsh reality of judgment.

This enactment of the parable is exemplary; though it begins as communal celebration it ends in didactic demonstration. It stresses the punishment of the damned rather than the community of the saved. This didacticism is one aspect of the attempt to give the parable an immediate human meaning for a lay audience through the use of vernacular language. To judge from the popularity of the motif of the wise and foolish virgins in sculpture during the next two centuries the lesson was memorable.[6]

The twin elements of didacticism and human emphasis distinguish the vernacular plays performed for popular audiences. An early fourteenth-century drama entirely in German, on the theme of the ten virgins, contains both an explanation of the symbolic meaning of the parable according to St Augustine and an attempt to justify the damnation of the foolish virgins in terms of their human behaviour: they are shown playing ball and dancing.[7] As they are taken to hell, they pass through the audience, lamenting, 'Alas, we shall never see Jesus Christ again'. Even the intercessions of the Virgin Mary do not succeed in reversing their fate. The effect of this play, performed by the scholars and clergy of Eisenach on 4 May 1321, is recorded in a chronicle. The little known story relates how the Marquis Frederick was so incensed by the erroneous doctrine and the injustice of the fate of the foolish virgins that he had the play suppressed, before his fury brought on a 'mortal apoplexy' which prostrated him for three and a half years.[8]

The *Sponsus* is remarkable for its early date and for the extent of its use of the vernacular, but it can hardly be said to provide a model for the development of an independent popular religious drama. And the same is true of the other liturgical plays which have vernacular elements. In the plays of Hilarius and in the Beauvais *Daniel* the French refrains are little more than stylistic flourishes. Mary's lament for Lazarus (in the *Resuscitatio Lazari* of Hilarius) and the court's jaunty macaronic summons to Daniel in the Beauvais play (*Vir propheta Dei, Daniel, vien al Roi!*) are brief modulations into a secular key.[9] They are not an attempt to interpret the action of the play for a lay audience. The more substantial vernacular interpolations in the *Carmina Burana* Passion play (*c.* 1200), however, constitute little scenes, designed to accommodate the secular world (e.g. Mary Magdalene's dancing-song, discussed above p. 58) and also to realize the human pathos of the crucifixion (in the Virgin's lament for the life of her lovely child: *Awe, mines shoene chindes lip!*).[10] The earliest Passion play, that of Montecassino (*c.* 1160), shifts from Latin to Italian vernacular for the lament at the foot of the cross. Unfortunately, only three lines of this poem survive in the fragmentary text, but they too promise human interest in Mary's reminding her son that she bore him in her womb.[11] An Easter play, composed *c.* 1284 for the nuns of Origny Sainte-Benoîte, surrounds a traditional Latin *Visitatio* with scenes entirely in vernacular French verse.[12] The French language gives secular feeling to the exchanges of the Marys and the spice merchant, reinforced by the sprightly *pastourelle*-like melody, and the words in which Mary Magdalene expresses love-longing for Jesus have courtly connotations. But both these elements are modified by the melodic pattern and graceful stylization of the whole play. The Origny playwright respects the integrity of liturgical tradition and moulds secular elements to its norms: the play is still performed during Easter night and actors and choir hold lighted vigil candles.

Neither the Origny play nor the other examples cited can be seen as evidence of an *incipient* popular religious drama. For all their 'human touches', they are lyrical expansions or interpolations in a celebratory drama. They are ecclesiastical cousins, not progenitors, of the popular drama which had existed in highly developed forms at least since the mid-twelfth century. The plays which used the spoken language of their lay audiences were, as we shall see, often directly representational, concerned very much with 'telling a story'. Their concept of drama, as one might anticipate, comes much closer to the mimic tradition of secular acting than do any of the sung Latin or macaronic plays we have looked at.

Spanish: 'El Auto de los Reyes Magos'

The oldest of the spoken play texts may be the mid-twelfth-century Castilian fragment usually referred to by this title of *Auto* (auto < actio: performance). The dialogue is recorded for private reading rather than future performance and has no rubrics, no indications of the speakers' names and no music. A thumb index provides the heading: *Caspar. Baltasar. Melchior.*[13] The three Magi, anonymous in Latin play tradition, have names attested in Spanish legend since the tenth century. These kings in the *Auto* are 'characters', capable of wonder, fear and scepticism. Most strikingly, they are shown as professional astronomers.

Caspar speaks first, proceeding by a series of abrupt clauses, exclamations, statements and questions. The halting and contradictory statements force the reader to imagine an actor impersonating the sage in detail, pausing frequently in his speech, gazing at the star, using his instruments and consulting his books:

> Dios criador, qual maravila!
> No se qual es achesta strela!
> Agora primas la e veida,
> poco timpo a que es nacida.
> Nacido es el Criador
> que es de la gentes senior?
> Non es vertad—non se que digo,
> todo esto non vale uno figo;
> otra nocte me lo catare,
> si es vertad, bine lo sabre   (*pausa*)
> Bine es vertad, lo que io digo?
> en todo, en todo lo prohio.
> Non pudet seer otra sennal?
> Achesto es i non es al;
> nacido es Dios, por ver, de fembra
> in achest mes de december.
> Ala ire o que fure, aora lo e,
> por Dios de todos lo terne.   (1–18)

(God, creator, what a portent! I don't know what kind of a star this is! Now is the first time I have seen it, just a little while after it is born. Is the Creator born, he who is lord of all peoples? That is not the truth; all this is not worth a fig— I don't know what I am saying. I shall examine it for myself another night; I shall know properly if it is real. In every part I [must] examine it. Could it not be another sign? It is the same one—it cannot be another: God is born, in truth, from a woman and in this month of December. I shall go, whatever happens, and adore him, for the sake of the God of all, the eternal one.)

Balthazar, too, is anxious to relate the observed star to book authority and he resolves to watch for three nights, puzzled how 'it has come into being so completely'. Melchior swears there is no such star in the heavens, as he is a good astronomer:

> Tal estrela non es in celo,
> desto so io bono strelero.   (36–7)

Just as the kings are individuated so is their meeting. In most of the Latin plays the meeting is simultaneous and completely stylized; the *Auto* has two of the kings meeting first, to verify each other's observations. They are then joined by Melchior, who asks if they wish to travel with him. The three determine to 'talk with' the Creator, whom they seem to envisage as a sage like themselves. Melchior still thinks they may be deceived:

> Cumo podremos provar si es homme mortal
> o si es rei de tera o si celestrial? (65–6)

(How shall we be able to prove if he is mortal man or if he is king of earth or a heavenly king?)

At this point the traditional threefold symbolism of the gifts is invoked, but in a manner which totally inverts the meaning and purpose of the offertory of the Epiphany Mass and the liturgical plays. Gold, incense and myrrh are to act as magical touchstones, tests of the true nature of the infant:

(*Balthasar*)
> Queredes bine saber cumo lo sabremos?
> oro, mira i acenso a el ofrecremos:
> si fure rei de terra, el oro quera;
> si fure omne mortal, la mira tomara;
> si rei celestrial, estos dos dexara,
> tomara el encenso quel pertenecera. (67–72)

(Do you want to know how we shall know it? We shall offer to him gold, myrrh and incense: if he is to be a king of earth, he will seek the gold; if he is to be a mortal man, he will take the myrrh; if a heavenly king, he will put aside those two and take the incense which will be his due.)

This motif, unique among Magi plays, is found in a number of poems on the infancy of Christ written in French in the twelfth century and based on the apocryphal pseudo-Matthew.[14] It is well suited to the scientific scepticism of the three astronomer sages; it can hardly have 'derived from' a liturgical play.

The poet's interest in giving human features and motivation to the figures of the drama continues in his presentation of Herod as a self-pitying, blustering tyrant who asserts that he is 'not yet buried' (*ni so la terra pusto*) and that 'the world is going to pot' (*El seglo va a caga:* literally, 'to excrement'). He has a large Spanish medieval court and orders his *mayordomo* to summon abbots and potentates, scribes, grammarians, astronomers and rhetoricians:

> Idme por mios abades
> i por mios scrivanos
> i por meos gramatgos
> i por mios streleros
> i por mios retoricos;   (119–23)

to discuss the truth of the prophecy. His rabbis argue comically among themselves; one, swearing by Holy Allah, taxes another with ignorance:

> Hamihala, cum eres enartado!
> por que eres rabi clamado?
> Non entendes la profecias   (138–40)

(Holy Allah, how ignorant you are! Why are you called rabbi? You don't understand the prophecies . . .)

With the second rabbi's admission of the lamentable lacuna in his own books of prophecy the lively fragment unfortunately ends.

The use of actors speaking vernacular language carries inevitably with it an idea of drama and of acting that is altogether different from that in the liturgical plays on the same subject. The impersonation of flesh and blood is unmistakable. The characters converse with one another in a simple and natural way and there is no grotesque in the comedy. They form a medieval social structure that has the stamp of Castilian Spain: the Magi are professional astronomers (in a country where, in the twelfth century, the astronomers led the world); Herod's entourage has both the Jewish and Mohammedan characteristics of contemporary Spain. The keynote of the play is its reasonable scepticism, as if the author were always aware of writing for an audience composed of pagans, neophytes and mere sceptics. By allowing for incredulity through the figures of the astronomer-sages and their touchstone test, he gives an original cast to the story, presenting it to the audience *as if they had never heard it before*. This is not celebration but entertaining representation and re-creation. In almost every respect the *Auto* is distinct from and independent of liturgical tradition: in its plot and manner of telling a story through dialogue, and in the personal emphasis required of the actors; by changing voice and explanatory gesture they must mimic 'real people'.

Anglo-Norman: 'La Seinte Resureccion'

The scope, content and dramatic method of the Anglo-Norman *La*

Seinte Resureccion are comparably distinct from those of any known liturgical play. Two incomplete texts, one of English and one of continental origin, give a fraction (possibly a quarter) of an ambitious dramatic spectacle performed by more than forty actors.[15] The action begins with Joseph of Arimathia's request to Pilate to be allowed to bury Christ's body and proceeds through apocryphal scenes of Joseph's arrest, imprisonment and miraculous delivery, to the Resurrection, the appearance of Christ at Emmaus, and finally the Ascension.

Performance is explicitly 'before the people' and 'in a large enough space'. The two versions of the prologue refer to the play in two different terms:

> En ceste manere *recitom*
> La seinte resureccion ... (Paris MS 1–2)
>
> (In this manner let us *recite*
> the holy resurrection ...)
>
> Si vus avez devocium
> De la sainte resurrectium
> En l'onur Deu representer
> Et devant le puple *representer* ... (Canterbury MS 1–4)
>
> (If, devoutly, you intend,
> For God's honour to *represent*
> The resurrection before a crowd
> And to speak each part of it aloud ...)

The apparent contradiction between recitation and representation is resolved by the agency of a narrator. Though the precise nature of the verse 'stage directions' linking the dialogue is obscured by the fact that both texts are versions for private reading rather than for acting use, the evidence for such an 'on-stage' narrator here seems conclusive.[16]

In the spoken prologue the narrator introduces the audience to the acting area, which has seven structures (*maisuns:* Heaven, Hell, Jail, Tower, Crucifix, Tomb, Emmaus Castle) and eight stations (*lius* or *estals*), each occupied by a character or group.[17] The arrangement of these is either in two parallel 'V's', open to the audience, or possibly on a circular plan, with the *petit chastel* of Emmaus *en mi la place*. To speak to one another the characters must leave their own 'islands' and travel through neutral space to visit one another, so that the action is described by a series of journeys. Apparently the narrator remains within the acting area and interprets these movements for the audience, explaining who the characters are and where they are going, redirecting attention to the appropriate 'house', or pointing out the sudden appearance of a new character, not met previously, whose presence is instrumental in furthering the plot. The significance of what is happening in this spacious acting area with more than forty characters is thus always clear. The drama is representational *and* expository, with the narrator explaining the play's conventions to the audience in such a way that the narrative line is continuous.

Unlike the liturgical dramatists, the playwright has treated his historical subject as 'story', to be represented in time and in geographic space. His concept of representation demands the simultaneous presence of all the characters and all the separate locations of the entire action. This is obviously very wasteful of actors and playing space, but he follows the principle faithfully. The arrangement of the 'houses' is symbolic, with the crucifix central and Heaven and Hell on opposite sides of the place. But the acting space also incorporates geographical features of the contemporary medieval world. The Canterbury text calls for a 'Tower of David and Bartholomew' (the keys of the medieval Tower of David standing at the west gate of Jerusalem had been granted by the Patriarch to Henry II of England in return for aid promised in the second crusade; St Bartholomew was specially revered at Canterbury).[18] The same medieval colouring is used for characterization: Joseph of Arimathia, for instance, is shown as a *seignur*, granted the privilege of burying Christ's body as a reward for feudal service rendered to Pilate.

More unusual than the 'medievalization' of character and place is the playwright's attempt to interpret the historical situation. When Joseph invokes the blessing of the god of Moses and Aaron on Pilate, the Roman governor answers gravely, returning the compliment 'by Hercules'. When he is blamed by Joseph for his part in the crucifixion of Christ, Pilate's self-justification shows the poet unusually aware of the nature of Pilate's office in Jerusalem:

> Li Jeu, par lur grant envie,
> Enpristrent grant felonie;
> Jo.l consenti par veisdie,
> Que ne perdisse ma baillie:
> Encuse m'eussent en Romanie,
> Tost en purraie perdre la vie.   (Paris MS 59–64)

(The Jews in their great hatred undertook this vicious crime. I consented out of policy so as not to lose my authority. If I had been accused at Rome I could have lost my life for it.)

In this taut political situation Joseph must obtain a warrant of safe conduct from Pilate before he can remove Christ's body; later he must obtain the same permission for Nicodemus to help him. Joseph is a man of authority with his own servants who carry the implements and ointment for the task of deposition; yet he is afraid to visit the tomb at night except disguised in a cape. When he is discovered by the guard it is plainly an embarrassment to have to arrest him, as the soldiers' shift from *tu* and *vassal* to the respectful *sire* and *vus* indicates in the following exchange:

Unus Miles
    Ki es tu, vassal? es tu espie?
Josephus
    Einz, sui Joseph de Arithmathie.
Alter Miles
    Ahy sire, ke fetes vus ci? (Canterbury MS 497–9)

First soldier
    Who are you, my man? Are you a spy?
Joseph
    No indeed. I am Joseph of Arimathia.
Another soldier
    Oh, *you*, my lord. What are you doing here?)

With Caiaphas's expression of pleasure at having proof of Joseph's complicity with Jesus, the longer of the two play fragments ends.

The suspense is that of a well-handled adventure story with Joseph as its hero. No resurrection play from a later period is so free in its treatment of the Gospels and it is attractive to surmise that Joseph's role was prompted by his popularity in contemporary didactic romance. Robert de Boron's late twelfth-century *Roman de l'Estoire dou Graal*, for instance, tells of Joseph's imprisonment and liberation after three days from a tower in Jerusalem, through the miraculous power of the Grail, a vessel containing Christ's blood.[19] Longinus, the blind beggar who accepts 'xii deniers' from Pilate's soldiers for piercing Christ's side and who recovers his sight from the stream of blood and water, is another figure in the play who may owe his apocryphal importance to popular legend.

The chief interest here is in the historical events themselves and in re-creating the minute, practical details of their accomplishment. Simple, single lines of dialogue accompany the work of deposition, Joseph suggesting that Nicodemus take out the nails first from the feet, assuring him that he has the weight of the body, ordering his (mute) servant to hand him the box of ointment. There is little that recalls the liturgical plays on the subject. The use of one rare detail whose origin is liturgical may serve to illustrate the radically different orientation of this drama. In the Canterbury text Joseph is given a long speech in which he relates a dream concerning the sepulchre. He tells how six or seven angels visited him in his sleep, alighting with great splendour on a rock, singing sweetly; they unfolded a great funeral pall, white inside and outside red as blood. His father has interpreted the dream to mean that a very sacred body is to be entombed in the stone and Joseph has consequently had a sepulchre freshly cut there. All this is used to explain how Joseph could have had the tomb ready in time (Matthew xxvii, 60). The images in the dream may have been suggested to the playwright by the displaying of the *sudarium* by the angels at the sepulchre in a liturgical *Visitatio* play. In English churches Easter sepulchres were often hung with crimson palls whose white underside, revealed on Easter Day, symbolized the miracle of resurrection after the blood of the Passion.[20] This liturgical symbolism is recalled remotely in *La Seinte Resureccion*, not for its own sake, but to fulfil the demand in a popular representational drama for causality and personal motivation and to satisfy a popular interest in miracles.

The play has little linguistic sophistication; the dialogue is rather formal, correct and colourless. In contrast to the celebrated *Mystère d'Adam* with its colloquial exchanges, stately rhetorical laments and touches of courtly lyricism, it appears modest and a little drab. The achievement of *La Seinte Resureccion* lies in its fidelity to a principle of representational stagecraft in setting forth so ambitious an action *devant le puple*. The two plays are as different from one another as both are from any known liturgical plays.

Anglo-Norman: 'Le Mystère d'Adam'
The so-called *Mystère d'Adam* is an astonishing work, a fusion of disparate traditions: ecclesiastical and popular, liturgical and apocryphal, sung and spoken, Latin and vernacular.[21] The thirteenth-century continental manuscript calls it *Ordo representacionis Ade*, suggesting by means of the two words for 'play' both its reliance on an order of liturgical procedure and its directly representational concerns. The play begins with the intoning of the *In principio* (Genesis i, 1–27) by the choir. The Word of Genesis is then made flesh in represented action and

is elaborated in the subtle French dialogue between God and Adam and Eve and Satan. This vernacular action is punctuated periodically by the choir's singing of liturgical responsories based on the Genesis text. The siting of the playing place, a *platea* (apparently a churchyard or public square) [22] flanked by a church, reinforces the impression of sacred history set in the secular world. As the uniquely elaborate 'stage directions' tell us, a raised structure with a curtain-walled garden represents Paradise; Hell is a devils' kitchen equipped with cauldrons and kettles; Earth is a patch of dug ground on a level with the audience. God appears from and retires to the church. It is likely the choir stands on the church porch or on steps behind or to the side of Paradise. There is no reason to doubt that performance was ecclesiastically organized, though the play's auspices are not known. Possibly it was put on at a cathedral school in northern France or southern England (experts are still disputing whether the play's language is continental or insular), where the attendance of aristocratic visitors would give some point to the feudal and courtly colouring of the story.

The debt to liturgy is deep and pervasive but, because many scholars have insisted on the play as an example of the natural development of *liturgical drama*, neither the true nature of this debt nor the differences between the dramatic method of *Adam* and true liturgical drama have always been properly appreciated. First, there are no known liturgical Latin plays on the subjects of the Fall or Cain and Abel. Secondly, the play's construction and its manner of performance have no precedent in the liturgical Latin drama. Consider first the structure.

The play does not present a continuous story, but, rather, a continuous theme—fall and redemption—through an episodic structure. Adam and Eve are dead and taken to hell before their children Cain and Abel are introduced on stage. The final part of the play is a procession of prophets of Christ. This three-act form (supposing the play to be more or less complete in the manuscript text) was created by joining two liturgical forms: the outline of the Genesis (Adam and Cain) sections is provided by the responsories which belong liturgically to Matins of Sexagesima. [23] Second, a model for the prophet-play existed in the sermon-based *Ordo Prophetarum* (see above p. 72). Each 'half' of the play finds its authority in a traditional text, and each half begins with a choral lection. The initial solo singing of the *In principio* is followed by the antiphonal singing of the responsory, *Formavit igitur Dominus hominem de limo terrae*, based on the Genesis account of Adam's creation ('And the Lord God formed man of the dust of the ground').

When this is over, vernacular dialogue commences with God's summons, 'Adam!', and his reply, 'Sire'. After the departure of Cain and Abel, 'the prophets are made ready in a hidden place', and the opening words of the prophet sermon are read in the choir: *Vos inquam, convenio, O Judei* ('I conjure you, therefore, O Jews'). The prophets are then called by name and speak their prophecies, first in Latin prose and then in French verse. The figures who appear do not in fact correspond exactly to those cited in the *Sermo*, but the sermon serves as their authority for appearing. The method of construction can be seen, in one sense, as the provision of vernacular dramatic gloss upon two liturgical texts. How much this description leaves out will be discussed in a moment.

Liturgically speaking, Adam and Cain belong to Sexagesima, the pre-Lenten period of emphasis on the necessity for atonement for sin; and the prophets belong to Christmas. In joining the two the playwright snapped the threads of liturgical occasion and composed a 'cyclic' drama whose theme and structure proclaim both death and renewal. The play anticipates, though it does not enact, a triumphant ending. In the depths of his despair Adam is given prophetic insight which allows him to see that 'No aid will ever come to me, unless it be from the son who shall be born of Mary' and as devils approach her Eve predicts that 'God will cast us out of hell by his might'. Abel's sacrifice of a lamb and his own sacrificial death, kneeling towards the East, show him foreshadowing Christ's Passion. The choice and wording of the prophecies of the last section are similarly suited to this new framework. Seven out of the ten figures are made to refer explicitly to the rescue of Adam from the power of hell. Yet each prophet is led to hell to join his forefather Adam. At the end of the play most of the significant Old Testament patriarchs and prophets await Christ's coming there (Adam, Eve, Abel, Cain, Abraham, Moses, Aaron, David, Solomon, Balaam, Daniel, Habakkuk, Jeremiah, Isaiah, Nebuchadnezzar).[24] The figures of Adam and Eve, Abraham, Moses and David reappear in the early Middle English dramatic fragment (*c.* 1250) known as the *Harrowing of Hell* ('A strif . . . of Jesu and of Satan') where they greet Christ after he has told of his sufferings on earth, has broken hell gates and bound Satan.[25] Abel appears among the group whose exit from Limbo Virgil describes to Dante in the *Inferno* (IV, 51–61).

The action of the play, then, points forward to a known conclusion. In this respect its performance would be suitable to the period before

Easter. But its emphasis is exemplary. Recurrent diabolic sallies into the place to remove the 'dead' underline the persistent effects of the Fall upon mankind. The hell-fire sermon on the fifteen signs of judgment which in the manuscript follows the prophecy of Nebuchadnezzar (in the place one might expect the *Signs of Judgment* told by the Sibyl) may well be an authentic ending, referring as it does to the prophecies of Jeremiah, Isaiah, Moses, Aaron, and David, and to Christ's sufferings for Adam's sin. Whether or not performance concluded with the sermon, the construction of the play to that point shows a well worked out didactic plan, which, while making use of liturgical models, is highly original. And this form, perhaps because it begins at the beginning, proved decisive in determining the course of the popular religious drama of the Middle Ages.

The manner of performance which the *Adam* demands is original and quite distinct from that of known liturgical drama. There are three categories of performers: singers, speakers and mimes. As singers, the choir do not speak or take part in the action. There are no directions for dressing them (presumably they wear choir robes) nor for their gestures. They are familiar and ecclesiastical, providing in their intoned lections and musically more ornate responsories the narrative authority of the drama. The second group, the historical persons of the Old Testament drama, speak to one another (God, Adam, Eve, Satan, Cain, Abel) or speak in isolation (the prophets) and do not sing. There are extensive rubrics concerning their costuming, speaking and gestures, showing the author's desire for emblematic dress and stylized, formal gestures which will convey the literal sense of the spoken words:

Adam shall be well trained not to answer too quickly nor too slowly, when he has to answer. Not only Adam but all the actors shall be instructed to control their speech and to make their actions appropriate to the matter they speak of; and, in speaking the verse, not to add a syllable, nor to take one away, but to enunciate everything distinctly, and to say everything in the order laid down. When anyone shall speak of Paradise, he shall look towards it and point it out with his hand.

This explicitness may be interpreted as an insistence on the proper gravity and decorum of ecclesiastical drama in the face of other, popular traditions. It contrasts markedly with the license implicitly allowed in the play to the third group of performers, the silent and mimic *demones*.

No costumes are specified for the devils nor for Satan. Their dress may already have been traditional. A twelfth-century Latin *Dispute of the Body and Soul* describes quasi-human figures with animal parts, claws, hair and wings, smoke and fire coming from their anatomies, manhandling souls into cauldrons with pitchforks and chains.[26] The structure for hell in the play calls for cauldrons and kettles which must be banged together causing clatter and 'great fumes'. The details of costume could presumably be left to the director. A distinct set of conventions governs the devils' theatrical behaviour: they are not historically limited, but are always at hand, creating diversions and fulfilling a practical need in removing 'dead' bodies to hell. They have no set lines, using dumbshow gestures to convey their meaning. They also enjoy a special relationship with the audience, a freedom to roam through the open spaces (*per plateas*) between the structures and to run in among the audience. Running is their characteristic activity. The *demones* are purveyors of entertainment as well as objects of doctrinal terror: Satan plays a stage trick on the fallen Adam, planting thorns and thistles in his garden while his back is turned; the demons are always full of energy and hilarity, dancing with glee at the imprisonment of Adam and Eve, 'shouting to one another in their joy'— apparently *ex tempore*. In contrast to the historical personae, the devils can improvize both words and gestures, a legacy, maybe, from 'the sub-literary tradition of antique mime'.[27]

How far the poet's techniques for representation have been influenced by secular tradition is hard to say. It is possible that the dramatic conception of Paradise as a raised stage 'surrounded by curtains and silk cloths, at such a height that the persons who are in Paradise can be seen from the shoulders upwards' owes something to the curtained booth stage of street *spectacula* (see above p. 25). But, though it seems odd to conceal so much of Adam and Eve, the garden wall of Paradise is attested in iconography.

A modern reader of the stage directions is struck by the representational, almost 'scenic' nature of paradise:

Fragrant flowers and leaves shall be planted there; there shall also be various trees with fruit hanging on them, so that it looks a very pleasant place.

Yet this impression would be superficial. The poet's concern is not primarily representational, but rather to express doctrinal meanings. Paradise is high because it is an elevated spiritual state; its aesthetic pleasantness denotes the joy which Adam and Eve know there. It is adjacent to the church, from which God and all life created by his words flow.

The 'figure' of God is priestly and wears a dalmatic (deacon's outer garment, usually silk). The reference to him throughout the textual rubrics as *Figura* indicate that the actor is a mere cipher not an impersonation of the Creator. One reference to him as *Salvator* shows that the author is thinking of the Old Testament God creating Adam as a *figura Salvatoris*, foreshadowing his own act of redemption that is necessitated by the sin that Adam will commit. Instead of being 'naked', Adam and Eve wear 'splendid clothes'. Adam's red robe denotes in patristic etymology that he is made from red earth while Eve's white woman's dress and white silk head covering may signify her creation from bone. As a contemporary Anglo-Norman poet puts it:[28]

> Os saunz char en sei est pure,
> Sec e nette, redde e dure;
> Os est blaunche come flour de may . . .
> Qe femme est natureument
> Blanche, nect e fin e pure.

(Fleshless bone in itself is pure, dry, clean, perfect, lasting; bone is white as may-flower . . . Thus woman is by nature white, clean, fine, pure.)

Red and white together anticipate the vestmental symbolism of Easter, red associating Adam with the blood of Christ's Passion, Eve's bridal white suggesting the Church, bride of Christ, taken from Adam's 'wounded' side.

The meaning of the Fall is shown not as the discovery of nakedness (which might have presented difficulties for the actors) but as the loss of fine clothes. After tasting the apple, Adam stoops behind the curtain wall of Paradise and 'removing his fine robes, puts on a pauper's garb sewn with fig leaves'. Hildegard of Bingen explains the symbolism in her *Book of Divine Works for the Simple Man* (I, 14):

By consenting to the persuasion of the devil in his envy of them, Adam and Eve lost the glory of a heavenly garment (*gloriam coelestis vestimenti*), that is to say, immortality.

The explanation for the stole which God dons before expelling Adam and Eve from Paradise lies in an extra-liturgical ceremony for the expulsion of sinners on Ash Wednesday, in which the same two responsories used in the play ('By the sweat of thy brow' and 'Behold, the man is become as one of us') are sung.

The author's 'realism' is almost always in the service of doctrinal symbolism. Thus the life-like quarrel of Cain and Abel, the skilful evocation of Cain's envious cunning, his ill-concealed fury, freeze into a tableau at the moment of Abel's death:

Then shall Abel genuflect towards the East. And he shall have a pot hidden in his clothes, which Cain shall strike as if he were really killing Abel. Abel, moreover, shall lie prostrate, as if dead.   (s.d. 722)

The repeated demand for verisimilitude here (with the added horror of red 'blood' on the white garment) is part of a total vision of Abel as sacrificial victim, whose murder prefigures that of Christ.

In the procession of prophets, costume symbolism reveals the same figural principles at work. Each is identified by an iconographic feature. Abraham is an old man with a profuse beard, dressed in flowing garments; Daniel, a youth in old man's robes (denoting his precocious wisdom); David and Solomon are dressed alike with royal insignia, crowned with diadems. The genealogical importance of the procession is stressed through the iconography of the stem of Jesse, at that time newly fashionable in art.[29] Moses carries a rod, Aaron a bough with fruit and flowers, explaining the symbolism of the rod (French *verge*, Latin *virga*) which like the virgin of Isaiah's prophecy (*vierge*, *virgo*) 'may make flowers and bear fruit without planting'. These figures are 'prophets' not only in the sense that they foretell Christ's coming, but also in being themselves his typological precursors, genealogical antecedents. The visual effects of the whole play are designed to give thematic coherence to its episodic events, to make the spectacle rich with doctrinal meaning.

So far, in discussion of the construction of the play's action and of its acting and staging conventions, the remarkable range of techniques at the author's disposal will be evident. His greatest achievement, as most students of the drama have recognized, is in his presentation of the human agents of the drama through their language. They are flesh and blood creatures with plausible human motivation; they speak French and inhabit a social world whose ideals are recognizably feudal, courtly and clerical, or anti-clerical. Considering the sheer bulk of exegesis that clung to the simple but enigmatic myth of Genesis by the twelfth century, the achievement of the *Adam*-poet in presenting the story of the Fall as a profoundly human tragedy is without precedent. His insight is apparent in the skill of the dialogue, and also (a fact less appreciated) in his reshaping of the received story. Hardison's perfunctory comment that 'the dramatist turned to an already extant outline and filled it in with dialogue based partly on suggestions in the responsory itself and partly on relevant passages in Genesis'[30] overlooks both the playwright's richness of invention and his use of independent vernacular tradition.

If the Sexagesima responsories formed the essential base of the structure, then why did the playwright omit the fifth and sixth responsories, which refer to the creation of Eve? In the play she is already created before Adam and she are placed in Paradise. This sequence of action plainly contradicts that of Genesis and of the responsory, where Eve is created *in Paradise* from Adam's side. Again, if the poet observed only liturgical authority, where in it did he discover that Satan was distinct from the serpent of the Paradise tree and assumed a quasi-human form? Why did he make Satan tempt *Adam*— twice, at that—and be rejected, before the successful temptation of Eve? That is not in Genesis either.

Part of an answer lies in the poet's familiarity with popular and apocryphal versions of the Fall, whose existence helped him to form his own clear conception of the story as a human tragedy with an intimate domestic meaning for a medieval lay audience. In the following account of the Adam and Eve section of the play, I shall try to make clear the extent and nature of the poet's originality.

At the beginning of the play Adam and Eve are *already* apparently both living; and the fact of their creation is subordinated to the poet's interest in the relationship between them and their creator. God's first act is to marry them. The Creator's statement that he has formed Adam according to his own image leads into an admonition with feudal overtones:

Figura
>A ma imagene t'ai feit de tere:
>Ne moi devez ja mais mover guere.   (5–6)

>(Of earth I have made you, in my image:
>you ought never to make war against me.)

Adam promises obedience. God then refers to Eve, who stands further from the Creator, her face lowered, indicating her proper inferiority and submissiveness:

>Je t'ai duné bon cumpainun:
>Ce est ta femme, Eva a noun.
>Ce est ta femme e tun pareil:
>Tu le devez estre ben fïel.

> Tu aime lui, e ele ame tei,
> Si serez ben ambedui de moi.
> Ele soit a tun comandement,
> E vus ambe deus a mun talent. (9–16)

> (I've given you a good companion:
> She is your wife, her name is Eve;
> She is your wife and partner,
> You must stay faithful to her and true.
> May you love her and in turn
> She love you; both will be loved by me.
> She must answer to your command,
> The two of you obey my will.)

The key words, *aime* and *ambe*, repeated within a formal pattern, emphasize an ideal of mutual love. God reminds Adam that they are created one flesh and that though Adam is given the government of Eve, the law of marriage is a bond mutually respected and without constraint:

> Tu la governe par raison.
> N'ait entre vus ja tençon,
> Mais grand amor, grant conservage:
> Tel soit la lei de mariage. (21–24)

> (Govern her with reason
> And let there be no dissension between you,
> Only mutual love and mutual comfort:
> Let such be the law of marriage.)

Turning to Eve, as a twelfth-century priest might to a young bride (she is dressed in white, her head covered), he teaches her her matrimonial duty:

> A tei parlerai, Evain!
> Ço garde tu, nei tenez en vain . . .
> Adam aime, e lui tien chier.
> Il est marid, e tu sa mullier:
> A lui soies tot tens encline,
> Nen issir de sa discipline!
> Lui serf e aim par bon coraje,
> Car ço est droiz de mariage. (25–38)

> (Now to you, Eve, will I speak.
> Keep this well, don't hold it light . . .
> Love Adam and hold him dear.

He is your husband, you his wife.
To him remain obedient;
Do not go beyond his government.
Serve him, love him with your heart,
For that is the due of marriage.)

Eve's promise, acknowledging God as *seignor*, Adam as her equal yet
stronger partner (*paraille e a forzor*) completes the harmonious relationship that God proposes as the condition of happiness. God now bestows
his gift of everlasting life, free from pain and distress, in return for
obedience freely given, for, he says, they are not tied to a stake (*liez a
pal*). Again Adam promises obedience.

At this point God leads the pair into Paradise; it is his dowry, the
realization of the promises they have sworn. It is not merely a place of
physical plenty (this is passed over in four lines of God's speech) but a
state of perfect individual and mutual happiness:

Femme de home n'i avra irur,
Ne home de femme verguine ne freür.   (93–4)

(No woman shall a husband's anger know,
No husband for his wife feel fear or shame.)

Confronted with the classic difficulty of realizing the unfallen state, the
poet presents ideal marriage in terms of its opposites, only too familiar in
the world of the audience. God's warning, spoken 'so that Eve may hear,
for if she does not then she falls to folly', pointedly directs attention to
the Fall that the audience anticipates. In a further oath, Adam condemns himself by feudal law if he should ever be traitor to his Lord for
the sake of an apple. The act of sin which has been adumbrated is seen
as perjury (because of the oath) as well as treachery (disobedience against
one's lord). God now returns to the church, leaving Adam and Eve to
walk about in Paradise, gesturing their innocent delight, whilst the
devils crowd against the curtain wall on Eve's side, pointing out the
forbidden fruit to her.

The play shows three forms of the diabolic temptation: the demons,
the quasi-human Diabolus whose appearance does not frighten Adam
or Eve and who addresses them 'with smiling face' and easy familiarity;
finally, there is a *serpens artificiose compositus* upon the forbidden tree.
The serpent is licensed by Genesis; the demons, I suggest, are licensed
by the nature of the entertainment as 'play', their function already well
established by a tradition of popular religious drama now lost. The

loquacious flatterer who accosts both Adam and Eve is suggested by the apocryphal tradition which appears in Avitus of Rennes' eighth-century Virgilian poem *De Originali Peccato*[31] and in the ninth-century Anglo-Saxon heroic poem known as *Genesis B*. In the Anglo-Saxon poem and in *Adam* (and nowhere else in medieval literature) Satan tempts Adam twice and is rejected before he convinces an 'innocent' Eve of the necessity of picking the apple.[32] The *Adam*-poet, if he lived in England, may well have been able to read Old English, for some of his contemporaries both read and wrote it.[33] Whatever the case, he gave a triple structure to the tempting scenes because it suited both his domestic and doctrinal themes.

The Devil is presented as having no specific knowledge of God's prohibition. His initial concern, through his solicitous inquiries, is to make the unresponsive Adam discontented. He suggests, in a knowing way that 'things could be better' in Paradise, and finally by means of calculated indifference ('I'm not in a hurry to tell you how') elicits Adam's curiosity. It is Adam who, alternately cajoled and scoffed at, reveals the condition of his tenure of Paradise. The Devil is thus able to provide a reason (God does not care about the other fruit) as if it were his own secret. Pointing to the forbidden fruit with his hand he identifies it:

> Ço est le fruit de sapïence:
> De tut saveir done scïence. (157–8)

> (This is the fruit of knowledge,
> It gives insight into everything.)

This first temptation is specifically of the desire for knowledge which will make Adam God's equal (*per*), and is rejected. Satan leaves him with a parting taunt:

> Kar tu es soz!
> Encore te membrera des moz. (171–2)

> (What a fool you are!
> One day you'll remember my words.)

After rejoining the demons and making a diversion by running about the 'place' with them, the Devil returns, 'happy and glad' to Adam, casually taking up the conversation ('I meant to say the other day . . .'). This second temptation is of the desire for power. The Devil calls Adam God's *provender*, his recipient of alms, the mere eater of his fruit, urging him to claim a higher honour:

> Tu regneras en majesté.
> Od Deu poez partir poësté! (193–4)

> (You shall live in majesty,
> Sharing power with God himself.)

In Adam's dismissal of him, the Devil is named for the first time, as if to show Adam's perception of his nature:

Adam
> Fui tei de ci!
Diabolus
> Qui dit, Adam?
Adam
> Fui tei de ci! Tu es Sathan:
> Mal conseil dones ... (195–7)

But the words, 'Get thee hence, Satan', are a clear 'pre-echoing' of the triumph of Christ, the second Adam, over the devil in the wilderness. They provide a justification for the triple pattern of temptation as prefiguration of that later event. At the same time, the language gives a feudal colouring to the episode; Adam calls Satan a *traïtres, e sanz foi*, accusing him of trying to embroil him with his *seignor* through 'bad advice' (*conseil* being a duty of the vassal to his lord).

Whereas for Adam the naming of Satan is the final outcome of reasoning about the nature of his advice, Eve greets her visitor by name, but clearly has no idea of his nature:

Diabolus
> Eva, ça sui venuz a toi.
Eva
> Di moi, Sathan, or tu pur quoi? (205–6)

> (Eve, here I am, come to see you.
> Tell me, Satan, now why have you?)

She appears pleased by his attentions, and gives him God's blessing when he reveals his concern for her *pru* and *honor* (worthiness and status), the attributes of a well-born lady. He piques her curiosity, refusing to satisfy it until she has sworn secrecy. Then, from expressions of his trust of her and praise of her upbringing (*Tu as esté en bone escole!*), he proceeds despite her initial protest to a denigration of Adam in contrast to her. The graceful lyricism of Satan's praise is a mirror held up to Eve, in which she is shown a courtly image of herself:

Diabolus

    Jo vi Adam: mais trop est fols.

Eva

    Un poi est durs.

Diabolus

             Il serra mols.

    Il est plus dors que n'est emfers!

Eva

    Il est mult francs.

Diabolus

              Ainz, est mult serf!

    Cure nen voelt prendre de soi;

    Car la prenge sevals de toi!

    Tu est fieblette e tendre chose,

    E es plus fresche que n'est rose;

    Tu es plus blanche que cristal,

    Que neif que chiet sor glace en val.

    Mal cuple em fist li criator:

    Tu es trop tendre, e il, trop dur!

    Mais neporquant tu es plus sage:

    En grant sens as mis tun corrage.

    Por co fait bon traire a toi:

    Parler te voil.

Eva

             Ore i ait fai.   (221–36)

(*Devil*

    I've seen Adam—but he's a fool.

Eve

    A bit severe.

Devil

             He'll soften up.

    Harder than hell he is just now.

Eve

    He's a gentleman.

Devil

             A menial rather.

    Even if he neglects himself,

    At least he might look after you.

    You're delicate and sensitive,

    Sweeter to look at than a rose;

A crystal-clear complexion, like
Snow in an icebound valley falling.
You two! God made a bad match there:
You have feeling, Adam has none.
But still, you are the wiser one,
Your instinct full of great good sense.
That's why it's better to deal with you.
I'd like a word.

Eve

You can trust me now.)

The image of superior beauty implies social superiority and, by the
insidious logic of *courtoisie*, superior wisdom. As an expression of
character, the speech suggests Satan as a courtly lover, insinuating
himself between a happy couple, arguing by courtly standards that the
flower of God's creation is a *mal cuple*. The sentiments are precisely
those of a humorous courtly defence of women written, in Anglo-
Norman, against the mainstream of clerical anti-feminism (see above
p. 117). The poet of *Du bounté des femmes* argues in scholastic manner
from Eve's creation; because the bone was 'blaunche come flour de
may', she and all women are 'blaunche, necte e fin e pure'. Adam, by
the same logic, is a mere clod. A homely eighth-century catechism goes
further, asking 'Who was the first woman to commit adultery?'
Answer, 'Eve, with the serpent'.[34]

Eve's acceptance of Satan's flattery and false logic leads to her disobedience: she promises to defy Adam and not to reveal Satan's
secret. The same arguments that the Devil used against Adam are now
repeated, and Eve is offered knowledge and power. But she is shown to
hesitate. For her the fruit must have a more immediate sensuous
appeal:

Diabolus

En celui est grace de vie,
De poëste e de seignorie,
De tut saver, bien e mal!

Eva

Quel savor a?

Diabolus

Celestial!
A ton bel cors, a ta figure
Bien convendreit tel aventure
Que tu fusses dame del mond,
Del soverain e del parfont ...   (249–56)

Devil

> In this is the gift of life itself,
> Of strength, and of authority,
> Of all knowledge, both good and evil.

Eve

> How does it taste?

Devil

>   Heavenly!
> With your figure and your face
> You deserve a chance like this
> To be first lady in the world,
> The queen of heaven and of hell . . .)

In the pun which links *saver* and *savor* the reduction of 'natural' knowledge of all things into 'revealed' knowledge of specific physical
objects points the downward path from man's first pure understanding.[35] Eve's hesitation gives Satan the chance for his most daring flight
of deception, and the irony latent in the earlier extravagant praise of
Eve turns almost to parody. Beginning with physical appreciation of
Eve's *bel cors*, he offers her an imaginative vision of herself as queen of
heaven. The titles, of course, belong properly to the Virgin Mary,
redeemer of the curse on mankind that Eve, her antitype, will bring.
Having elicited a promise from Eve to taste the fruit when Adam is
resting, Satan makes a mocking farewell ('Only children put things
off'), leaving her 'gazing longingly at the fruit'.

  The final movement of the Fall is presented as a domestic quarrel in
which husband and wife each try to assert mastery. The subtle psychological progression here has been sensitively analysed by Erich Auerbach[36] and only its general lines need be sketched here. Adam, 'angry
that she has spoken with the Devil', remonstrates with Eve, calling her
muiller, wife, to remind her of her place. She defends herself and
Satan. He insists that Satan is a traitor whom he has tested, and cites the
attempt to usurp the seat of his lord in heaven. Eve asserts, possibly in
mockery of her husband, that she will not believe Satan until she too
has tested his advice. The impasse is broken by the movement of the
mechanical serpent up the trunk of the forbidden tree. Silently Eve
listens to its advice and defiantly picks the apple. This simple action
overthrows Adam's authority. Eve assumes control, exulting in her
power and contemptuous of Adam's scruples. Her pattern of speech,
alternately bullying and turning away, reveals how thoroughly she has
become the devil's advocate:

Eva

> Gusté en ai. Deus, quele savor!
> Unc ne tastai d'itel dolçor!
> D'itel savor est ceste pome—

Adam

> De quel?

Eva

> D'itel nen gusta home.   (303–6)

(Eve

> I've tasted it. Oh, God, the flavour!
> I've never tasted such a sweetness.
> This apple has a taste like—

Adam

> Like what?

Eva

> Like no one's ever tasted.)

Finally, Adam reaches for the fruit, saying,

> Jo t'en crerra. Tu es ma per.
>
> (I will trust you. You are my companion.)

His gesture of trust in their equality (*Tu es ma per*) surrenders his *con-servage*, his natural authority in marriage.

For Adam, eating the apple precipitates immediate understanding. Possibly the poet wished to show Eve's rapture as deception, or perhaps she perceives the good and he the evil knowledge the fruit contains (it is Eve who later speaks the final words of expectation and hope of salvation). Also, theological tradition stressed Adam's sin; as 'reasonable man', the nature of Satan's advice was clear to him, though he was blinded by trust of Eve. Impervious, like Paris, to the temptations of wisdom and power, he succumbs to the voice of love.

Now that the Fall is accomplished there is a sharp shift in tone: Adam's lengthy speeches, architecturally wrought in their rhetorical structure, stress the moral of broken feudal trust and the misogynistic wisdom—after the event—that is so widespread in medieval clerical writing.

> Vers mon seignor sui si mesfait,
> Nen puis contre lui entrer en plait,
> Car jo ai tort, e il ad droit.   (343–5)
>
> (Against my lord I have done such ill
> I cannot begin to plead against him,
> Since I am wrong and he is right.)

Ai, Eve! Ai, femme desvee!
Mal fussez vus de moi nee!   (357–8)

(Oh, Eve! You foolish woman!
Cursed that you were ever born of me!)

The overthrow of Adam's *discipline* is shown as the loss of *raison*, that is, the right to justice or to protection by his lord. God's judgment is that of a lord threatened by a rebellious vassal: exile from the fief of Paradise with no right of appeal (*n'i avez rien que chalengier*). Adam's reproaches are directed against Eve, accusing her of treason, and of having stolen his *sens* and *raison*; she will never bring good to men because she will be 'always opposed to reason'. The psychological verisimilitude is directly exemplary.

Adam's reiterated curses have the venom of centuries of clerical anti-feminism. The proverbial wisdom which insists that Eve should have been ruled by Adam complements the poet's earlier use of the courtly ideal. For the courtly image of female superiority propounded by Satan was shown to contain a direct threat to the primal ideal of marriage. The protracted nature of the rhetorical *planctus* and re-criminations allows the audience to dwell on the implications of exile to 'earth' in familiar and domestic terms. The dialogue has a model in anti-feminist poetry that has not, to my knowledge, been noted. An early twelfth-century Anglo-Norman poem, *De Conflictu Corporis et Animae*, is distinguished from the tradition of such poems by the fact that the reproaches of Body and Soul take the form of an argument about the responsibility of each for the Fall. The Soul at first assumes a self-righteous identification with Adam which the Body later criticizes. As they look forward to diabolic torments and heap blame on one another, the idiom is distinctly domestic.[37] While I do not suggest the *De Conflictu* as a literary 'source' for this part of the *Adam*, such an early vernacular poem may have helped the playwright to establish the domestic meaning of the Fall in his play.

Adam's laments are not really appeals for sympathy, since, after all, he voices only the common lot of the fallen audience. The exaggerated quality of this protracted anti-climax seems, however, to be deliberate. It is not Adam but Eve who has the last word. She acknowledges the justness of his reproaches and accepts the burden of guilt which he has avoided both in his incomplete confession of his own responsibility and in his casting blame on her.

> Adam, bel sire, mult m'avez blastengee,
> Ma vilainnie retraite e reprochee.
> Si jo mesfis, jo en suffre la haschee.
> Jo sui copable: par Deu serrai jugee . . .
>
> Nen a raison que vers Deu me defende,
> Que peccheriz culpable ne me rende.
> Pardonez le moi, kar ne puis faire amende:
> Si jo poeie, jo frai par offrende.   (559–70)
>
> (Adam, my lord, on me reproach you've bent:
> You blame me for my crime and castigate.
> If I did wrong, I feel the punishment;
> I am to blame, God is the magistrate . . .
>
> I've no excuse; to God how could I defend
> Myself? No grounds can clear me of this sin.
> Forgive me, since I cannot make amend:
> If I were able, I would—with offering.)

Eve's complete confession, her desire for pardon and her wish to make restitution by offering (the obligation of Cain and Abel in the next 'act') constitute an exemplary pattern. It is she and not Adam who, as the Devil and demons approach from Hell with chains and manacles, expresses the hope of salvation:

> Deus me rendra sa grace e sa mustrance;
> Gieter nus voldra d'emfer par pussance.   (589–90)
>
> (God will show me his favour and his grace;
> From Hell he will wish to snatch us with his strength.)

The 'realism' of this extraordinarily human play is functional; there is no concern to represent the *mise-en-scène* or the teeming physical reality of contemporary everyday life. The eternal truths are located firmly in the medieval world chiefly through the language of the characters. The wonderfully supple dialogue expressing intentions, relationships and feelings of the characters, creates a network of social assumptions and religious attitudes that are those of a Norman culture in its feudal, clerical and courtly aspects. Composed at about the time when marriage was instituted as a 'sacrament', the play shows the Fall as the failure of the Christian ideal and, in a wider social context, as an act of feudal treachery. Its consequences are shown and an act of penitence is recommended by example, with the promise of salvation. This human and moral interpretation, which I believe to be highly original in the play, is set within frames provided by ecclesiastical tradition: the overall structure, the use of liturgical authority, Gregorian chant, symbolic costume and action, force the audience to view the action as part of the divine plan of salvation, containing within itself the seeds and shadows of that total fulfilment. The human insight, the sure sense of stagecraft and the keen sense of relevance that the poet brings to selecting and fusing liturgical and popular traditions make the *Adam* in my view the richest and most humane work of the early medieval drama.

7

PLAYS OF ARRAS

In the early medieval drama direct representation of the physical detail of the life known to the audience is quite rare; yet it is common in the urban plays of Arras and is characteristic of them. Arras, a manufacturing town with a thirteenth-century population in the region of twenty thousand inhabitants, had enough prosperous and educated burgher-patrons to support a group of resident poets and *jongleurs*.[1] Some of these entertainers were practitioners of the traditional mimic skills; many had clerical schooling; some had acquired a knowledge of ecclesiastical drama as well as of the epic and love-poetry of the feudal courts in northern France. Their own dramatic compositions were, as we shall see, suited to the practical interests of their business-minded audiences and usually had a firmly 'realistic' basis in the mimic style. The earliest Arras play that is purely secular in its material (Adam de la Halle's *Le Jeu de la Feuillée*, c. 1276) looks something like a modern satirical revue. But, much earlier than this, the distinctive features of an Arrageois tradition were stamped on the material of saints' legend by Jehan Bodel.

Jehan Bodel: 'Le Jeu de Saint-Nicolas'
Bodel's play (c. 1200) contrasts with *Le Mystère d'Adam* in the thoroughly *secular* nature of its realism: however bizarre the persons or actions of the story, the play-world is always recognisably the streets and taverns of Arras, and the characters are intimate with local people and affairs. Unlike the *Mystère*, Bodel's play shows almost complete indifference to the traditions of liturgical drama. Latin miracle plays of St Nicolas had existed for a century before Bodel wrote, but all who have studied

Bodel's play and his possible sources have stressed his independence and originality in virtually every aspect of episode and technique.[2]

The basic plot of the play (recounted briefly in Wace's *Vie de Saint-Nicolas*) concerns a miracle performed by an icon of the saint. It belongs to the crusading era. During a war between Christians and Saracens, the Saracen king captures the icon. To test its power he leaves his treasure in its keeping. The treasure is stolen but, at the intervention of St Nicolas, is returned and the king is converted. Bodel, who, according to his own confession, planned to go on crusade before he contracted leprosy, turned these brief suggestions into a complex double action, interweaving and playing off against one another the imaginary worlds of the epic *chanson de geste* and knockabout, low-life *sotie*.

There is an element of festivity in the dramatization of this bizarre plot that accords well with what can be conjectured of the play's auspices. The hundred-line prologue telling the story, spoken by the 'preacher', refers to the night of performance as St Nicolas' Eve (5 December). There were several charitable guilds dedicated to St Nicolas, patron of scholars, in Arras. Later records show that the *Confrérie des clercs de Saint-Nicolas* annually attended Mass on their patron's day and feasted whilst the Life of the Saint was read aloud.[3] As a *clerc* who worked for the city government, Bodel probably belonged to such a guild. At meetings of the *Confrérie des Ardents de Notre-Dame*, a guild of *jongleurs* and poets of Arras, opened to bourgeois membership in 1194, vast amounts of food and wine were consumed; professional entertainers performed either in a public square or, in winter, in a nearby guildhall. On such nights of revelry the links between the players and their audience would have been intimate, and wine their common indulgence. The picture of vicious life in the play may have served to license the audience's own more staid amusements. Two centuries after Bodel's death, on St Nicolas' Day 1417, his play was revived by the scholars of Notre-Dame de Saint Omer before an enormous crowd in the town square. After the play the scholars dispersed to the adjoining taverns, abandoning themselves to wild drinking and dicing (normally prohibited them), apparently in imitation of the play.[4]

But one must not romanticize the social setting by extrapolating from the play; after all, an audience actually engaged in the vicious pleasures shown with such relish in the play would hardly find 'straight' representation amusing. The drinking and dicing of the idealised low-life characters of the play presupposes an audience socially and morally

superior to them. A good corrective to the 'romantic' view is to read in
the *De Naturis Rerum* of Bodel's English contemporary Alexander
Neckham an account of dicing and drinking.[5] This may have been
observed during his school days in Paris; more to the point is Neckham's interpretation. For him, dice-players (because the soldiers cast
lots for Christ's garments) epitomize the vicious life of men enslaved to
Fortune. He describes in vigorous language the eagerness with which
the gamester follows each throw, his changes of expression, his vows to
heaven, his imprecations, his accusations of unfairness against his
opponents (though he himself uses false dice). The wrangling and
fighting always end, says Neckham, in the victim playing away his
clothes. The same theme is pursued in Neckham's ensuing story of the
prodigal son. This chapter of Neckham's encyclopaedia may stand as a
warning against too strictly sociological a reading of the Arras plays,
not only of Bodel's *Saint-Nicolas* but also of *Courtois d'Arras*, a treatment
of the parable of the prodigal son.

Bearing in mind that the *clercs* who composed plays for the guild feasts
were men learned in *moralitas*, it is still hard to avoid the overwhelming
sense of specifically *local* enjoyment that the plays offer. *Saint-Nicolas* is
presented to its audience as 'play'; its conventions of staging are an
object of fun, the preacher's preamble suggests:

> Pour che n'aiés pas grant merveille
> Se vous veés aucun affaire;
> Car canques vous nous verrés faire
> Serra essamples sans douter
> Del miracle representer
> Ensi con je devisé l'ai.   (106–11)

> (And so do not be too much amazed
> if you see some funny business here;
> for whatever you see us doing
> will be a faithful attempt, it's certain,
> at representation of the miracle
> just as I have recounted it.)

Aucun affaire may refer specifically to the quarrels (*li affaires* of line
1169) which have the appearance of improvisation. It is all part of the
show.

Bodel's stage represents an infinite kingdom with several distinct
loci of action: the Saracen king's palace with its shrine of the god
Tervagan, the tavern, the prison, the distant lands of the four vassal
emirs, the battlefield, and, possibly, a 'heaven'. Of the structures the

tavern is most clearly outlined in the dialogue; it seems to be a porch-like house opening on to the 'place'; it has a doorway at the back through which wine is brought to the tables and dicing board; on the roof is a barrel-hoop sign. The characters move freely from one locality to another, so that action is continuous, the abrupt shifts and juxtapositions causing delight. Action is divided sharply between epic conflict and riotous living, with a predominance of the latter. High and low plot characters remain separate, except for the messengers who post about the world in a Puck-like way with lightning speed.

The play begins with high plot: the King's herald Auberon announces the Christians' attack. The gilded god Tervagan is consulted and the Saracen army summoned. Auberon is sent to summon the vassal emirs, 'swifter than a camel can run a league'. As he rides to the furthest out-posts of empire Auberon meets a taverner of Arras, who is advertising hot bread and herring and wine of Auxerre. At once the taverner and Auberon, the Saracen emperor's courier, fall into a technical discussion over the legal price of city wine and an argument develops about whether Auberon shall pay a penny and have a farthing's worth on credit or pay a halfpenny and owe a farthing. One of the tavern regulars, Cliquet, proposes a dice game to settle the bill. Auberon wins, escapes and summons the emirs gravely to the king's presence. They assemble, bringing tribute. The combined army advances to meet a group of Christian knights.

In the ensuing action the conventions of Old French epic, already hinted at in the pagan idol worship, are dramatically recreated. The Christian knights are outnumbered a hundred to one and are exhorted with promises of heavenly reward:

> Paradis sera nostres et eus sera ynfers!

The line might be uttered by Roland or Turpin. An angel appears, promising the crown of martyrdom. When the emirs have killed them, the Christians are apparently escorted to 'paradise' by the angel. A Good Man, owner of the icon, is captured and taken to the king, who proposes to hazard his treasure. Connart, an Arras city crier, is sent out to proclaim that the king's treasure is guarded only by the icon. At this point the depraved world of the tavern is reasserted by repetition of the earlier device: as Connart passes the tavern, the taverner's boy Raoul is sent into the 'place' to advertise the wine. The two meet and quarrel over territorial rights. The old routine of two performers disputing which has the right to be 'on' is given a realistic

and satirical turn, with Connart explaining that he has a licence from
the magistrates of the *cité*, Raoul that he is employed as wine crier by
men of the *ville*, a different jurisdiction. Their fight is interrupted by
the taverner and they make peace. Raoul now 'cries' the wine formally:

> Le vin aforé de nouvel,
> A plain lot et a plain tonnel,
> Sade, bevant, et plain et gros,
> Rampant comme escureus en bos,
> Sans nul mors de pourri ne d'aigre;
> Seur lie court et sec et maigre,
> Cler con larme de pecheour,
> Croupant sur langue a lecheour;
> Autre gent n'en doivent gouster.   (645–53)

> (New wine, just freshly broached,
> wine in gallons, wine in barrels,
> smooth and tasty, pure, full bodied,
> leaps to the head like a squirrel up a tree.
> No tang of must in it, or mould—
> fresh and strong, full, rich-flavoured,
> as limpid as a sinner's tears;
> it lingers on a gourmet's tongue—
> other folk ought not to touch it!)

The images, which may be those of a convention in advertising wine,
recur in at least two later Anglo-Norman alliterative formulae used
for this purpose.[6]

The tavern scene continues for five hundred lines, and is broken only
by the brief visit (twenty-four lines) of the three thieves, Pincedés,
Cliquet, Razoir, to steal the king's unguarded treasure. Their visit to
the royal palace is made possible by the sleep of the royal household;
by extension of the same convention, the theft and its later return are
discovered through the seneschal's dream—a further device which
the high plot shares with epic (e.g. Charlemagne's dreams in *Roland*).
The rest of the lengthy central scene is taken up with the vicious
pleasantries of the tavern folk, their slick banter, drinking, quarrelling
(two more fights follow the pattern of the first) and dicing. Details are
minutely observed. The gamblers accuse one another of jogging the
dice board, and it is tested for level by placing a pea in the centre.
Standard dice passed by the local authorities are borrowed from the
barman. Pincedés, the professional cheat, recommends that Razoir
check his sweaty palm with dust. Each throw is followed by cries of

delight or dismay, swift calculations, boasts, attempts to cheat or claim 'no-throws'. From the cryptic exclamations of these exemplary slaves of Fortune, an audience familiar with the rules of *hazard* is expected to follow the course of the game.[7] Tavern reckonings are kept in mind. In contrast to the sumptuous vagueness of the gold treasure hazarded by the king, the exact amount of each dice player's debt is recorded. In accordance with Arras practice, the barman charges for candles used and reckons interest on loans.

When sleep finally closes the scene at the tavern, the high plot recommences with the discovery that the treasure is lost. St Nicolas visits the tavern and orders the return of the gold. Cliquet's coat is stripped off as pawn for the night's bill before the three depart, shaken but unregenerate. The play concludes in its loftier tone with the discovery of the returned treasure, the liberation of the Good Man, conversion of the king and his emirs, the breaking of the idol Tervagan. The singing of the *Te Deum*, by recalling liturgical play practice, reaffirms that the miracle of St Nicolas has been played as an act of piety.

Although in many respects the miracle is 'straight' the element of parody is marked. Satire of overblown literary conventions is apparent in the outlandish practices of the Saracens, their creeping up the temple steps to the gilded idol on bare knees and elbows, in the emir's boast that in the land of Orkenie the dogs excrete pure gold. The spirit of mischief touches also the representation of Christian subjects: the icon of the mitred Bishop Nicolas is referred to as *un mahommet cornu* and a *cornu menestrel*. The august saint himself speaks a broadly vernacular idiom, calling the thieves *fil a putain*. The solemnity of the conclusion, in which the king orders the emirs to kneel and swear allegiance to St Nicolas is enlivened by the refusal of the emir from the Land beyond the Withered Tree and a subsequent tussle. This is not to say that the whole play is 'a parody' of a saint's legend, for medieval sensibility in such matters was complex and could tolerate large elements of ridicule. Bodel is master of the grotesque juxtaposition. Thus, a devout tribute to the power of St Nicolas takes the form of a litany of praise by the Good Man:

> Il fait ravoir toutes les pertes,
> Il ravoie les desvoiés,
> Il rapele les mescreans,
> Il ralume les non voient,
> Il resuscite les noiiés. (521–5)

(He is able to retrieve all losses,
  he puts lost travellers on their road,
  he calls the faithless back to God,
  he gives a light to those who are blind,
  he brings the drowned to life again.)

A moment later the prison is opened and the Good Man welcomed by
his ghoulish jailer. 'What a big club you have!' (*Sire, con vo machue est
grosse!*), says the Christian. The jailer threatens to pull out his molars
with a pair of tongs. An angel appears and comforts the Christian with
thoughts of the Saviour. Such abrupt transitions and juxtapositions of
tone are often found in the later dramatic art of the passion plays.
What is unusual about Bodel's technique is the tongue-in-cheek verbal
sophistication. His dialogue is rich in slang and puns. His rogues speak
in proverbs, always 'putting on the style'. It seems appropriate that the
thieves should receive only a warning and should part planning fresh
schemes for robberies in villages near Arras. Exuberant word-play and
delight in stage antics keep reminding the audience that the play is a
game not to be taken too seriously, and that its rules are arbitrary.

Anon: 'Courtois d'Arras'

The image of the tavern is skilfully recreated in *Courtois d'Arras* as the
scene of the prodigal's riotous living.[8] The play is a few years later than
Bodel's. The anonymity of its author, in a society where poets made
names for themselves, suggests that by Arras standards he was un-
distinguished. *Courtois* has not the imaginative range of *Saint-Nicolas*,
but the poet's handling of 'realistic' situation and dialogue are equal to
Bodel's. These qualities, found in all the Arras plays, argue for a high
level of professional competence in handling favourite dramatic
situations and stock characters.

The continuity of the tradition is unmistakable. The tavern is again
the chief structure, opening on to a garden with grass and rush mats.
Courtois is persuaded to go into the garden to relieve himself, so that
the two prostitutes can plan his deception; on his return he admires the
courtyard and its flowers. The landlord and barman complete the tavern
ensemble. Courtois is robbed of his money and, after a scuffle, is made
to leave his clothes, including his breeches, in pawn. Courtois is told
that his vanished sweetheart lives at Bethune some twenty miles away
and that two of her recent victims are Damagrin and Baudet d'Estruem
(apparently real Arrageois). There is thus precise social satire here,

whilst the coarser touches bring the play close to the world of *Le Garçon et l'Aveugle* (see above p. 23): the savage mimicry of physical hardship, the obscenity and stage 'tricks' involving dressing and undressing, suggest the strength of that tradition beneath the religious drama of Arras.

The duping of *le cortois vilain*, who fancies himself to be a Sir Gawain, by two common whores is presented with unblinking focus as a harsh satire of all courtly pretensions. Attracted to the tavern by the crier's extravagant boasts of luxury and the promise of everything on credit, the country-raised Courtois succumbs at once to the gay flattery of the girls. That their *courtoisie* is a glittering veneer, transparent to all but the prodigal bumpkin, is shown by the skilful dialogue, the repeated use of 'asides' and the rapid alternation of courtly formulae with blunt vernacular terms. In the following scene the three share a 'loving cup':

Pourrette

> Mais vostre amie et vostre ancielle,
> qui bien vous ainme de cuer fin,
> vous done par amors le vin
> et, saciés, pas ne vous dechoi.

Courtois

> Damoisiele, jou le rechoi
> de bon cuer et de bon corage.

Pourrette

> Et j'en apiele le bevrage
> de ceste amor ki s'afruite.

Manchevaire

> Taisiés, dame; tout estés cuite;
> chou doit dire une fole garche.

Pourrette

> Nous avrons qanke tiere carge
> se l'on truist encore anuit.
> Esgarde, pute, quel deduit!
> Fu ainc mais feme si a aise?
> Dieus! que doit or qu'il ne me baise?
> Com je le truis viers moi eskiu!

Courtois

> Taisiés, dame, assés arés liu:
> ce faz jou pour le gent deçoivre.

Manchevaire

> Il a bien dit; donés nos boivre.   (214–32)

(*Pourrette*
> I am your sweetheart and your mistress;
> I love you truly with a gentle heart.
> I give you this wine as a token of love—
> believe me, dear, I won't deceive you.

Courtois
> My dear young lady, I accept
> with a trusting heart and in good faith.   (*he drinks*)

Pourrette
> And now I ask for a loving advance
> upon our ripening amour.   (*she takes the cup back and drinks*)

Manchevaire
> Hush, now! Be careful what you say;
> you are talking like a silly girl.

Pourrette [*to Courtois?*]
> We will reap whatever the plot will yield,
> if you can find the place tonight.
> (*Aside to Manchevaire*)
> Look, you slut! What a lark this is!
> Did ever a woman have such a chance?
> (*Aloud*)
> Oh, Lord! Why doesn't he kiss me now?
> I think he is most unkind to me.

Courtois
> Hush, my lady, time enough for that.
> I am doing this to deceive the other people.

Manchevaire
> Spoken wisely. Give us a drink.)

A scene like this demands a high degree of *mimic* skill from the actors if it is to be understood by the audience, and the tone, ranging from elaborate pastiche of courtly phrases to sly indelicacy to downright crudity, needs clever vocal handling.

The real world is kept constantly before our eyes in this play. There are no miracles and no religious conversions. Courtois decides to return to his father's farm simply because he will be better fed there. His long monologue, delivered as he 'drives pigs' aimlessly about the acting place, envying them their mast, retching as the chaff and rye husks from his own crust stick in his throat, dreaming of bowls of hot peas cooked in lard, is one of the most unusual pieces of writing in the vein of medieval realism. Everything here is concrete. In the course of the play, the moral of the parable has been changed from ever-ready divine forgiveness into one of worldly prudence: distrust the world, especially women; keep your head clear and your hand on your wallet. The implicit anti-feminism, the materialism and cynicism of this world are not necessarily personal to this author; they are found, for instance, in the *fabliaux* of Rutebeuf and Gautier le Leu.[9] These qualities are the stock-in-trade of the old mimic tradition, relying on the accurate observation of real life, obscene antics and the playing of stage 'tricks' for its satirical effect.

Adam de la Halle: 'Robin et Marion'

In contrast to the poet of *Courtois*, Adam, the greatest of the thirteenth-century Arras poets, seems at once more learned and more courtly. Born about mid-century, he was a celebrated musical composer and the author of witty debate poems on questions of love. His subtle, allusive, mock-autobiographical poetry is the source of most speculations about his life. Probably he studied polyphony in Paris and was a tonsured *clerc*, who, because he married, was caught between the laws and taxes of ecclesiastical and secular powers. As a professional minstrel he depended on the patronage of a patrician class he distrusted. He became court musician to Count Robert II of Artois in about 1283, dying, apparently in the count's service, in about 1289, and leaving two plays among his works.

Neither of Adam's plays is what both seem at first sight—folk drama. They are, rather, a professional entertainer's sophisticated adaptations of folk forms, and they show his art serving both courtly and plebeian audiences. The musical play *Robin et Marion* has already been discussed briefly as a crowning achievement of the traditions of *bergerie* and of pastoral dancing-games (see above p. 53). In the present chapter I shall simply suggest some ways in which the play is related to the common achievement of Arras.

Although it is composed in Adam's native Artésian dialect and makes use of songs of a typical northern French *pastourelle* kind, *Robin et Marion* is a transplant.[10] For, when, in about 1283, Adam was employed by Count Robert, he moved to southern Italy with the French army of occupation set up after the Sicilian Vespers massacre, and spent the rest of his life between Naples and Sicily. It seems that *Robin et Marion* was composed for an expatriate court and, though nothing is known of the actual circumstances of production, it may give an idealized image of the homeland several removes from reality. Adam did not compose his own music, but instead he incorporated traditional melodies, dances and snatches of refrains to be recognized by his audience, lively and attractive 'popular' tunes, easily learnt and easy to dance to.[11] The plot, to recapitulate briefly, is that of many *pastourelle* lyrics: Marion is wooed by a knight and rejects him, preferring her rustic Robin. (Is there perhaps some autobiographical playfulness here, particularly if Robin were played by Adam and Marion by his wife Marie?[12]) The path indicated by traditional plot and marked out with traditional song-and-dance stops short, halfway through the play. The remainder of *Robin et Marion* is devoted to a party of rustic boys and girls: they sing and dance, chatting, flirting, playing games, describing with relish the food they have hoarded for their picnic. The hero Robin soon forgets his discomfiture at the hands of the sarcastic knight and demonstrates his bravery (dashing off to rescue Marion's sheep from a wolf), his devotion to Marion (by ostentatious hugs and kisses), and his dancing skills. The 'wedding' (*noches*) of the pair is celebrated before the whole party dance their way 'out', 'along the path to the greenwood'.

As in all *pastourelle*, sense of class consciousness is an essential part of the play's charm. The shepherds and shepherdesses with their straw hats, apples and cheeses, their bagpipes and dances, comic brawling, dainty exchanges of love tokens and vows, are a refined aristocratic image of idealized country sports.

The rustics are 'quaint'—objects of delight and ridicule through whom the audience participate critically in an idyllic and erotic fantasy world. They are both innocent and ignorant. Ignorant of courtly behaviour, in that Marion cannot recognize the knight's hooded falcon and asks why its head is made of leather, mistakes his pursuit of heron for herring (*hairon, hairens*) and compares his spirited horse unfavourably with Robin's docile plough horse. Yet she is too much a lady to touch a sheep for fear of dirt! Robin is shown as a boastful but endearing coward who hides in a bush to watch the knight attempt to make love to his sweetheart, and has his ears boxed for mismanaging the escaped falcon. They are also innocent in sexual matters. The whole party is adolescent and Robin and Marion engage in hugging and kissing. In the quizzing game the boys ask questions about 'country matters', trying to make the girls blush. In contrast to the serious threat posed by the knight who tries to drag Marion away on his horse, it is all very innocent. The dialogue between Robin and Marion contains flickers of double meanings, but these are put there for the sophisticated audience by the author; they are not intended or understood by the characters themselves. When Marion produces two round cream cheeses from the front of her bodice or when Robin complains of strain from playing ball it is the knowing audience who recognize the latent sexuality of innocent children's talk. If this double awareness, this condescending irony implicit in the pretence of such an innocently paradisal existence is missed, then the play's social meaning is greatly impoverished.

My interpretation can to some extent be corroborated by noting the changes made to the play when it was revived, some years after Adam's death, for an audience of burghers in his native Arras. The delicate balance of courtly idyll and satirical realism was shifted to suit the coarser palates of urban dwellers whose chief occupation was commerce, wine, wool and law. There is a prologue (*Li jus du Pèlerin*) designed for the occasion and presenting the play in a new perspective.[13] It is spoken by a pilgrim who claims to have visited the tomb of Adam in Sicily and who praises Adam's poetry, songs and plays. A low-born *vilain* and three youths appear and contradict him, denigrating Adam's talent and singing some of his melodies to their own obscene words. Finally they beat the pilgrim and drive him away. When the play properly begins the three youths, Guios, Warniers and Rogaus reappear for the picnic party, cracking jokes and fighting over the wine. The nature of the two interpolated scenes totalling eighty-eight lines can be sampled in Robin's greeting of them:

Robins
> Warnet, tu ne sès? Mehalos
> Est hui agute de no prestre!

Warniers
> He! Tout li diale i puissent estre!
> Robert, comme avés maise geule!　(61–4)

(*Robin*
> Warnet, don't you know the news? Today
> Mehalos has had a child by our priest!

Warnier
> Ha! May all the devils take you!
> What a filthy mouth you have!)

In this way the well cultivated pastoral turf is thoroughly trampled by dungy hobnail boots.

These late alterations illustrate a curiously cyclic process of cultural phenomena. The 'folk' culture (here the popular dance games) has been idealized by an aristocratic court culture and then repopularized for less exclusive audiences (the progression is similar to that of Celtic story to courtly romance to folk-ballad). The figures of Robin and Marion were not the sole property of Adam de la Halle and existed in popular tradition too. But what they did there is largely beyond recovery. In the centuries following Adam's play they became thoroughly assimilated into popular revels. In an Anglo-Norman *Dispute of Wine and Water* (*c.* 1300) the Wine of Auxerre (pride of the taverners in *Le Jeu de Saint-Nicolas, Courtois d'Arras,* and *Le Jeu de la Feuillée*) speaks feelingly of the couple. Before the court of the god of love, Wine of Auxerre claims that it should become king of vintages: 'My strength makes people sing of Robin and Marion in every region: I make people dance and leap, and quarrel and fight one another.'[14] The names Robin and Marion, introduced into England by Norman minstrels, stuck to the lord and lady of traditional May games and became associated too with the plot elements of popular romance. A printed sixteenth-century play of Robyn Hode in which the Friar ('a wagger of ballockes when other men sleepes') wins the 'Lady', suggests that anti-clerical satire was a recurrent element in the tradition.[15]

The *bergerie* picnic, which Adam presents in his play with such accomplished ease and gaiety, served too as a model for clerical dramatists in their characterization of the biblical shepherds. *Pastourelle* touches are quite frequent in the later French Nativity plays. One of the earliest, the fourteenth-century *Nativité Jhesuchrist* from the Liège area, in Walloon dialect, shows a *pastourelle* scene entirely in the idiom of *Robin*.[16] The shepherds all have girl-friends and the air is filled with excited youthful exclamations and the sound of dancing feet. They carry with them to Bethlehem a basket of nuts and apples left over from their yesterday's supper. Eylison insists that her boy-friend produce his flute so that he shall appear *ung tres gentils pasturiax*. The girls agree to walk together, letting the *jollis pasteur de renon* dance ahead of them. They make their exit 'following the little path' reminiscent of 'the path beside the greenwood' in the final song of *Robin et Marion*.

The biblical shepherds, 'keeping their flocks by night', are scarcely recognizable in the delightful summer games of these courtly young rustics, who infiltrate several of the later French Nativity plays (see below p. 188). Adam de la Halle did not invent the *bergerie* tradition, though he is its best, and also one of its earliest, exponents. Working as a professional entertainer, responsible for a self-contained 'show', he took the games of the folk and the court and turned them decisively into drama. With great delicacy *Robin et Marion* gathers up the pastoral fantasies of the courtly world, pushing them gently back in the direction of the real world.

Adam de la Halle: 'Le Jeu de la Feuillée'

Adam's earlier play satirizes life in Arras in about 1276. *Le Jeu de la Feuillée* is the strangest of medieval plays. In its emphasis on folly, its bizarre stock characters and its shrewd satire of the ecclesiastical and civic establishments, it anticipates by two centuries the Parisian law clerks' theatre of the *basoche*. In its medley of fairies and rude mechanics and its play-within-a-play, it looks towards *A Midsummer Night's Dream*. But the very topicality of the play requires a fuller account of Arras itself than has been necessary so far.

The exact auspices of the play are not recorded, but have been postulated in Marie Ungureaunu's sociological study of medieval Arras.[17] Mlle Ungureaunu finds social division to be the key-note of Arras life and a principal impulse behind its vigorous literature. Rule of the city was divided between the *échevinage* (a magistracy of patricians and wealthy bourgeois), the count of Arras, and the abbot of St Vaast's. Until the end of the thirteenth century, when the communards won some administrative and judicial reforms, clashes of jurisdiction concerning property and taxation were a major cause of civil violence. The quarrel of the criers in *Le Jeu de Saint-Nicolas* is a humorous but typical example. Amidst periods of rioting and recession in the woollen industry, physical clashes of civil and ecclesiastical interests were common; several times angry mobs desecrated public shrines and more than once a pitched battle took place between the canons of the cathedral and the monks of St Vaast's over the exhibition of relics on disputed territory. The situation in the 1260s and 1270s was particularly frustrating for those tonsured *clercs*, like Adam and some of his friends, who had married and so by recent papal decree forfeited their rights of clergy. As 'bigamists' (supposedly previously married to the Church) they were no longer exempt from secular courts and taxation. In social and literary recreation the citizens were divided too. The patrician families patronized their own literary society, the *puy*, which organized feasts, tournaments (*tables rondes*) and poetic contests in which debates on amorous and frivolous subjects were fashionable. Ordinary citizens belonged to the *Confrérie* or *Carité des Ardents*, the guild of jongleurs and bourgeois already mentioned. As a professional Adam apparently performed for both kinds of audience, choosing his tune to suit his patrons. The *puy* elected a yearly *prince* of poets, the *Confrérie* a *maior* of minstrels. In August, on the eve of the feast of the Assumption of the Virgin, the *Confrérie* held its major summer festival outdoors and it seems that the newly elected *maior* was responsible for the entertainment. *Le Jeu de la Feuillée* may be Adam de la Halle's show for just such a plebeian occasion: the manuscript titles the text *Li jus Adans*—Adam's play.[18]

At the end of the text, the *explicit: li jeus de le fuellie* conceals a typical Arrageois pun. According to Mlle Ungureaunu, the play was probably performed in a public square known as *la place de la fuellie* ('Mad Square'), the scene of public executions and other diversions of Arras life; there is a strong vein of folly in the make-up of the play. *Fuellie* refers also to the *feuillée* or canopy of greenery beneath which the shrine of the Virgin was exhibited publicly during the summer and to which the characters of the play go, at the end of the show, to light devotional candles. The play too has its *feuillée*, a decorated bower standing, it seems, outside a tavern porch, and containing a table set with three places for the fairies whose visit forms the centre-piece of the entertainment. (Was it perhaps through familiarity with such 'folk-play' stages that medieval commentators came to define the Roman word *scaena* as *umbraculum*—a shaded place or arbour?[19]) In the course of the play it is revealed that this bower with its inviting banquet is the work of the author Adam and his friend Rikiers.

The play, rich in interwoven themes, is virtually plotless, having the air of a series of improvisations performed by the author and his friends to amuse themselves. There is thus constantly an inner audience of actors as well as the real audience. In the manner of a student revue, it is probable that Adam and some of the other actors 'played themselves' while others took off real people known to the audience, and others played completely fictional 'stock' characters. As in the folkplay tradition, the arrival of new characters generates new 'acts'. The cast list, a motley of real and fanciful persons, set down in order of appearance, reveals the structure to have five major acts.

(1) *Adam's farewell and 'turn'*   (1–199)
  Adam (poet and husband)
  Rikiers Auri (his friend)
  Hane the merchant
  Gillos le Petit
  Henri (Adam's father)

(2) *The doctor's 'turn'* (200–321)
    Doctor
    Rainelès (his helper)
    Dame Douce

(3) *The monk's 'turn'* (322–589)
    Monk (bearer of relics of Sainte-Acaire, patron of madmen)
    Walès (a madman)
    Fool ('dervish')
    Fool's father

(4) *The fairy show* (590–857)
    Crokesos (Puck-like messenger to Hellekin, king of fairies)
    Morgan-le-Fay (fairy queen)
    Arsile (good fairy)
    Maglore (bad fairy)
    Fortune (mute)

(5) *Tavern scene* (876–1099)
    Raoul (Watchman, Taverner)

Adam dominates the first act. He announces his intention of going to
Paris to resume his clerical education, leaving his young wife in Arras.
His friends mock his plan and fidelity, and he tells in detail his dis-
illusionment in love, the transformation of his lovely sweetheart into a
dowdy wife. Adam's father complains of his financial burdens and the
talk turns to misers and women. For the second act the doctor commands the stage. He diagnoses greed and avarice in various local
people. Then, aided in a farcical 'test' by Rainelès, he pronounces the
outraged Dame Douce pregnant. The arrival of the monk initiates the
third act. Claiming to cure lunacy by means of his relics he extorts
offerings from various madmen brought to him, while the more
sophisticated characters talk of taxes and the pope's revocation of
rights of clergy from married *clercs*. All the characters then withdraw
to form an audience as the fairies come in to occupy the centre-piece.
The fairies make wishes for the organizers of the banquet and then
discuss the lives of the great and wretched in Arras with the illustration
of a tableau of Fortune's Wheel. They then disappear to meet the
townswomen at the nearby *Crois ou Pré*. The actor–audience move to
the tavern for the finale. After drinking and quarrelling, the monk is
tricked into leaving his relics in pawn for the wine. The male company
exits to light candles at the shrine of the Virgin, leaving the monk and
the incurable dervish.

The play action takes place overnight; the fairies must disappear before dawn, the company breakfasts in the tavern, the monk hears the Matins bell calling him away. It is a waiting-up, a night watch (the Midsummer show in medieval Chester was known as 'the Watch', see below p. 182), a vigil before worship at the Virgin's shrine. As we have noted earlier, these vigils were notorious occasions of folk revels, particularly when the Christian feast had been instituted on the occasion of a pagan feast. Among the ancient women's practices condemned as diabolical and obscene by Burkhard of Worms (*c.* 1025) is the custom of 'setting a table with three places and food and drink, with three knives upon the table, so that those three sisters, whom ancient peoples and ancient foolishness named the *parcae*, might come and eat there'.[20] The other abuses in the list for which Burkhard prescribes penances are sexual ones practised by women (the next in order concerns a *molimen aut machinamentum in modum virilis membri*). The Penitential of Bishop Iscanus (1161–86) interprets this diabolical practice as a charm to bring luck to an unborn child and Robert of Brunne says the same in his *Handlyng Synne*.[21] In Arras, this women's ancient rite may perhaps have coincided with the Eve of the Assumption, and so have been in part a deliberate obverse of the men's pious devotion to the Virgin. In any case, hostility between the sexes is a pervasive theme of the play. Adam sets the tone of anti-feminism with his virtuoso piece renouncing the pleasure of love and marriage. On the other side, Dame Douce enlists the help of the matriarchal fairies and leads the women of the town to take revenge with tooth and claw upon the man responsible for revealing her pregnancy. One may perhaps see in the militancy of the Arras women a dramatic folk custom similar to the Coventry 'hocking' (see above p. 42).

But the existence of folk custom alone cannot explain its use in the play. It must be that *impersonated* fairies made traditional visits in Arras (like Santa Claus or Halloween witches nowadays). For Adam's use of the fairies is simultaneously both traditional and a complete spoof. It is evident that the fairies are eagerly awaited by the characters: they hush one another, listening for the ringing of bells on the fairies' folk-play costumes, and reminding one another of the order of appearance:

> Char ch'est droite coustume estavle
> K'eles vienent en cheste nuit. (566–7)

> (For it is the well established custom
> for them to come upon this night.)

The poet adds fun to this suspense in several ways. He plays an elaborate trick on the tradition of folk-drama with its secret meeting place, which to reveal would 'break luck'. He makes Rikiers ask the monk to leave, pretending that his relics are keeping the fairies away from this hallowed ground. Again, Dame Douce seems to think that the fairies will be somewhere else and she leaves the acting place to look for them. When the fairies approach, Rainelès is so terrified of them (though Adam the character tells him that they are ladies dressed up, *Che sont beles dames parées*) that he runs away. When Crokesos the messenger enters he asks the actor-audience if *they* have seen the fairies, as if he has made a mistake about the rendezvous. Finally, to crown all this mischief, after the banquet, as Morgan-le-Fay tells her fairies to leave before dawn light makes them visible to men, Dame Douce reappears, out of temper, to scold them; she claims that she and the other old women of the town have been waiting up for them at the *Crois ou Pré*. Adam pretends that *his* play has waylaid the fairies from their traditional tryst and has kept the old women of the town waiting up all night. Adam's play seems to have no bounds, to be one corner of a carnival of make-believe which stretches out into the streets of Arras and into the night.

Dame Douce wants the fairies to help her catch and beat up the man who has humiliated her before the company. This man must be Rainelès, who, as helper in the doctor's farcical 'thumb-test', pro-claimed aloud *Dame, je voi c'on vous fout!* ('I see someone screwing you!'). In the scuffle which followed, the male company prevented the Dame from taking her revenge. But now the fairies, traditional champions of the weaker sex, come to her aid. The reason for Rainelès' fear of the fairies is now clear. As the fairies leave the acting place to marshal an army of women Bacchantes, Dame Douce threatens to mutilate the poor fellow *en sen lit*, in bed. How far the make-believe continues beyond the acting place can only be a guess, but there is an ominous note in Dame Douce's mention by name of two of her victims from the previous year.

All this suggests to me without the shadow of a doubt that the fairies and Dame Douce were permanent features of a traditional 'show'. The realistic dialogue of the play and its topical satirical references, its biographical postures, are like fresh paint on masks saved from the year before. I think that other elements in the play were also traditional. Some have the stamp of true folk-drama. There is the doctor, whose diagnosis of an illegitimate pregnancy from urinoscopy is a well known motif in folklore. Dame Douce is a lively incarnation of the folk-play 'dame' and was probably played by a man. Like Old Dame Jane of the Bassingham plough play (see above pp. 37, 39), she tries to blame her child on one of the principal men (Rikiers) and he denies the bastard. The fool (*Dervés*) of the *Feuillée* also has a model in the plough-play tradition and preserves some of the obscenity of his folk prototype. The plough-play fool usually wears a cow's tail and carries a phallic stick with a bladder of peas tied to it. In Adam's grotesque portrait the *Dervés* is roused by the 'mooing' of the sadistic crowd to try to mount his father. This 'baiting' lasts some time:

Hane
  Or en faisons tout le veel,
  Pour chou c'on dist k'il se coureche.
Li Communs
  Moie! (376–8)

    . . .

Li Derves
  Escoutés ke no vake muit.
  Maintenant le vois faire prains.
Li Peres
  Ha! sos puans, ostés vos mains
  De mos dras, ke je ne vous frape. (418–21)

(*Hane*
  Let's all play the cow for him—
  They say that gets him all worked up.
Crowd
  Moo!

    . . .

Fool
  Listen how our cow is mooing!
  Now I'm going to get her pregnant!
Fool's father
  You stinking fool! Get your hands
  Off my breeches—or else I'll thrash you!)

Hellekin's fairy-folk (*la maisnie Hellekin*), mischievous night-spirits, are a recurrent feature of European folk-tales. The king himself, who does not appear on stage but sues for Morgan's love through his messenger, may be related to the fairy Herla known to Walter Map.[22]
  In the play the fairy troupe wear bells on their costumes as in Morris dance and in the Thracian plough-play (see above p. 35). The

messenger Crokesos introduces himself by singing a refrain that is his leitmotive and draws attention to his costume:

> Me siét il bien li hurepiaus? (590–836)
>
> (How does it suit—my *hurepiaus*?)

The mysterious *hurepiaus*, possibly a cape, I believe to be some kind of headdress, perhaps even an animal head (O.Fr. *hura*: boar's head; *hureper*: to bristle). Crokesos is later teased with the appellation *barbustin* ('whiskers'). In providing welcome for the luck-bringing fairy triad, Adam and Rikiers forget to put a knife at one of the places and incur the curse of Maglore. This episode of the 'fairy who wasn't invited' is also common in folk literature. Similarly with Morgan-le-Fay's temporary infatuation for a mortal (Robert Sommeillons, the *prince* of the *puy* and possibly Adam's rival), a motif best known in Shakespeare's *Midsummer Night's Dream*.

Other 'turns' are of a civic and satirical nature. The cynical portrait of the mercenary monk with fraudulent relics is almost certainly a comment on the activities of the monks of St Vaast in the very spot that the play is performed. The monk's *Spiel* has the panache of an ecclesiastical counterpart to the quack-doctor of folk-play. Fortune's Wheel is a device that could well have been used from year to year to comment on the fortunes of the citizens of Arras, those in favour with the count and the self-seeking patricians, and on the hardships of plebeians who suffered from the arbitrary cruelty of local legislation or taxation. The tavern scene makes a traditional finale in the favourite Arrageois style.

Into these framing devices Adam also works themes and conventions drawn from courtly and learned poetry. His opening farewell to his friends is paralleled in his own lyrical *Congé* (addressed to the more exclusive *puy*) and also in the *congés* of Jean Bodel and Baude Fastoul.[23] His conflict of loyalties between love and learning is the theme of many of the *jeux-partis* (poetic debates) of Arras, and is a distinct topos in medieval Latin poetry. His cynical grumbling about marriage is paralleled in his Parisian contemporary Rutebeuf's complaints of a *mal marié*.[24] His playful speech on the delusions of love, comparing the slender-limbed wanton for whom he pined with the same pasty, jealous shrew who is now his wife, is a masterpiece in a conventional mode. The detailed description of an ideal type and antitype of feminine beauty in the Middle Ages is usually traced to Matthew of Vendôme's *Ars Versificatoria*, where verbal portraits of

Helen and Beroë are juxtaposed.[25] But, to me a more striking parallel to Adam's speech is in the eleventh-century romance *Ruodlieb*, in which the hero's mother urges him to marry soon, describing graphically the transformation of a young woman into an 'aged ape', her eyes bleared, her teeth loose, her full breasts like dried mushrooms, her pretty nails claws full of dirt.[26] The similarities of structure and detail are so remarkable that they suggest to me a minstrel's set-piece lying behind both. Adam's speech became famous independently of the rest of the play (two manuscripts contain it thus) and was commended by Brunetto Latini, Dante's teacher.[27] The knowledge of these conventions serves to qualify the impression of autobiography that the play offers. Whatever Adam de la Halle thought of his real wife we shall never know, for he is a poet who loved using masks.

A heap of gaily coloured shreds and patches, then—is the play no more than this? My gloss on the themes and conventions points to three layers of structure: first, a folk and religious watch; this then became the occasion of a yearly revue; finally, this in turn provided a platform for a professional poet. Adam uses the opportunity to offer the audience a playful commentary on his own life and troubles. The thread is an elusive one but rewarding to follow.

Adam begins the play by bidding his friends goodbye. He has donned a clerical gown and vows to return to Paris to his studies (*clergiét*), to fulfil an old dream of his:

> Seigneur, savés pour coi j'ai men abit cangiét?
> J'ai esté avoec feme, or revois au clergiét;
> Si avertirai chou ke j'ai piech'a songiét.
> Mais je voeil a vous tous avant prendre congiét.
> Or ne pourrant pas dire aucun ke j'ai antés
> Ke d'aler a Paris soie pour nient vantés.   (1–6)

> (My friends, you wonder at my change of clothes?
> I've been attached to a wife—now back to my books,
> To make my dream of long ago come true.
> But first I want to take my leave of you all.
> Now none of my friends can say my plans to return
> To school in Paris have only been idle boasts.)

The proposal meets with immediate ridicule and is clearly a long-standing joke to his friends. Rikiers says that Adam has delusions of grandeur (*grans abusions*) and Hane calls him a scatter-brain (*muavle kief*). One need not suppose that the play takes place on the eve of Adam's actual departure, for the very terms in which Adam expresses his resolve imply that it has been made many times before. And in fact Adam treats the same 'autobiographical' problem in a totally different vein in his lyrical *Congé*.

The common theme is Adam's projected departure to realize his ambition of a nobler life in which he will reconcile his aspirations as a *clerc*, a poet and a lover. The courtly attitudes expressed in the *Congé* and intended for the ears of his patrician patrons are in sharp contrast to the cynicism of the *Feuillée*. The difference merely illustrates the poet's versatility in pleasing two kinds of audience and in arguing any side of a moral problem concerning love and poetry. This skill was learned by composing and performing dozens of *jeux-partis* (debate-poems in which the joke is divided between two contestants) for the *puy* 'courts of love'. The 'autobiographical' problem of the *Feuillée* and the *Congé* is compounded of problems debated in a forum of poets.[28] In one poem Jehan Bretel asks Adam if he would like to live all his life in Arras, enjoying prosperity and the lady he loves, on condition that he must remain faithful to her and never leave town. Adam says he would; the gay world Bretel describes is full of *envie* and he would rather enjoy secular life than go to an abbey. Jehan de Grieviler asks Bretel if a poet makes better songs before or after he has obtained his lady's favours. Rogiers proposes to Adam that they exchange wives. Adam refuses. He is not attracted by Rogiers' wife and does not think him attractive enough to seduce his own. Guillaume le Viniers asks the monk of Arras if he will love his lady less after he has obtained her ultimate favours; the monk says no. De Givenci asks Guillaume le Viniers whether it is worthier to have a great but transient joy or a high ideal which he can never realize. Guillaume prefers the latter.

It would be foolish to look for consistency of attitude in such playful social poetry. It may well be that some details of Adam's life are to be found in his verse, that he found his *métier* in writing about a genuine conflict between his marriage, his poetry and the Church. But it must be acknowledged that in common with dozens of less talented poets of his native town he cultivated an image of himself as a lover and a *clerc*.[29]

The most striking difference in the attitudes of the *Congé* and the play is in Adam's treatment of his 'lady'. In the *Feuillée* he shows himself as a spent lover, now *mal marié*, fleeing domesticity to develop his true talents. In the *Congé* his lady is his Beatrice, his source of inspiration and he laments that he has wasted his bloom 'in the world', too much amongst laity (*Trop ai esté entre les lais*). He praises his lady as his Eve and his Mary, Adam's Fall and his salvation.[30]

Adieu, amours, tres douche vie,
Li plus joieuse et li plus lie
Qui puist estre fors de paradis.
Vous m'avés bien fait en partie
Se vous m'ostastes de clergie:
Je l'ai par vous ore repris,
Car j'ai en vous le voloir pris
Que je racate los et pris
Que par vous perdu je n'ai mie,
Ains ai en vo serviche apris,
Car j'estoie nus et despris,
Avant, de toute courtesie. (49–60)

(Farewell, my love, my sweetest life,
the most joyful and delightful
there may be outside paradise.
You made me lose that
when you took me from the clergy.
But now through you I have recovered it
for in you I have found the will
to earn again my honour and worth,
so that through you I have lost nothing;
for when I took to serving you
I was naked and outcast,
barren of all courtesie.)

He then takes leave of many of the patrician members of the *puy* who
have been his patrons, and of the gay carnival world of Arras tournaments, feasts and games. In the final stanza he defies those who are
cynical of his vow:

Mais il i a maint faus devin
Qui ont parlé de men couvin
Dont je ferai chascun hontex,
Car je ne serai mie tex
Qu'il m'ont jugié a leur osteux
Quant il parloient apres vin,
Ains cuellerai cuer despiteus
Et serai fors et vertueus
Et drois quant il gerront souvin. (148–56)

(But there are many false prophets
who have spoken of my oath
whom I shall make ashamed, each one,
for I shall never be such a man

> as they have judged me in their taverns
> talking, after wine.
> I shall bear a proud heart
> and be brave and virtuous
> and honoured when they lie dead.)

In *Le Jeu de la Feuillée* Adam tosses his *courtois* ideal into the tavern and lets the cynics have their say.

Adam's opening speech in the play continues with two lines which provide key metaphors in the ensuing action:

> Cascuns puet revenir, ja tant n'iert encantés;
> Après grant maladie ensuit bien grans santés. (7–8)

> (Any man could return, however deep the spell:
> 'After sickness cometh perfect health'.)

His domestic entanglement has been an enchantment, a sickness, but clerical life in Paris will cure all that. The themes of sickness and enchantment pervade the play and are reflected in the actions involving the doctor and Dame Douce, the fairies, the various madmen and the monk.

His friends mock Adam's resolve, telling him that he is too attached to his bed and, besides, when Holy Church joins two people they cannot be separated. Adam tries to justify his infatuation with his wife and his present disgust by ascribing it to the delusive power of Love:

> Mais Amours si le gent enoint
> Et cascune grasse enlumine
> En feme et fait sanler plus grande,
> Si c'on cuide d'une truande
> Bien ke che soit une roïne. (82–6)

> (It's Love, who so anoints his people
> that he lights up every grace and feature
> in a girl, and makes them seem the finer;
> so that you'd think a beggar woman
> as lovely as you would a queen.)

The point is brilliantly illustrated in the ensuing rhapsody on his sweetheart, a reverie of sensual detail that is periodically punctuated with grosser images of her as his wife. Adam concludes that he must come to his senses again before his wife becomes pregnant:

> S'est drois ke je me reconnoise
> Tout avant ke me feme engroisse,
> Et ke li cose plus me coust,
> Car mes fains en est apaiés. (171–4)

   (I must know myself again
   in time, before my wife gets pregnant
   and this 'thing' becomes expensive;
   my appetite for that has cloyed.)

Adam's friend Rikiers immediately offers to look after Marie, whom
he would find 'tasty enough'. Adam does not doubt it and prays God
that his troubles will not arise in that way. He may well be disturbed,
for we soon have clear proof of Rikiers' lecherousness. The doctor
reveals Dame Douce's stomach pains as pregnancy and Rikiers,
despite his denials, is to blame. Dame Douce, pregnant, common as
dirt, out to get her man, is something of a scarecrow. As the company
names various local shrewish women Adam's wife is casually mentioned, to keep the theme in mind.

   It is at this point that the monk exhibits his relics of Saint-Acaire
patron of madmen, claiming to cure all forms of lunacy, male and
female. The delusions of the madmen brought to him for cure are
curiously similar to Adam's own. Walès claims that if he had tried to
be as good a minstrel as his father, 'they' would have cut off his head.
The dervish is more grotesque but his comments also have an elliptical
pertinence. He denounces the hypocrisy of the worshippers and claims
first that he is king, then prince of the *Puy*; he claims that he can play
better than Robert Sommeillons, the newly elected prince, and to
prove this he trumpets in the usual coarse *fabliau* manner (squeamish
antiquarians usually record in their folk-play texts that 'the fool
trembles'). His sexual perversion too is pertinent, since, as already
noted, he purports to make his father pregnant. As the father strikes
his son away, the dervish stares at Adam and asks, 'Who is that clerk in
the gown?'. Told that he is *uns parisiens*, the dervish claims that he
looks more like a dried pea—the fool's own token. As his father tries
to quieten him 'for the sake of the ladies' (in the audience or, possibly,
the fairies) he continues to provoke Adam, accusing him of bigamy.
Whilst this comment opens up a wide ranging discussion of the evils
of the papal revocation of rights of clergy from married *clercs*, its
personal point is to make a mockery of Adam's intention of leaving his
wife to 'remarry' with the clergy. The dervish continues his fantasy of
being a great minstrel, adding to it the conviction that he is pope.
Given an apple to quiet him, he tries to throw it to Paris. The parody
of Adam's aspirations is clear. The dervish and his father are sombre
shadows of Adam and Henri. Both old men complain of their sons'
crazed fantasies and sexual preoccupations, and grumble about the

expense of keeping them. Adam and his father think that the way to a cure is through the Church. The idiot's father turns for help to the charlatan monk.

As Rikiers complains that the whole evening has been taken up with the *riotes* of fools (*sos et sotes*), the fairies approach. Morgan learns from Crokesos that Adam and Rikiers are responsible for the decorations and feast. She and Arsile pronounce gracious rewards: Rikiers shall become richer and Adam will fulfil his dream—he shall be 'the best lover that may be found in any country' and also 'gay, and a wonderful maker of poems'. But Adam's good fortune is short-lived, for Maglore, the 'uninvited' fairy, concludes with curses.

Maglore

> Je di ke Rikiers soit pelés
> Et k'il n'ait nul cavel devant.
> De l'autre, ki se va vantant
> D'aler a l'escole a Paris,
> Voeil k'il soit si atruandis
> En le compaignie d'Arras
> Et k'il s'ouvlit entre les bras
> Se feme, ki est mole e tenre,
> Si k'il perge et hache l'apenre
> Et meche se voie en respit.   (682–91)

> (I say that Rikiers shall go bald
> and have no hair at all in front!
> and Adam, who's been bragging around
> about going off to study in Paris—
> I hope that he becomes disgraced
> By joining the riff-raff of Arras;
> and that he so forgets himself
> in the arms of his sweet and loving wife,
> that he wastes his time, hates his studies,
> abandons his projected journey.)

The spiteful fairy, who jumps at the chance of helping Dame Douce in her obscene rites, reasserts the traditional claims of women. Adam shall not leave his wife a prey to Rikiers, whose attractions (and by implication sexual potency) will disappear with his hair.

With the departure of the fairies into the dawn, the midsummer night's dream is over. The male company rouse themselves and the monk wakes from sleep. The acting place becomes the tavern and the leftovers of the fairy banquet mere scraps in the taverner's pantry to be quarrelled over. Adam's midnight fantasy is tested out in the hard cynical light of the tavern. At first Adam does not join the group of drinkers and Hane calls out to him:

> Vois ke maistre Adans fait le sage
> Pour chou k'il doit estre escoliers.
> Je vi k'il se sist volentiers
> Avoeques nous pour desjuner. (949–52)

> (I see that Adam's being virtuous,
> because he's going to be a scholar.
> I've seen the time that he has been
> glad to join us for his breakfast.)

Adam's father pulls him towards the tavern group, but he resists, remembering his oath:

> Biaus sire, ains couvient meürer,
> Par Dieu! je ne le fach pour el. (953–4)

> (Good sir, I'd rather break my covenant,
> by God. I won't for anything!)

Again Henri urges and Adam refuses. At the third attempt, he gives in and enters the tavern. Hane comments:

> Aimi! Dieus! Con fait escolier!
> Chi sont bien emploiét denier!
> Font ensi li autre a Paris? (960–62)

> (Well, for Christ's sake! Look at the scholar!
> That's a fine way to spend your money!
> Is that what the others do in Paris?)

Adam has been tempted and has fallen.

At this point Rikiers notes that the monk has fallen asleep. The timing is apt. The monk, representative of a fraudulent and impotent clergy, is tricked and beaten; his relics, left in pawn, are 'worshipped' by the company, led by the innkeeper. The doctor now reappears and chastises them all for dissolute drinking, but he is quickly induced to join them. The tavern claims all. The dervish and his father return, the father pleading with the monk to cure his son. Helpless and humiliated, the monk sends them away. The dervish upsets the wine, causing chaos in the tavern, and the characters take their own belongings and leave. The dervish is led away, beaten and blubbering, claiming he is his father's bride. Someone urinates on him from above the tavern porch. Finally the monk is all alone in the street, clutching his re-claimed but powerless relics, listening to the sound of St Nicolas' morning bells. The lofty cathedral of Adam's dreams lies a heap of rubble from which stares out the gargoyle face of the folk-play *Dervés*, obscenely leering at the architect.

The resounding defeat of the charlatan monk in the parodic adoration of his pawned relics in the tavern gives public voice to the strong anti-Church feelings in contemporary Arras, which also found outlets in social violence. The truly secular life and attitudes of most thirteenth-century cities are mostly lost to us, because the records and the dramatic texts are biased in favour of the clerical perspective. Adam's *Jeu de la Feuillée* is unique in that it recovers and preserves in the words of a learned and literary poet a whole spectrum of secular (and in many instances sub-literary) forms of drama—from market place and village green, guildhall and courtly feast. Lacking 'plot', though bursting with themes and images, the play veers wildly between courtliness and cynicism, intellectual display and grossness, deep sophistication and pure inanity. A modern reader's sense may well be of bewildering ephemera, for this is the most ephemeral of all medieval plays. Yet, as I have tried to show, its patterns and meanings can be understood in relation to acting traditions which stretch back into the early Middle Ages. Of all medieval plays *Le Jeu de la Feuillée* comes closest to putting the real life of its contemporary audience on stage. In view of the fact that this is what the Arras dramatists, whatever their starting point in plot or dramatic genre, tried to do, the play can be seen as *the* achievement of the secular drama of Arras.

PART III
The Traditions in England

8

THE EARLIEST ENGLISH DRAMA

England under the Angevin kings shared largely in the literary culture of northern France. Minstrels and clerics as well as the court moved to and fro across the Channel, spreading the traditions of church and popular drama. At the instigation of Henry I, Geoffrey of Le Mans was summoned from Normandy to be master of the school at St Albans. While he lodged nearby at Dunstable, Geoffrey organized a play of St Katherine. A fire during the night following its performance destroyed both his library and the vestments he had borrowed from the abbey at St Albans and, according to the chronicler, precipitated Geoffrey's entry into monastic life.[1] Illustrations in the *Saint Albans Psalter* (*c.* 1123), executed shortly after Geoffrey rose to the position of Abbot, suggest that he may have introduced plays of Herod and of Easter subjects there.[2] In a more popular vein, songs of Robin and Marion were imported from Picardie and Artois together with the wine and wool shipped from these regions.[3] Among the 'minstrel kings' at the feast for the knighting of Prince Edward in 1306 was 'Maistre Adam le Boscu', a performer who seems to have inherited the professional name of the famous Adam of Arras.[4]

It seems unlikely that England ever nurtured a dramatic tradition comparable with that of Arras. The absence of comparable urban literary guilds and the socially divisive use throughout the country of two vernacular languages—English and French—may have inhibited the development of such socially-oriented forms. Examples of early English drama in all three languages have already been discussed (the *Book of Cerne* 'Harrowing' and the Winchester *Visitatio Sepulchri* in Latin; *La Seinte Resureccion* and *Le Mystère d'Adam* in French; the

Interludium de Clerico et Puella in English). These texts give some idea of three distinct social milieus, one ecclesiastical, one both courtly and clerical, one purely secular and popular. Beyond these plays so little survives from before the fifteenth century that it is hard to present a coherent picture of English medieval drama. The conveniently 'evolutionist' view of this dark period as a time of 'gradual secularization' of liturgical drama, preparatory to the invention of Corpus Christi play cycles in the late fourteenth century cannot be documented. Perhaps as a result of the Reformation, relatively few of the service-books in which one would expect to find liturgical plays have survived. As a result records of liturgical plays are rare and refer to a very limited range of subjects. With the exception of the tenth-century *Visitatio*, the only liturgical Latin texts from the British Isles belong to the late fourteenth century. The other play texts and fragments of the thirteenth and fourteenth centuries are either Anglo-Norman or English: they are strikingly popular in nature; some are definitely the work of the preaching orders. If one grants the existence of histrionic traditions separate from those developed in liturgical drama, then many of the records and fragments make sense as clerically organized attempts to transmute devotional material into popular dramatic modes.

What was this lost popular drama like? The performance of a 'representation of the Lord's resurrection' in St John's churchyard, Beverley, in about 1220, is described in some circumstantial detail in a chronicle.[5] Though the subject was the resurrection, it was played in summer (i.e. it was *not* connected to its appropriate feast), and outdoors. Performance was on the north side of the church (*ex parte aquilonari*), a fact the chronicler would hardly have mentioned unless he wished to connect the occasion with those folk dances and practices which the medieval church dedicated to the devil by allowing in that relatively unhallowed location. The Beverley play was performed 'by masked actors, as usual' (*larvatorum, ut assolet*). Masks, mentioned in clerical writings with inevitable condemnation, because of their association with folk dramatic practices, were forbidden to clergy by the Council of Nantes (A.D. 890) and by a series of later decretals, as William of Wadington reminds English clerks in about 1300.[6] The play at Beverley was apparently 'in the round', since the crowd, gathered together, the writer says, by delight or curiosity or devotion (*variis inducta votis, delectationis videlicet, seu admirationis causa, vel sancto proposito excitandae devotionis*), formed a ring (*corona*). Some boys climbed into the church tower to get a good view of the costumes, actions and dialogue. Outdoor performance, in the round, in a place associated with folk *ludi*, by masked actors, although the play is of the resurrection—these are some distinguishing marks of the 'rival tradition' in England. No doubt there were many more rival traditions than we know of. It seems important, at least, to stress that neither the Beverley play nor *La Seinte Resureccion* was connected with a church service. Neither were the miracle plays (*miracula*) of saints' lives, which, boasted William Fitzstephen (*c.* 1170–82), were performed in London streets 'in the place of secular shows' (*pro ludis scenicis*).[7]

Within the church, at English monasteries and cathedrals, a number of liturgical plays became traditional. According to William of Malmesbury, his abbey had a Peregrinus play in about 1125.[8] In the mid-thirteenth century York minster had properties for plays of the three kings and the shepherds, and for a 'Boy Bishop of Fools' in connection with Epiphany or New Year revels.[9] At about the same time Norwich cathedral possessed a *Visitatio Sepulchri*, while in the fourteenth century Lincoln had an Easter play of St Thomas of India and a Christmas play of the Three Kings.[10] Lichfield statutes of the thirteenth or fourteenth centuries made provision for a *Pastores*, a *Resurrexio* and a *Peregrinus*; these same three traditional plays were apparently updated in the early fifteenth century by provision of some English text to form the so-called 'Shrewsbury Fragments'.[11] From the limited evidence available, it looks as if the popular religious plays established at a very early date traditions separate from those of liturgical drama.

What can be recovered of this lost vernacular drama? One important clue is the recurrent connection of plays and sermons. G. R. Owst has argued for the importance of preaching friars in developing entertaining forms of instruction during the thirteenth century.[12] In the surviving texts, sermons and plays are linked in a number of interesting ways. The homiletic attempts to capitalize on the popularity of dancing-song plays by describing *La bele Aelis* abducted by the devil or by explaining her allegorical significance as the Virgin Mary have already been mentioned (see above p. 58). But a sermon might also form an expository prelude to a play (as with Bodel's *Saint-Nicolas*). Indeed, a thirteenth-century English Dominican sermon for St Nicolas's Day promises the congregation, 'boþe þis lewed and þis clerkes', that a play is to follow. The sermon tells a tale of a rich king and of 'saresines' that has similarities with Wace's *Vie de Saint Nicolas* (found in the same manuscript) and with Bodel's play.[13]

A sermon itself could also be a dramatic performance; in a lively verse monologue (*c.* 1300) the preacher impersonates Caiaphas.[14] The role is conceived (as in the later cycle plays) as that of a Jewish bishop. 'Bysschop Cayface' addresses a large crowd in Palm Sunday procession, expounding his 'prophetic' text ('it is better that one man should die') and inviting the audience to join him in singing. He refers to his performance as a 'god game, god y-pleyd' for, he says, belief is a matter for joy ('lovelych & lyȝt ys leve'). The punning assurance that he has obtained '*leve* of þe grete' to preach and his request to the dean for permission to sing, suggest the uneasy position of a preaching friar at, or rather outside, a large secular cathedral. Beyond his exposition of the meaning of the palms and of Caiaphas' part in the Passion of Christ, the preacher's purpose is to bring the audience to a sense of sin and to shrift. The economic motive is not explicit but it appears to be the point of recommending all 'unshriven wretches' to his partner, one 'Symon Cumpayngnoun', who has 'power of discipline' and who gives shrift and administers penances. As in the folk play tradition, the performance concludes with a collection.

Caiaphas is an equivocal figure, offering a new style of instruction, playing his sermon-game by special permission of cathedral authorities. The preacher's caution seems to have been well placed, for by the middle of the thirteenth century there had developed an ecclesiastical hostility towards the unlicensed performance of religious plays by clergy. Between 1236 and 1244 Bishop Grosseteste of Lincoln issued a series of disciplinary pronouncements to his clergy forbidding folk *ludi* ('drinkings', 'ram raisings' etc.) and also 'plays which, we have heard, have been made by clerics and are called *miracula*'.[15] Writing about 1300, William de Wadington refers to these decretals and condemns miracle plays as 'plain foolery' contrived by 'foolish clerks who disguise their faces with masks'. William goes on to contrast miracle plays, performed in churchyards after feasts, with liturgical plays performed within the office of the Holy Church. The latter (he cites the sepulchre as an example) are allowable to clergy, but performances in churchyards and city streets are diabolical, even though, William says, their instigators claim that they are done to the honour of God. Robert Mannyng of Brunne, who adapted William's remarks in

---

god good

his own *Handlyng Synne* (1303), makes the same distinction between devotional plays and performances under secular auspices in the street or on village greens.[16]

Two verse play-prologues of the late thirteenth century give a hint of what these miracle plays may have been like. Both texts are bilingual, having Anglo-Norman and English verses, so presumably they were portable commodities, capable of appealing to audiences made up of French-speaking gentry and common people (the herald in the Cambridge text bullies the 'hardi man' but politely requests silence of 'tes lordes'). The alternative texts may be for use in different parts of the country, since English or French speaking depended on place as well as on class and occupation. Both pieces are boisterous and popular in tone, calling for silence in minstrels' formulae. The Cambridge prologue is spoken by the messenger of 'the emperor', who commands silence in the name of his lord and of Mahomet. The Rickinghall fragment is spoken by a *rey coronné* who makes a similar gesture on his own behalf. This gesture is apparently an established convention and is one that is later used many times in the fifteenth-century cycle plays (by Herod or his Nuncius in *Towneley Plays* XIV and XVI, and by Pilate in XX; by Octavian and his herald in *Chester Plays* VI).

The Cambridge messenger orders the audience not to venture into the acting area or disturb the play, on penalty of imprisonment:[17]

> S'il i a nul que noyse face,
> U que entre en cete place
> Pur nostre ju ren desturber
> Prendre le frun saunz demorrer
> E juter leyns la prisun.

> (If anyone here makes a noise
> or enters into the acting place
> to disturb our play for any reason,
> we shall have him taken without delay
> and thrown into the prison.)

Penalty for escape from prison will be hanging or beating at least, he swears by Mahound. The English lines are more explicit about the physical proximity of actors and audience which forms the basis of performance. The audience must sit well spaced and allow the actors to pass among them:

> And sittet rume and wel atwo
> Þat men moȝt among eu go.

Their idle chatter must not impede the play ('lette hure game'). The messenger promises hanging, though more lenient tortures for children and simple folk ('vitles man þat mannes wit ne can'). This curious touch is hardly explicable as Mahoundish humanitarianism, but makes good sense as a hint of things to follow in the play itself. The whole dramatic function of the conventional exhortation to silence and good order seems to be a positive invitation to frolic—a challenge to a 'game' in which actors and audience provoke one another and the audience's misdemeanours are punished 'in play' by the lackeys of a pagan emperor using a stage prison. The mingling of actors and audience necessitated by the arrangement of the playing place and the evident scope for improvization first noted in the devils of *Le Mystère d'Adam* here forms a basis of a 'game' drama, in which both actors and audience have a physical part.

Further evidence of the tradition of popular religious drama earlier than the institution of the Corpus Christi play cycles is found in *Pride of Life*, which has recently been dated mid-fourteenth century on linguistic grounds.[18] This earliest English morality on the stark theme *memento mori* is probably the work of an Anglo-Irish religious house. The sparse stage directions are in Latin. Performance is outdoors and the audience is asked 'Teryith (or *Prayith*) al for þe weþer' and 'distourbith no3t oure place'. The relation of audience to 'place' is intimate, for when the King of Life's messenger goes to ask if any man will fight with his master he delivers the challenge to the audience: 'Pes and listenith to my sawe . . .'. The king too uses this vaunting form of address, commanding silence and threatening violence.

Both king and bishop occupy a throne. The king's is a curtained tent which is closed to let him sleep. The acting place may also be divided or bounded by a ditch or stream (as in the *Castle of Perseverance, c.* 1405); as the messenger comes running, the king praises his ability to 'lepe oure the lake'. A more usual meaning for *lake* in the later Middle English drama, however, is the pit, or prison, of hell. So perhaps one should imagine Nuncius skipping over a hole in the ground similar to the Devil's Spoon in the medieval Cornish 'rounds' or to the prison of the Cambridge fragment. Such a focal lake of hell is appropriate to a play concerned with the certainty of death.

The dramatic method makes much of posting to and fro between the thrones, and of direct address to the audience. Dialogue is rarely an exchange, the text consisting rather of monologues, vaunts, proclamations of challenge, satirical homiletic complaints and straightforward commands. The messenger Mirth is principal agent of action. He is a tumbler and a minstrel, singing on his way. The formally patterned vaunts promise the main action of the play to be a conflict between Death and the King of Life. Behind the heroic boasts of the king's champions may be heard the simple vernacular formulae of the sword and mumming plays. The king's first 'wonschild' (champion, or defender of his household) is called Strength and boasts:

> Ic am Strent, stif and strong,
>> Nevar is suc non,
> In al þis world brod and long,
>> Imad of blod and bon. (147–50)

He brandishes his sword, hailing the king as another who 'florresschist with þi briȝt bronde'. 'Flourishing' is the technical term for the sword display in the earliest sword-dance text.[19] And Strength's boast goes on in mummers' tones:

> I wol withstonde him with strife
>> And make his sidis blede,
> And tel him þat þou are King of Life
>> And lorde of londe and lede. (251–4)

The King of Life is shown as the ruler of a worldly entertainment played in defiance of the voice of the bishop with its *memento mori* and lasting, like the dance of Franciscan *exempla*, until the intervention of Death:

Rex
> I wool let car awey
>> And go on mi pleying.
> To hontyng and to oþir play
>> For al þi long prechyng. (427–30)

The concepts of 'prechyng' and 'pleying', upon which the structure of the drama depends, are here contrasted. Playing is pure entertainment, diversion, patently worldly and ultimately unreal. Preaching contains the word of truth.

The modes of play used in *Pride of Life* betray their origins in a popular, non-ecclesiastical drama: the vaunt and combat, audience intimidation, running about the 'place'. As we have seen, these modes were established in the popular religious drama of the thirteenth

---

lede men

century. They survive most purely in the stylized combat of the mummers' plays, from which they may originally have been adapted.

The recurrent association of sermon and play or game in the thirteenth and early fourteenth centuries testifies to the agency of preaching orders in developing a distinct concept of popular religious drama long before the Corpus Christi plays. The tradition continues alongside the great community Corpus Christi drama in *Duk Moraud* (*c.* 1400), an exemplary play on a story of incest, in the spectacular *Castle of Perseverance* (*c.* 1405), and in *Mankind* (*c.* 1465), a high-spirited professional morality which will be discussed in the final chapter. How far this tradition was 'professional' is hard to say. In *Mankind* the actors collect, in character, from the audience. *Caiaphas* also seems to require a collection of sorts. The purpose of the 'folde' (enclosure) to which Duk Moraud refers in his vaunt—[20]

> No yangelyngys ʒe mak in þis folde
> To-day—

may well be to keep out non-paying audience; and Richard Southern has argued the same for the ditch and fence illustrated in the manuscript diagram for staging *The Castle of Perseverance*.[21]

Whether these plays are the work of professionals, of friars licensed to beg, or of worldly clerks such as were condemned by William of Wadington and Robert of Brunne, the plays which survive from the period before the Middle English cycles (setting aside the 'Shrewsbury Fragments' which are from about 1400) are quite free of liturgical influence and constitute a distinctly popular tradition.

---

yangelyngys chattering or quarrelling

9

THE CYCLE PLAYS

Play 'cycles' are first recorded in England towards the end of the fourteenth century. Those at York (1376) and Beverley (1377) were for the feast of Corpus Christi. Those in London (one at Skinners Well in 1384 lasted five days) were apparently not. By the fifteenth century more than a dozen cities had Corpus Christi plays. Four complete English cycles survive (the *York Plays, Chester Plays, Towneley Plays* from Yorkshire, and 'N-Town' plays—known in an old edition as *'Ludus Coventriae'*—which belong to East Anglia, as well as a western Cornish cycle, the *Ordinalia*. Little is known about how these plays were composed or first instituted, but it is clear that such encyclopaedic spectacles of sacred history were not derived from any comparable known Latin drama. There is no sure evidence that cycles of plays on subjects from Creation to Judgment were ever played in Latin at all. In England the total range of liturgical play subjects was small, and in any one city very small. This point is made emphatically by V. A. Kolve in his lucid study of the cycles:[1]

It will not do to argue as though the whole range of Latin liturgical drama in Europe was at the disposal of any local versifier asked to produce an episode for a cycle: texts of sufficient variety and adequate distribution were not available as models.

Kolve argues that the impulse towards cyclic form was lacking in the liturgical drama, where each episode belonged to a specific day's worship and so relied on the Church year for its 'contextual completeness'. He locates the cyclic impulse in the institution of the feast of Corpus Christi (established in 1311, generally adopted in England,

1318), the rationale of this feast being a day of joyful remembrance of the Passion in its complete doctrinal meaning, seen as the fulfilment of a divine purpose prefigured in certain Old Testament episodes. Kolve's account of the structure common to the Corpus Christi cycles is full and generally convincing, and need not be reiterated here. One may add, however, that *some* plays of a cyclic nature performed during the summer season were unconnected with Corpus Christi—for instance, those in London, Cornwall and in France. So that Corpus Christi should be seen not as an 'original source' but rather as a symptom and a regulating focus of a wider movement. This movement was a popular demand for 'contextual completeness' and was linked with the clerical attempt at explaining to the laity in the vernacular the meaning of the Christian stories. The same impulse informs the twelfth-century *Mystère d'Adam* (see above pp. 113–15): Old Testament episodes are selected and organized according to a doctrinal and figural pattern so that they point forward to a known conclusion (the Redemption, even though this is not shown), stressing the legacy of the Fall, the necessity for salvation; the play ends (in the extant manuscript, at least) with a sermon on judgment at the world's end. If only by beginning at the beginning, *Adam* provided a model for popular drama and it is notable that all the British cycles stage Adam and Cain, while three of them stage the prophets. The fourteenth-century Maastricht *Paachspel* shows Adam, Cain and the prophets as a prelude to the Incarnation and Passion. The tradition may be continuous in other ways, too. The practical and doctrinal use of devil-stagehands to punctuate the action by removing Old Testament bodies to hell is continued in the fifteenth-century Cornish *Origo Mundi*. The twelfth-century Anglo-Norman *La Seinte Resureccion* provides a different sort of narrative completeness, anticipating by two centuries the expansive, stiffly 'realist' approach to continuous narrative that is characteristic of the Cornish *Resurrexio*, the French *Passions* of Semur and Autun and the corresponding sections of the Middle English plays. The impulse to create cyclic completeness is at work also in cycles of pictures (e.g. the *Holkham Bible Picture Book*, *c.* 1330) and roof-bosses, as well as in encyclopaedic vernacular poems—*Cursor Mundi*, the *Passion des Jongleurs*, the *Northern Passion*, the apocryphal gospels of Nicodemus, lives of Jesus and Mary, the legends of the Rood—which formed the immediate story matter of the Middle English cycle plays. Dramatic 'sources' for the English cycle plays are much harder to establish with any certainty.[2]

The debt to liturgical drama

While recognizing the general independence of the Middle English
drama from liturgical Latin drama in its selection of material and
manner of playing, one must acknowledge the debt to a limited number
of liturgical play models.[3] English plays of the prophets, shepherds,
Magi, Herod, the Easter sepulchre and garden scenes, Emmaus, the
Annunciation and other Marian subjects, all show signs of indebtedness
to typical (though hardly ever *specific*) liturgical plays on these subjects.
Brief discussion of some examples will serve to indicate the nature
and extent of this debt and to provide a contrast with the dramatic
techniques which were inherited from the popular and secular
drama.

The liturgical *Ordo prophetarum*, though only a handful of texts
survive, proved an influential model. This most didactic of liturgical
plays was, as we have seen, a realization of the processional potential of
its sermon source, a mere pageant of self-explanatory historical figures.
The form is clearly recognizable in the Chester and N-Town plays.
The latter has twenty-seven prophets; Chester is limited to six, though,
as the expositor says, 'Moe prophetis, lordinges, we might play'. The
form is almost infinitely expandable. But, though the liturgical form is
observed, the manner of presentation is different. The audience is not
assumed to be familiar with the sermon in its liturgical context and
the Chester expositor interprets the significance of each prophecy to
them after it has been pronounced. The same concept of drama as a
'speaking pageant' extends beyond the prophet plays themselves.
Thus in the N-Town plays Abraham and Moses introduce themselves to the audience by name, while Noah presents his whole
family:[4]

> Noe serys my name is knowe
> my wyff and my chyldere here on rowe.

The *Visitatio Sepulchri*, of which hundreds of versions survive,
provided a widespread and readily available model of a more complex
action. The extreme stylization of the liturgical form is imitated in the
vernaculars, even where this means a departure from narrative consistency. The Chester Marys are not individualized in their responses;
they are rather three-in-one. Each begins eight lines of lament with
'Alas', and each then addresses four lines concerning the sepulchre to
her 'sisters'. The typical liturgical play conflation of two gospel

accounts leads to the same inconsistency in the role of Mary Magdalene. First she must express joy at the angel's message:[5]

> A! hye we fast for any thinge,
> and tell Peter this Tydinge;
> a Blessedfull word we may him bringe,
> sooth if that it weere. (361–4)

but immediately she finds Peter and John she must adopt her other role:

> Ah! Peter and Ihon! Alas! Alas!
> ther is befallen a wondrous case;
> some man my lord stollen hase,
> and putt him I wott not where. (369–72)

The Towneley play, too, follows a ceremonial pattern. Liturgical texts rather than the gospel narratives lie behind the question 'And which shall of us systers thre/remefe the stone?', the 'whome have ye soght?' dialogue, and the angels' singing of *Christus resurgens*. Yet in both these plays the model has also been adapted through speech which is both descriptive and expository. The characters draw attention to one another's features and gestures:

Maria Solome
> Two Children ther I see sittinge,
> all of whyte is ther Clothinge,
> And the Stonne besyde lyinge;
> goe we neare and see!
>   (*Tunc ibunt et in Sepulchrum circumspicient*)

Angelus Primus
> What seeke ye, women, what seeke ye here,
> with weping and with unlyking cheare? (341–6)

Outside the context of the Easter liturgy the action is not self-explanatory and these speeches insist that the audience notice the properties and persons of the play, even if this entails 'giving away' that the Angels are played by children.

The most elaborate development of a liturgical style in the English vernacular is in the plays concerning the Virgin. In most of these plays the singing of liturgical texts is crucial to the devotional effect, while in the York, Chester and N-Town plays of the Salutation and Conception, the action is designed to illustrate the meaning of an antiphon,

---

unlyking cheare sad countenance

Ave Maria, gratia plena, and a canticle, the *Magnificat*. These plays are close in form and method to the contemporary Latin plays of the Virgin from the continent (no Latin texts from England are extant). But the English vernacular plays are again more didactic and expository than the Latin. The N-Town Gabriel glosses his *Ave* for a lay audience, explaining how 'here þis name Eva is turnyd Ave/þat is to say withowte sorwe ar ȝe now'.[6] As he leaves Mary, he and the other angels sing the *Ave Maria* sequence a second time. The play shows Mary composing the 'holy psalme' *Magnificat*, while her cousin Elizabeth glosses each two lines of Latin in English. At the conclusion the expositor promises those in the audience who say our Lady's Psalter daily for a year that they will have ten thousand and eight hundred years' pardon.

If the true liturgical drama was, as Mary Marshall has said, 'too deeply rooted in belief for intellectual didacticism',[7] then the instructional method used here is not 'liturgical'. Yet the use of service texts and music, the concern for structural pattern and the purpose of inducing an act of worship in the beholder are all part of the experience of liturgical drama. The N-Town play of the Annunciation is designed as a communal act of worship, in which the expositor Contemplacio has a priest-like role. His passionate invocation of the threefold God sets in motion the process of the Incarnation:[8]

> Gracyous lord, Gracyous lord, Gracyous lord, come downe!

The triple cry for grace is taken up in the angels' prayer of 'Mercy, mercy, mercy, we crye' addressed to a three-personed God. Here, as in the Latin drama, gesture and stage effects have symbolic form. We are told that Gabriel 'makyth a lytyl restynge and Mary be-holdyth hym', in order to emphasize the momentousness of her decision and the necessity for her free assent to the divine plan. The incarnation is denoted by intricate stage iconography: three gilded beams each jointed in three and held vertically by the hierarchically-seated members of the Trinity, are passed down to touch Mary's bosom:[9]

here þe holy gost discendit with iij bemys to our lady, the sone of þe godhed nest with iij bemys to þe holy gost, the fadyr godly with iij bemys to the sone. And so entre All thre to here bosom.

Symbolic meanings attached to the numbers 3, 5 and 7 recur throughout the Marian plays of this cycle, just as they form part of contemporary fifteenth-century devotions to the Virgin. Their purpose in both

---

nest next

contexts is to provide a highly wrought mnemonic structure, a store-house for the ordering and remembering of devotions. The method is far more scholastic and 'Gothic' than is found in the earlier liturgical drama, but it is clearly indebted to that tradition. It is at once highly intellectual and also concerned to stimulate an emotional human response. The Presentation of the infant Mary at the temple (a subject from apocryphal legend) is a perfect example of this Gothic art. The three-year-old child must climb unaided fifteen steps (*grees* or degrees) to the waiting bishop; her precocious success will indicate that she is indeed blessed by God. The mixture of pride and sorrow which Mary's parents express at seeing the only child of their long-barren marriage leave them, and Anna's motherly concern that her daughter shall not fall, are the exquisitely realized human features of a scene whose basis is symbolic mathematics. Mary enacts a ceremony used for the dedication of girls to a virgin life. At each step she must sing one of the fifteen 'gradual psalms' explaining its Latin text in English. The pageant is given further meaning for the audience by the bishop who asks them to see it as a mnemonic device and to join in an act of communal prayer, resolving to amend their lives, and to see in the little girl's ascent every man's journey from the earthly city of Babylon to the heavenly Jerusalem.[10]

Episcopus
> Come gode mary, come babe I þe call
> þi pas pratyly to þis place pretende.
> Þou xalt be þe dowtere of god Eternall
> If þe fyftene grees þou may Ascende.
> It is meracle if þou do. Now god þe dyffende.
> Ffrom babylony to hevynly jherusalem þis is þe way,
> Every man þat thynk his lyff to Amende
> þe fiftene psalmys in memorye of þis mayde say.

As in Gothic architecture, the shape of the whole is apparent in each homologous component.

Neither this over-articulate scholastic structuring nor the sensitive, 'feminine', feelings evoked in the N-Town Marian plays are typical of the liturgical drama of the early Middle Ages. But they were not features of *early* medieval liturgy either. These vernacular plays of the fifteenth century, wearing their structural design on the outside, inviting a response both intellectual and strongly emotional, draw their inspira-

---

pratyly prettily   *pretende* direct   *dyffende* protect

tion rather from the liturgical Hours of the Virgin which occupied religious women, noble families and Marian guilds in their private chapels, and which formed an increasingly important part of cathedral and parish worship in the later middle ages.

Folk elements in the cycle plays

Immediately after the communal singing of *Ave regina coelorum* in the N-Town plays, comes a rude reminder of the drama's debt to popular traditions of playing. A satirical figure, Den the Summoner, pushes his way through the crowd, acting as presenter to the bishop who will try Joseph and Mary for infidelity. Like the folk-play presenter, he must clear the 'place':[11]

> A-voyd Serys. And lete my lorde þe bischop come . . .

He summons the audience to appear in court together with a list of stock characters such as inhabit Glutton's haunt in *Piers Plowman*: Johan Jurdon and Geffrey Gyle, Malkyn Mylkedoke, Jak-at-the-Style, Tyffany Twynkelere, and all. As in folk-play the actors come to the audience, and the stage direction says that the 'pageant of the trial of Joseph and Mary is brought into the place'. The action begins with a comic detractor teasing the audience because they do not know his name, yet claiming that they know him:

> Aa! serys god save ȝow all!
> here is a fayr pepyl in good ffay.
> Good serys telle me what men me calle.
> I trowe ȝe kan not be þis day—
> ȝitt I walke wyde and many way . . .
> bakbytere is my brother of blood.   (p. 124, 1–8)

He promises that if his brother would appear they would raise some mischief and 'slawndyr'. The second detractor duly appears and is asked, coyly, to tell the audience his name. Out of their casual and crude banter is generated the slander that Mary is lecherous ('tekyl under þe too'). Later, at the trial itself, they mockingly tell the tale of the snow-child, conceived by his mother's swallowing a snowflake. When Den the Summoner goes to call Joseph and Mary to court, the game with the audience is resumed. He is apparently on horseback and

---

A-voyd make room   *ffay* faith   *bakbytere* backbiter

threatens to trample them if they do not show reverence and give him money:

> Do of ȝour hodys with an evyl grace!
> Do me sum wurchep be-for my face
> or be my trowth I xal ȝow make
> if þat I rolle ȝow up in my race
> ffor fere I xal do ȝoure ars qwake.
> But ȝit sum mede and ȝe me take
> I wyl with-drawe my gret rough toth
> gold or sylvyr I wol not for-sake
> but evyn as all somnorys doth.   (pp. 127–8)

The 'gret rough toth' that he draws out, to threaten the audience with, is a comic property straight from folk-play.

Earlier we saw that the constant motifs of folk-play are combat and 'death', and its characteristic manner of acting aggressive and comic. Despite many factors inhibiting the clerical dramatists from following folk-play models for their treatment of sacred subjects, it is notable that the cycle plays often do show death and its aftermath in a comic mode. The cycles include three sacred killings: the death of Abel, the Slaughter of the Innocents, and the Crucifixion (as well as the death of Herod and Judas's suicide, both usually played as comedy). The manner and circumstances of Christ's death by crucifixion were most explicit in the Bible and, of the three major episodes, might seem to offer the strongest proscription against unauthorized elaboration. The dramatists' problem was to translate narrative into impersonated action and in doing this they turned, naturally enough, to ideas of 'acting' that they already knew. Kolve has shown how the authors of the Passion sequences confronted the practical problem of showing the torturers working and talking together by developing action and dialogue as a series of 'games'.[12] The models for these 'games' (blindfolding and buffeting, 'guess-who-struck-you', the pretence that Jesus is a fool or jester, that he is a mighty lord mounting his wooden horse for battle) lie very often in the realm of folk games ('hot cockles', the making of a 'summer king' and so on). However, in the case of the Towneley *Mactatio Abel* and the Chester *Slaughter of Innocents* I shall suggest that the cycle-play treatment was determined by models in the pre-existent folk *drama*.

---

rolle ȝow up in my race trample you in my rush
But ȝit sum mede and ȝe me take unless you give me money

In the Towneley *Cain and Abel* a peculiar spirit of nonsense and buffoonery, a grotesque jesting in the face of death, accompanies a more radical (and, I think, previously unnoticed) debt to the agricultural folk-drama. The distinctive dramatic quality of the Towneley play is established by presenting Cain driving a plough team and by giving him as his accomplice a saucy ploughlad. The name of Cain's boy, Pikeharnes, connects him with the plough gear ('plough harneys') which occupies the playing place for the duration of the play, as well as suggesting that he is a thief of personal apparel. A further pun on harneys as sexual parts ('privy harneys') may also be intended.

Pikeharnes' opening address to the audience introduces both his master Cain and the action of the play. At the end he takes his leave. His hail and farewell provide a framework of familiar festive mirth within which the violence and blasphemy of Cain can appear comic and absurd. Pikeharnes' manner of speech contrasts strangely with the words which introduced the previous play (God's *Ego sum alpha et O*) and follows the formula of the folk-play presenter:[13]

> All hayll, all hayll, both blithe and glad,
> For here com I, a mery lad!
> Be peasse youre dyn, my master bad,
> Or els the dwill you spede.
> Wote ye not I come before? (1–5)

As the speech continues, the tone becomes coarser and more abusive than that of the prologues to early vernacular plays that we have examined. But the function is the same; it generates a dramatic game in which the audience are the servants of this great master ('Som of you ar his men'). As in the mummers' plays, the presenter then withdraws:

> For if my master com, welcom hym then.
> Farewell, for I am gone— (23–4)

as Cain enters. Cain drives a ploughing team:

> Io furth, Greynhorne! and war oute Gryme!
> Drawes on! (25–6)

Does this mean that a 'complete' plough team is brought before the audience? A. C. Cawley[14] thinks so and proposes that Cain's team consists of four oxen and four horses. But, in fact, nine animals, not

---

Be peasse youre dyn hush your noise   *dwill you spede* devil prosper you
Wote know   *war oute* look out

eight, are named. We saw earlier how in the Scots plough play (discussed above pp. 40–2) dancers represented, or were imagined to represent, a single plough ox which was also, as here, given nine names.[15] There need not be eight beasts 'on stage' here, then, or nine, or even one. The ox-team, however indicated dramatically, is a mere excuse for the first conflict between Cain and Pikeharnes (just as in the Towneley *Prima Pastorum*, the First Shepherd threatens to drive 'a hundreth' sheep over his fellow's pasture, see below p. 191). Four of the animal names are used by Cain, the remaining five are in turn uttered by the boy who, returning to the place, tries to curse the recalcitrant 'team' to move on. The ox-play ends with Pikeharnes unharnessing the plough and leading or driving 'the animals' from the place:

Garcio

> Harrer, Morell! io furth, hyte!
> And let the plogh stand.   (*aside*)   (55–6)

No further mention is made of the animals. The plough remains idle until after the murder of Abel. Thus the ploughing action makes a self-contained processional prelude to the conflict between Cain and Abel. As in the folk-drama, the plough marks the spot of ground chosen for the performance.

The oddity of this prelude is set off by the introduction of Abel. He enters the playing place unannounced, incurring Cain's reproach for breaking the rules of the game:

Cain

> As welcom standys theroute.
> Thou shuld have bide til thou were cald.   (60–1)

He is conceived as a simple, expository character and Cain mocks him twice for preaching. Abel speaks the homiletic text—the necessity of tithing—upon which Cain will improvise. This juxtaposition of 'sermonyng' and 'game' extends to the dramatization of the offerings: Abel's brief, prayerful offertory is contrasted with Cain's extensive 'game', played with evident relish and provocative crudity beneath his brother's admonitory eye (Cain chooses the worst sheaves of wheat to burn, he miscounts, he shuts his eyes and pretends 'by chance' miraculously to arrive at the right number). It is unlikely, though possible,

---

hyte gee up

that the clowning continues through Cain's 'killing' of Abel with the grotesque animal's 'cheke-bon' club. Certainly the clowning is resumed in the comic proclamation which follows Abel's death. Cain proposes to proclaim the king's peace for himself and Pikeharnes, his 'crier', whose interrupting asides refer to the emptiness of his own stomach and reduce any notion of justice for murder to an absurd 'sick' joke (why not eat the man?):

> Yey, cold rost is at my masters hame . . .
> My stomak is redy to receyfe. (422–32)

To avoid Cain's anger, Pikeharnes scampers aloft, out of reach, and delivers his 'blessing' on the company apparently from the eminence of the stage 'heaven':

> Now old and yong, or that ye weynd,
> The same blissyng withouten end,
> All sam then shall ye have
> That God of heven my master has giffen. (444–7)

Our attention is now redirected to the plough. Threatening to hang the boy upon it ('By hym that me dere boght') Cain forces him down from his perch and orders him to 'take yond plogh'.

Through the processional use of the plough, the biblical events are linked to an agricultural dramatic ceremony and its modes of playing. The mimetic action accompanying the Scots 'plough song' showed the harnessing of an idle plough and driving of the team; it played a death and resurrection—the bystanders are involved in a jolly sport causing the death of the ox-man; the play ended with an invocation of blessing on the audience and crops. The plough ceremony was also a ritual of social relationships, an act confirming the bonds and obligations of master and 'hynd'. In the Towneley *Cain* the plough is unharnessed and left to stand; death is made a sport. The social obligations of servant and master are parodied in Cain and Pikeharnes and in Cain's farcical tithing. In conclusion, a curse is pronounced over the audience who have been bullied into being accomplice to the act. The Wakefield Master may be indulging in 'literary parody' here. Alternatively, the popular motifs uncovered may not even be employed consciously. But it seems clear that the inherited material has been recast in a dramatic mould which was originally forged for an altogether different and

---

weynd go away

quite secular drama. And this may account for the oddly festive tone
of much of the play's dialogue and of the grotesque clown-like antics
of the unregenerate ploughman and his merry lad, a tone which makes
God's intervention and Cain's recognition of evil perfunctory, to say
the least.

As an example of the third of the cycle play subjects concerned with
violent death, the Chester play of the *Slaughter of the Innocents* is strikingly 'popular'. Its freely invented episodes and grotesque knockabout
comedy contrast markedly with the formal, liturgical character of the
Magi play which precedes it in the cycle, and with the restraint and
non-naturalism of the Latin liturgical treatments of the Slaughter. In
the 'Fleury playbook' version (discussed above pp. 80–3) the Innocents
are not shown as babes in arms, but as singing choirboys. Their death
performed in dumbshow (save for the single line of intercession sung
by the mothers communally), is shown as preceding a joyful resurrection into the choir. Herod's death, alluded to by St Matthew, is
shown only in mime. The whole mode of the Chester play is distinctly different: Herod vaunts, parades, and brandishes a sword; his
messenger boasts of his speed. More radical than these stylistic elements,
reminiscent of *Pride of Life*, is the patterned structure given to the actual
slaying. There are two parallel actions, each involving a soldier, a
woman and her child. Each of these actions follows the stylized
sequence of the mummers' combat. First the knights make vaunting
presentations of themselves to the audience:[16]

Primus Miles
>   If you will wot what I height,
>   my name is Sir Waradrake, the knight,
>   against me dare no man feight,
>   my dentes they be so dreede.   (X, 201–4)

The legendary boasts and topical allusions, the repetition with simple
inversion, the threats to the audience and the sword flourishing are all
in the same tradition:

Secundus Miles
>   And I also, without bost,
>   though the kinge of Scotis and all his host
>   were here, I set not by their bost,
>   to dryve them downe bydeene.

---

dentes strokes   *bydeene* at once

> I slue ten thowsand upon a day
> of kempes in their best aray,
> there was not one escaped away,
> my sword it was so keene.
>
> therfore to me you take good keepe,
> my name is Sir Grymball Launcher deepe;
> they that me teenen I lay to slepe
> on everych aside.
>
> I slew of kempes, I understand,
> more than a hundred thousand ... (217–30)

Each slaying is preceded by a flyting between knight and woman. A challenge is answered by abuse and counter-challenge. A child is snatched and lamented. After a further challenge and defiance, physical combat begins ('I shall cracke thy crowne'). The child is then run through and is lamented by its mother. Fresh combat commences.

The element of grotesque humour and pathos is emphasized both by the nature of the weapons the women use (here a boot but one of the Coventry play women uses a 'pott-laddull' threatening to make the soldier's 'braynis addull') and by the obscenity of their desperation:

Secunda Mulier

> Nay! freak, thou shalt fayle,
> my child thou shalt not assayle,
> he hath II holes under the tayle,
> kyss and thou may assay! (365–8)

One section of the text is very incoherent as it stands in the manuscripts and seems to imply that the First Woman, accused of being a 'quean', denies the charge and claims that her infant daughter is the soldier's bastard, pointing out that her companion's babies were all boys.[17] The motif of denied parentage in the ploughing play (above p. 37) may possibly lie behind this garbled passage. A variation of the same theme forms the basis of the play's major structural alteration to the model suggested by liturgical drama. The Second Woman reveals that her slaughtered babe was really the king's son. After recommencing battle with the soldier, she takes the child before Herod and the two of them lament his death. Herod's grief is for a slain champion:

> for in gould harnes he was dight,
> paynted wondrous gay (403–4)

---

kempes champions   *me teenen* annoy me   *freak* fellow

The reiterated reference to 'gould' in mourning the royal son, slain in this grotesque combat, suggests to the audience the survival of the true child-king living in exile in Egypt. The comic, 'folk' nature of the mode in which the episode is played justifies itself as festive parody: there is really no cause for sorrow. Herod's ranting gives way to comic death throes, and the sequence concludes with the satirical address of a demon who comes from hell to claim his body. Threatening to claw the audience's backs with his 'croked cambrock' (meat hook?) and warning tapsters who give short measure that they shall soon keep Herod company, the demon bids the audience good day.

Most writers on the Middle English drama have made the Chester plays out to be the 'simplest' and closest to a hypothetical liturgical 'source'. Yet popular motifs and apocryphal episodes abound in this cycle. Scholars with a preference for poetic sophistication have not seen that the lack of literary artifice and the popularity of the dramatic method go hand in hand. These popular modes were not, I suggest, a late development, but were integral to the plays when originally conceived as public entertainment in Chester. The date and circumstances of the institution of the play cycle in Chester are still disputed and the tradition that they are the oldest of the extant cycles called in question. But, I believe, not nearly enough serious attention has been given to the traditional association of the religious plays with the festive *civic* show known in Chester as the 'Midsummer Watch'.

Chester plays and Midsummer Watch

Since the eleventh century a Midsummer fair had been held in Chester, on Abbey ground outside the gates of St Werburgh's (the first of the stations at which the religious plays were later performed). In this connection Glynne Wickham has argued that the Chester guilds' 'vested interest in a Midsummer association with the Church preceded the Church's interest in the guilds as possible executants of its plays'.[18] Whether or not plays were performed at these Midsummer festivals during the early Middle Ages can only be conjectured. Midsummer Day (the feast of St John the Baptist) was a notorious occasion of folk *ludi* in England: a thirteenth-century Latin sermon refers to 'not only joy on the day of St John's nativity, but also foolery and profane love-making, bonfires, unlawful and lewd plays in public places (*per plateas turpibus et illicitis ludis*), eating and drinking.'[19]

A collection of records relating to Chester, made by Archdeacon Robert Rogers (d. 1595), contains some notes on the Midsummer

Watch, testifying that it was older than the religious plays and relating how, after the Protestant suppression of the religious plays (1574), certain improprieties in the 'Watch' were also reformed:

Of the showe at midsomer in Chester
The beginninge thereof beinge uncertayne, but it is more anchante then the whitson playes which weare played yearely there for about 200 yeares together, this midsomer showe had divers thinges in it which weare ofensive in anchant times as Christe in stringes men in womens apparell, with divells attendinge there called cuppes & cannes, with a divell in his shape ridinge there, which preachers of God's worde, and worthye divines there spake against as unlawfull and not meete . . .[20]

Other similar notes show that the Chester guilds were involved in presenting certain stock figures or set-pieces of pageantry in a processional entertainment of a carnival nature. In 1599, Mayor Hardware 'caused the giantes which use to goe at midsomer to be broken',[21] and

the maior caused the Graull not to goe at Midsomer wach, but in stedd a man in complet white Armore on horsback. He, at same show, put downe the divell Ryding for buchers, & caused a boy to Ride for them as other companies. nor cupps nor canns nor dragon & naked boys would he suffer at show . . .[22]

The Midsummer Watch may have been a mere processional 'riding' or it may have involved traditional dramatic turns such as, I have argued, must lie behind *Le Jeu de la Feuillée* of Arras. Only one such set-piece from Chester can be identified with certainty—'cupps and canns'. A scene concerning 'a man in womans apparell, with a divill waytinge on his horse [the whole scene], called cuppes and cans' is found in four of the extant manuscripts (including the oldest) of the Chester cycle of plays. It forms a farcical and satirical epilogue to the play of the Harrowing of Hell, performed by the guild of cooks, tapsters, hostlers and innkeepers. The central figure is a dishonest alewife of Chester, who, after the exodus of Adam and the patriarchs from Hell, is the one articulate soul left. Addressing the audience directly, she confesses to having given short measure and having watered her beer. She holds herself up as an example to 'taverners, tapsters of this cittie' against 'breakinge statutes of this cuntrey', and goes on to enumerate the finer points of selling small cups and 'casting maulte besyddes the combe'. The scene ends with her welcome by a triad of devils to a wedding and

---

the Graull the Dragon   *combe* brewing tub

everlasting 'cardes, dice, and cupes smale' in hell. The alewife identifies herself for the audience by shaking the tools of her trade (to advertise her torment:[23]

> Therefore I maye my handes wringe,
> shake my cupes and canes ringe.

The Chester alewife is apparently common property, the key figure in a satirical set-piece used by both the religious plays and the Watch. She is visualized for posterity in a misericord carving installed in St Lawrence's church, Ludlow, in 1447.[24] The misericord shows two devils, complete in the winged and feathered costumes of the drama, pitching naked souls into a gaping hellmouth, while a third devil with a grotesque head reads from a scroll. (Here, perhaps, is the point of the dragon and naked boys referred to in the accounts of the Watch.) The Ludlow alewife hangs upside down over the shoulder of one of the devils; she wears a fashionably 'horned' headdress, her bloomers and naked knees are revealed by her disarrayed skirt, and in her hand she holds the graduated measuring can of her profession.

This sermon-grotesque, which was also the advertisement of the taverners' company is close in spirit to parts of Bodel's *Jeu de Saint-Nicolas*; it is a rare English example of a purely satirical scene and was apparently much in demand with the Chester audiences. Upon its popularity depends the brief allusion of the devils who haul away Herod's body to Hell in the play of the *Slaughter of Innocents* already discussed:[25]

Demon
> you Tapstars, by my lewty,
> that fills ther measures falcly,
> shall bear this lord Company.

If the Chester plays were originally thought of (as they undoubtedly were in the sixteenth century) as in some sense a rival or alternative attraction to the Midsummer show, taking advantage of an established summer occasion of outdoor revels and folk-plays, then the festive style of much of the playing is placed in a new perspective. The use of formulae of presentation, the 'game' with the audience, the repeated cries of 'room!' are explicable as the inherited social framework of a popular drama, old secular bottles for a new ecclesiastical wine.

The first of the presenter-messenger figures, familiar from our examination of folk-play and of the thirteenth and fourteenth century popular fragments, identifies himself as a fairy spirit whose appearances and disappearances have an air of formulaic magic:[26]

Nuntius

> All peace, Lordinges, that be present,
> and herken now with good intent.
> Now Noe away from us is went
> and all his Companye;
>
> And Abraham through Gods grace,
> he is comen into this place,
> and yow will geve him rowme and space
> to tell you of storye ...
>
> My name is Gobet-on-the-grene,
> with yow no longer I maye bene.
> farewell, my Lordinges, all by dene
> for letting of your playe.

What is Gobet-on-the-grene doing introducing the sacrifice of Isaac? Surely, it is the nature of the occasion and of the audience's expectations, not the story, which demand that a perambulatory performance be presented by such a folk-loric creature. New characters are presented by a messenger, according to the formula:[27]

> Make rome, lordingis, and geve us waye,
> and lett balack come in and playe,
> and balam that well can saye ...
>
> Make rowme, lordinges, and geve us waie,
> and let octavian come and plaie,
> and Sybbill ...

The perplexing rapidity of action and the 'secular' nature of the Chester *Octavian* play, with its apocryphal 'miracles of midwyves', has often been noted, but not the direct line of its descent from the tradition of popular 'miracles' recorded in the Cambridge and Rickinghall bilingual fragments (see above p. 165). The Chester Emperor Octavian introduces himself to the audience, parading and boasting of his might, commanding their homage. He speaks first in Anglo-Norman, then in English, warning the people not to come too close to him. He then decides to prove his might by counting the heads of his subjects,

---

all by dene at once

and sends his beadle among the audience to collect a penny from each:[28]

> Each man one peny shall paye,
> therefore, my bedill, do as I saie;
> in mydds the world by any waie
> this gamon shall begin.

The action shown here is, of course, Caesar Augustus's taxing of 'all the world' before the birth of Jesus. Yet the manner of presentation, which incorporates the audience so physically into the action, strongly suggests here that the actors in fact take a collection from the audience. Is it a 'game' ('this gamon shall begin'), adapted from folk drama, for defraying the cost of production?

Among the motifs in the Chester plays which may owe their presence to the expectations of the audience rather than to doctrinal necessity I shall mention only one—the recurrent note of anti-feminism. As I have suggested, hostility between the sexes is a key-note in much of the folk-drama, while in the civic 'watch' drama of Arras the lament of a *mal marié* may well have been a traditional piece. In Chester, not only Noah, but Joseph and the Third Shepherd address the audience directly and moralize on the commonness of wifely domination. We may accept this as 'conventional', but *why* should the drama license such entertaining diversions? Perhaps there is more to Noah's complaint than meets the eye:[29]

Noe

> Lord, that women be crabbed aye,
> and never are meke, that dare I saye.
> this is well sene by me *to daye*,
> In witness of yow each one.
>
> Good wife, let be all this beere
> that thou makes in this place here;
> for all they wene thou art master,
> *and so thou art by St John.*

Oaths by particular saints are very rare in the Chester plays. Is it possible that Mrs Noah's *maistrie* is a state of topsy-turvy licensed by traditional practice on St John's Day, Midsummer Day? Her solidarity with her 'gossips' against the entreaties of her husband and sons makes her an apocryphal place in sacred history by playing out the impulses

---

gamon game   *let be all this beere* leave off this uproar

behind folk dramatic practices in Arras and Coventry, and leading her
to swear:

> they shall not drowne, *by St John*,
> and I may save their lyfe.

But, of course, she cannot. Noah's authority and God's put her in her
place.

My examples of popular motifs are deliberately suggestive, not
exhaustive, for I do not claim to have revealed proven 'sources'. The
very nature of the inquiry precludes fixed and definite debts. I am
pointing, rather, to dramatic traditions and social occasions which will
make sense of the rapport between actors and audience, in so far as this
exceeds what is strictly necessary for the demonstration and explanation of 'the story'. The English shepherds' plays, particularly those of
the Chester and Towneley cycles, contain the largest amount of
dramatic activity that is, strictly speaking, superfluous to the inherited
story. As we shall see the possibilities for invented action and dialogue
are very fully realized.

The shepherds' plays

It may be helpful to recall that the liturgical *Pastores* plays established
the number of shepherds as three, and provided them with three
structural functions which they performed in unison. They witnessed
the song of the angel (*Gloria in excelsis Deo*), sometimes also (a legacy
from the Magi plays) seeing the star. Secondly, they went to the
manger to worship the Christ-child. These two functions were linked
and explained by a third: the shepherds were made interpreters of the
meaning of the song or star. In the most extensive of the Latin shepherds' plays, that of the *Carmina Burana* manuscript, the three shepherds
respond to the angelic voice, discuss the meaning of its message,
proceed to the manger singing an antiphon based on the *Gloria*, and
adore the infant.[30] They are singers and they also do 'omage' as in the
relatively simple York version.[31] But the *Carmina Burana* shepherds
are in no sense naturalistic: they address one another as *frater* and
engage in a lengthy scholastic debate about the paradoxical reality of
appearances. They have not a whiff of sheep to them.

The achievement of the vernacular plays in English, French and
Provençal, was to naturalize the shepherds, showing them as humble

and if

men in whom the meaning of the incarnation is embodied. Their
simplicity, which is endowed with both an aesthetic and a moral
value, is insisted on to the point of comedy. Much earlier than the
extant Middle English plays, the Holkham Bible Picture Book (*c.* 1330)
shows a scene characteristic of the English drama. The three shepherds
tend long-haired sheep; one has a bagpipe; a dog attends them. As the
angel above sings *Gloria*, one of the shepherds comments (his words
in a 'balloon') '*Glum glo*, ceo ne est rien'. The two lines of English in
the Anglo-Norman text—

>   songen alle wid one stevene
>   Also þe angel song þat cam fro hevene:
>   Te Deum et Gloria—

tell us that the shepherds are rustic, English-speaking. '*Glum glo*' tells us
that the shepherd makes nonsense of the Latin. This comic incompre-
hension is found in elaborate form in the N-Town and Chester plays.

Once the figures of the shepherds were naturalized and located in a
recognizably 'real' world of sheep and vernacular language, exactly
how they spent their time 'keeping watch by night' became a matter
of concern for dramatists. What should they *do*, what should they say
to one another prior to the appearance of the angel? The French playwrights, as has already been mentioned (see above p. 143), filled the
vacuum by recourse to the materials of secular *bergerie*. Here was a
ready-made idiom and a store of gambits which could be adapted to
the biblical shepherds—dancing, singing, playing of instruments, the
greeting of friends, a pastoral picnic, to which all the young shepherds
and shepherdesses contribute food, quizzing and offering games,
satirical banter, the abduction and return of a sheep, boasts, quarrels
and reconciliations. In the fourteenth-century *La nativité de Nostre
Saveur Jesus Christ* in the Saint Geneviève manuscript we find Gobelin
vowing to compose a song for Marion, his *douce amie*, whilst in
Arnoul Greban's fifteenth-century *Mystère de la Passion*, Aloris,
Ysambert and Pellion discuss *la doulce saison* and sing *pastourelle* songs,
Rifflart tells how the wolf Ysangrin stole a sheep which was rescued by
Robin, and describes his own visit to the fair to sell three hundred
sheep.

Millicent Carey, who made a study of the background to the English
shepherds' plays, concludes that this pastoral tradition has 'no place in

---

stevene voice

the English plays'.[32] True the English shepherds do not have sweethearts nor any youthful, courtly daintiness; they are salty proverb-mongers, men who talk of winter and rough weather. Yet the English shepherds of the Chester and Towneley plays are characterized in a very similar manner: their night watch is filled by comparable series of plotless 'games' (boasts, quarrels, feasts, 'turns'). What is more, fourteenth-century shepherds in the north of England actually did meet seasonally, outdoors, 'to play by turns' (*invicem ludere*: perhaps wrestling, or 'ramraising' is implied?).[33] But let us return to the plays, to look at the Chester shepherds' games.

The first Chester Shepherd must enter the acting place through the audience, and he addresses them directly, boasting of his herbal skills. He points out that he is alone; then he drinks, whoops aloud, calls and blows his horn to summon his companions.[34]

> *Tunc flat cum Cornu et reddit 'Aho!'*

At last the Second Shepherd approaches, sewing a 'cloute' upon his heel with the feather of a crow. Still the play lacks plot. The two men agree that they require the presence of a third, Tud, so that they may then sit and feed. The shouting and hallooing is redoubled and Tud finally appears. Like the First Shepherd, he speaks more to the audience than to his fellows as he demonstrates the 'poyntes that longes to my crafte'; he has borrowed his wife's old pot in which to mix sheep salve, and he uses the fact as a pretext for observing how many husbands in the audience are cowed by their wives, 'for feare of a clout'. Now that the cast is assembled, the show can begin. 'Tud, will we shape us to some solace?' asks the Second Shepherd. Each of them produces his contribution to a communal feast: onions, garlic, leeks, ale, sheep's head, pig's foot, ox tongue, and much more are enumerated. Each item is introduced with a formula ('Ye shall se here . . .', 'And that is in my sachell to shake out'). Both eating and drinking are narrated: 'this flaggen will I tame', 'Now of this bottle will I bibble'. If this is a 'folk ale', then where are the sports and wrestling?

After the feast, fresh horn-blowing summons the shepherds' boy and his 'good dog Dotinowle'. He is a boastful idler, who drinks from a skull ('this Golgotha') and challenges his masters to a *flyting*, sitting apart from them on a hill and complaining of their mouldy food and their lateness in paying his wages. After some crude histrionics (he threatens to spew on the heads of the three below and to pull out the First Shepherd's testicles), he wrestles with each of them in turn.

Having thrown each of his masters, the servant retires to his hill with
the remnant of their feast and invites the audience, 'all the world', to
'wonder on the wach'. The expression would have peculiar point for a
Chester audience. This profane prelude thus leads to the enthronement
of a fool-king ('I pipe at this pot like a pope') who rules the 'watch'.

Kolve has drawn attention to the doctrinal themes which are played
'in game' here: the shepherds are pastors and healers of flocks, their
quarrelling precedes the angel's message of peace. (Kolve suggests, to
my mind a little implausibly, that the wrestling falls hint that the
mighty shall be put down from their seat by a child.[35] (By contact
with the mystery of the Incarnation each of their shepherdly functions
is consecrated as metaphor. Indeed, so is the whole concept of 'watch',
and we may note that it is the profane boy-fool who finally takes a
solemn oath that,

> shepheardes crafte here I forsake,
> and to an Anker hereby
> I will, in my prayers to wach and wake. (632–4)

In the boy's resolve to forsake secular shepherds' craft and to enter a
house of Anchorites, to watch and wake in prayer, the didactic and
devotional movement of the whole drama is epitomized.

So much has been written about the shepherds' plays of the Wakefield Master that I shall confine attention here to commenting on the
way in which the invented comic action is played rather than on
interpreting the thematic significance of each design. The fact that
there are two plays on the same subject (this is unique in the English
cycle drama) is itself illuminating. Were the two played consecutively,
or in alternate years? To me the most attractive suggestion is that the
Prima Pastorum concluded the first day's playing and the *Secunda
Pastorum* began the second day. When Mak is asked to name his
'child's' godfather, he mentions the first two shepherds of the first
play, and he recalls the quarrel ('all the garray') that they made in that
play. While this might perfectly well be a private joke of the author's,
it seems rather to be evidence of a playful rivalry between two casts
which have the same script writer.

An important structural innovation common to these two plays is
the shepherds' sleep, marking off the 'prelude' from the traditional
action of the biblical play, separating the strange antics of the night
watch from what is 'gospel'. In the first play this prelude is plotless.
The First Shepherd complains of mutability, the Second mumbles a

night-spell. Action is improvised on the basis of colloquial exchanges between the characters. The First Shepherd's proposition, 'I go to by shepe', starts a vigorous brawl, with the two men shouting contradictory commands, each trying to drive an imaginary flock of sheep past the other. The sequence is scarcely comprehensible as 'realism' or as social satire (though no doubt quarrels over grazing rights were common). Whether one chooses to see the actor or the shepherd instigating the foolery, it exists as pure make-believe. One game generates another. The Second Shepherd pretends that the First is a great lord whose postman (the Third) is approaching. The Third Shepherd empties out a sack to demonstrate the emptiness of his companions' brains. The late (and apparently unauthentic) introduction of Garcio into this scene is again for the purpose of 'showing up' the foolery of the other three. Following the suggestion that they drink, an elaborate fantasy is enacted. The Third Shepherd plays the lord:[36]

> Gett mete, gett,
> And sett us a borde!

disdaining, in Frenchified terms, to eat at the others' 'mangere' (table).

The extravagant parade of food which follows (is it perhaps only verbal?) has been variously interpreted as a miraculous plenty in winter and as a 'grotesque' banquet of aristocratic proportions.[37] A. C. Cawley has analysed the interlarding of aristocratic and plebeian dishes, of 'realistic fare with flights of culinary fancy which come straight out of cookery-books, resulting in a ludicrous gallimaufry that can never have existed except in the imagination'. What properties do the actors have? The pantomimic absurdity of the whole affair is suggested by the sobering words of the First Shepherd to the Third who has been 'putting on the style':

III Pastor
> Good sawse,
> This is a restorité
> To make a good appeté.

I Pastor
> Yee speke all by clergé,
> I here by your clause.
> Cowth ye by youre gramery rech us a drynk
> I shuld be more mery—ye wote what I thynk! (237–43)

---

by clergé by vote *gramery* book learning

They have, I suggest, only a bottle ('good ayll of Hely') and the only *action* implied in the next thirty lines of dialogue is drinking and handing round the bottle. All the more ludicrous then that after the feast their laudable impulse to give the left-overs to 'poore men' should take the form of an antic hand-out to an imaginary audience:

I Pastor
> Geder up, lo, lo,
> Ye hungré begers, frerys!   (285–6)

The shepherds of this play are preeminently role-players; they embody a concept of acting as improvised buffoonery, a fantasized version of real life. With the saying of a nightspell and the song of the angel, the mood and the mode change. The shepherds wake the wondering men of the gospels, become expositors of prophecy and find their traditional role as humble and joyous worshippers of the Christ-child.

In the *Secunda Pastorum* the author's purpose is different and the provision of 'entertainment' is concentrated in the shape-shifting figure of Mak. The three shepherds are 'straight'. Indeed, in a world of winter floods, strange spirits, moon-magic and eerie enchantment, the typical stance of the shepherds is one of bleak scepticism, a constant vigilance against deception. Each of the shepherds is presented by means of a satirical set, the first moving from a complaint about the weather through the abuses of purveyance (the requisitioning of food or vehicles by king or nobles) to the abuse of clothes. The second is the complaint of a *mal marié*, couched in the proverbial imagery of animal fable. It develops via a warning to the audience into a rollicking anti-feminist grotesque, such as we saw formed part of a satirical mimic tradition in *Ruodlieb* and in *Le Jeu de la Feuillée*, and which Shakespeare recast for Dromio of Syracuse's speech on the greasy kitchen wench. The Third Shepherd is an oppressed servant, whose complaint recalls the begging of the mummers for food:[38]

> Both oure dame and oure syre,
> When we have ryn in the myre,
> Thay can nyp at oure hyre,
> And pay us full lately.   (158–62)

The 'real' complaints of the shepherds are taken up and parodied in the series of roles which Mak adopts: he is cold, poor, badly married. When he enters, Mak is, significantly, cloaked. When the cloak is

---

nyp whittle away

pulled off him, the poor 'man that walkys on the moore' assumes the role of yeoman, messenger on the king's business, demanding reverence, affecting a southern accent until he is threatened with violence. Reduced to his recognizable self, Mak plays the *mal marié* for the still suspicious shepherds. Next he is a magician, casting a circle about the sleeping shepherds, then changing his role—

Was I never a sheperd, bot now wyll I lere—   (288)

in order to steal a sheep.

With the introduction of Gyll a *flyting* of man and wife is developed, each striking a pose and satirizing the other in proverbial language. Together they plan the centrepiece of the prelude: the deception of the sheep hidden in the manger, to be practised before a 'knowing' audience and unsuspecting shepherds. The trick is called a 'good gyse' and a 'far-cast', a 'gam', in which Gyll promises to 'play a fals cast'. The ensuing farce, a perfect example of 'mimic' drama, is too well known to need description and too delightful to gain from it. At the moment the shepherds recognize the deception, they appreciate it as a 'quantt gawde' and a 'hee frawde', and in their decision merely to toss Mak in a blanket, they accept the 'game' nature of the previous action. As in the first play, sleep closes the scene. The angel's song and the consequent adoration of the child in the manger work to 'place' the secular farce as harmless parody of the real Nativity and adoration.

Attempts to see Mak as a diabolic figure seem clumsy, for he is not diabolic in the terms established in the Towneley plays. He is not a grotesque clown, he never threatens the audience, he serves neither Mahomet nor Lucifer, he is neither obviously blasphemous nor crude in his humour (the shepherds are coarser spoken). We should, rather, take our cue from the shepherds and judge Mak no more harshly than they do. The reason for Mak's privileged position (after all, he is guilty of a serious crime) may be that he is an intruder from a tradition which conceived drama from the beginning as a make-believe in which mimic actors practise deceptions upon one another for the delight of an audience.

The Corpus Christi or Whitsun plays are usually seen as the secu-larized version of a drama developed from liturgical play models. There is, of course, much truth in this view. By drawing attention to the framing devices, the folk motifs and the manner of playing in

---

lere learn

some of the plays, I have tried to suggest some ways in which a popular and secular drama accommodated the Christian story. It is easy to overstate the 'folk element' in the cycles, but its case still needs to be made in order to explain as living, social drama some aspects of the cycle plays which would be ignored if we assumed, as some critics of the plays increasingly insist, that 'all that is writ is for our doctryne'.

10

EPILOGUE: MIRACLE AND MORALITY

In the last two chapters something of the inheritance of Middle English drama from liturgical drama, from the non-cycle miracle-play tradition, and from the folk-drama has been illustrated. It has not been part of my purpose to give an historical, social or doctrinal account of the Corpus Christi plays which are the most substantial Middle English dramatic achievement. The cycles are not in danger of critical neglect.[1] In this epilogue I shall review in miniature the achievement of the popular religious drama, by focusing on two crucial non-cycle plays, composed within a few years of one another, c. 1470. They are the Croxton *Play of the Sacrament* and *Mankind*.

Both the Croxton miracle-play and the morality have been praised for their comedy, their theatrical showmanship and popular appeal. Both were played by small companies (six or nine actors) and seem to anticipate the drama of the sixteenth century. The black comedy of the *Sacrament* with its perfidious Christian and its villainous Jew, gloating over his precious stones and spices shipped from overseas, with its slapstick devices and cauldron of boiling oil, may have provided a popular model for the stereotypes and gambits of Marlowe's *Jew of Malta*. In *Mankind*, the intimate rapport of the vices with the audience and the ridicule of scholastic language in knockabout obscenity smack of the Tudor interlude and anticipate university wit. Yet I think the two plays ought to be seen first in relation to the two distinct traditions which precede them: the Corpus Christi cycle and the sermon-and-game form. Each of the plays makes a different compromise with a popular audience's appetite for folk-entertainment.

The Croxton play, offered as the dramatization of a miracle of the host said to have occurred in Aragon and formally reported in Rome in 1461, illustrates the doctrine of the corporeal presence.[2] A group of Jews, sceptical of the Christian belief, acquire a sacrament through the treachery of a Christian merchant and the negligence of his priest, and put it 'to a new passyoun'. The host itself is the central 'character'; subjected to the 'new turmentry' of the Jews, it undergoes miraculous transformations (ingeniously contrived by stage devices) whose climax is the appearance of Christ himself. In the conclusion of the play the host, returned to its original form, is carried in procession into church and placed on the altar.

As the action unfolds, the form of this 'new passyoun' is revealed as that of the Passion cycle of the Corpus Christi drama in miniature. The Jews hold a council, planning to capture the host. A bargain is struck between the chief Jew Jonathas and the Christian merchant Aristorius. The host is stolen in the night. Jonathas then lays it on a table in mockery of 'hys sopere' and mimics the Eucharist in the words *Accipite* and *Commedite Corpus meum*. After they have rehearsed in mockery the tenets of the Christian creed from the conception to Last Judgment, the Jews enact the Passion:[3]

> Surely with owr daggars we shall ses on thy bredde,
> And so with clowtys we shall know yf he have eny blood . . .
> And so shall we smyte þeron woundys fyve. (451–8)

In the manner of Christ's torturers in the Passion plays (e.g. *York Plays* XXXV, 101ff.) they vie with each other in their cruelty and prowess:

Masphat
> And I yow plyght I shall hym not please,
> For with thys punche I shall hym pryke.

Malchus
> And with thys augur I shall hym not ease,
> Another buffett shall he lykke. (473–6)

In an attempt to unfix the bleeding host from Jonathas's hand (*Her he renneth wood with þe Ost in hys hond*), a closer parody of the Crucifixion is performed. Jonathas is bound fast to a 'poste':

Jasdon
> Here is an hamer and nayles thre, I seye;
> Lyffte up hys armys, felawe, on hey,
> Whyll I dryve þes nayles, I yow praye,
>   With strong strokys fast.

---

clowtys strokes *lykke* take *wood* mad

After a masterstroke of comic ingenuity (*Here shall thay pluke þe arme, and þe hond shall hang styll with þe sacrament*) the Jews retire to their chamber.

At this point there follows an interlude of a quack doctor and his impudent servant. Clearly, within the structure of the whole play, the episode serves to counterpoint the theme of Christ as the true doctor who will eventually heal the handless and penitent Jew. Yet the connection between the grotesque parody and 'moral' is oblique, and the interlude of comic diversion occupies an eighth of the total length. The conventions governing the playing of this scene are different from those governing the rest of the play. Master Braundysch and Colle do not 'belong' in the acting place. Whereas the Christians occupy Aristorius's 'hall' and the Jews Jonathas's chamber (both of these apparently raised booths) this folk-play pair merely 'happen into' the acting place from outside: '*Here shall þe lechys man come into þe place sayng. . . .*' Colle pretends to have stumbled on the audience as he attempts to give his master the slip, having left him in a tavern. Colle's confession is both a revelation of mutual knavery and a professional advertising *Spiel*. Master Braundysch, 'called þe most famous phesy-cyan þat ever sawe uryne', uses the traditional means of diagnosis:

> In a pott yf yt please yow to pysse,
> He can tell yf yow be curable. (647–8)

Like the doctor of Adam de la Halle's Arras, he is a frequenter of taverns and has a way with ladies. Colle stands up to make a proclama-tion, offering the audience a reward if they can arrest his villainous master. Of course, Doctor Braundysch appears and 'discovers' this impudence. The entertaining dialogue which ensues follows the pattern of boast and deflationary aside used by doctor and servant in the Cotswold mummers' plays and by the Towneley Cain and his boy. Observing the 'grete congregacyon' of the audience, the two get to work advertising their trade:

> Who hat þe canker, þe collyke, or þe laxe,
> The tercyan, þe quartan, or þe brynnyng axs . . .
> For hedache, bonache, and thereto þe tothache—
> The colt-evyll, and þe brostyn men he will undertake,
> All tho þat have þe poose, þe sneke, or þe tyseke—
> Thowh a man were ryght heyle, he cowde soone make hym sek.
>
> (610–19)

þe *laxe* diarrhoea   *The tercyan, þe quartan* tertian, quartan fever
colt-evyll swelling penis   *brostyn* ruptured   *poose* cold   *sneke* sniffle
tyseke phthisis   *heyle* healthy

In terms of plot the two characters scarcely impinge. Jonathas accuses them of coming to cause 'stryfe' and the four Jews beat them away, thus exorcising the ghost of a folk-play solution.

The miracle-play with its evident cyclic skeleton now continues with a 'deposition' and 'resurrection' of the host and a 'last judgment'. The three nails are drawn out with pincers and the host wrapped in a cloth. It is deposited first in a cauldron, then in an oven sealed with clay: '*Here the owyn must ryve asunder and blede owt at þe cranys, and an image appere owt with woundys bledyng.*' This image of Jesus speaks the words based on the Lamentations of Jeremiah (i, 12), which are used in the liturgy of Holy Week and are ascribed to Christ in both the resurrection and judgment plays in the cycles:

> O mirabiles Judei, attendite et videte
> si est dolor sicut dolor meus. (717–18)

> (O Jews who wonder, give heed and mark, if any suffering
> is equal to my suffering).

Jonathas is healed and praises Christ as the strong lion of Judah, the *leo fortis* of liturgical Easter play. The procession of the host, singing of *O sacrum convivium*, the baptism of the Jews and a general absolution follow. The bishop blesses the congregation and leads the *Te Deum*.

The didactic purpose of the Croxton play, like that of the miracles of the host related in *Handlyng Synne* and in Mirk's *Festial*, is to demonstrate the dogma of transubstantiation. Promulgated in 1215, this dogma can be seen as an important step in the establishment of the feast of Corpus Christi by decrees of 1264 and 1311. Wycliffe's attacks on transubstantiation, begun in 1381, may have stimulated the currency of such miraculous demonstrations and these may, in their turn, have become the object of fresh Wycliffite criticism, such as the *Tretis of Miracles Pleying*.[4] The advertisement to the Croxton play makes explicit the doctrinal purpose by relating the doubts of the Jews concerning the flesh and blood nature of the Sacrament to the audience's own doubts on the matter: they must show to the Lord 'no maner of dowghtys'. The Jews' mockery of the whole eucharistic ritual anticipates by over half a century the scorn of Protestant reformers for the sacramentalism of Rome.[5] In the context of the play itself, this iconoclastic element is strictly placed in two ways: first, by its attri-

---

cranys corners

bution to the Jews; second, by a total structure which is modelled on the cycle play drama and to which it refers for its own validation.

The Croxton play is unique in English, though it is of course possible that some of the Corpus Christi plays mentioned in town and parish records were miracle plays of the Host rather than cycle plays. The prologue makes clear this was not an amateur community drama but the property of travelling players. At King's Lynn in Norfolk, the chamberlains' accounts for the year 1385 record payment to certain players for an *interludium* on Corpus Christi Day. There are other similar records in East Anglia. The *Play of the Sacrament*, performed further south in Norfolk and providing as it does a 'miniature cycle' would have been suitable for performance under such auspices. It is economically designed: there are twelve parts, but the manuscript says 'IX may play yt at ease'. Performance depends on the slick manipulation of a few portable devices—the host, the false hand, the cauldron and oven used in conjunction with a 'furneys'. A child may have played 'God in the pot'. The attention given to kindling fire and the necessity for skilful handling of this element, together with the knowledge that Master Brentberecly lodges at 'þe colkote' (charcoal shed) points fairly specifically to the charcoal-burning part of Norfolk, at the centre of an area most frequented by professional players during the fifteenth century.

The contemporary morality-play *Mankind* has been described as 'the most indisputably popular play of the fifteenth century'.[6] Yet the sense in which it was popular as well as the auspices under which it was performed have been disputed. Like *Le Jeu de la Feuillée*, which it resembles in its self-conscious theatricality, *Mankind* is a paradoxical creation: highly sophisticated 'folk-drama'.

The string of East Anglian towns and villages referred to by the characters lie mostly in an arc to the east of Cambridge. If, as seems likely, the performers travelled about, then the ambiguous sense of season in the play's dialogue (a Shrovetide moral, Shrovetide football, and a 'Cristemas' song) is understandable. Performance is envisaged *indoors*, in a house or inn, where a 'master' or hostler presides, and which Mankind must leave, going into the 'yard' to relieve himself. In the arrangement of audience, social distinctions are preserved: *O ȝe soverens þat sytt and ȝe brothern þat stonde ryght wppe*. The actors jostle close to the audience and the vices improvise in the 'narrow space', tumbling ('Xall I breke my neke to schew yow sporte?'), tripping one another, playing football with Mankind's jacket. 'All þe yemandry' are invited to join in singing the scatological song omitted from early editions of the play. References to local worthies, made during the actors' collection from the audience, suggest that the auspices may have included manorial halls as well as taverns.

The winter season and the indoor location are social and occasional factors which the performance shares with mummers' plays. The same is true of the method of playing. No large structures are referred to. Instead, the actors keep clear a space among the audience and use merely properties that they bring with them or borrow from the house (a spade and board, net, fetters, rope, gallows and halter, a giant head). Minstrels are called on and play a 'Walsyngham wystyll' for dancing. Structural motifs from the Christmas mummers' drama have long been recognized in the bizarre medley of the action. Besides the repeated calls to 'make space', there is the formal presentation of the devil Tityvillus:[7]

> Cumme forth now yowr gatus!
> He ys a goodly man, sers; make space and be ware! (473-4)

The figure of Tityvillus is 'a man wyth a hede þat ys of grett omnipotens', a big-head-and-little-wit, Beelzebub character, who appears from 'off' at the summons of a flute and introduces himself with a typically gnomic folk utterance:

> I com wyth my leggys wnder me. (454)

His appearance is made contingent on the audience's contribution to a collection.

Neu Gyse
> Nos gostly to owr purpos, worschypfull soverence.
> We intend to gather mony, yf yt plesse yowr neclygence,
> For a man wyth a hede þat ys of grett omnipotens.

Nowadays
> Kepe yowr tayll, in goodnes, I prey yow, goode broþer!
> He ys a worschyppull man, sers, savyng yowr reverens.
> He lovyth no grotys, nor pens of to pens.
> Gyf ws rede reyallys yf ȝe wyll se hys abhomynabull presens.
>
> (459-65)

In a piece of sheer buffoonery, Myscheff plays comforting *mère sotte* to three 'babes' and then becomes swordsman in a beheading game which

---

now yowr gatus on your way   *gostly* quickly   *tayll* tally   *pens* coins
to pens twopence   *rede reyallys* gold 'royals'

is also a castration game. Nowadays' head is between Neu Gyse's legs:

Myscheff
I xall helpe þe of þi peyn;
I xall smyttt of þi hede and sett yt on ageyn . . .

Neu Gyse
ȝe xall not choppe my jewellys, and I may.

Nowadays
ȝe, cristys crose, wyll ȝe smyght my hede awey?

. . .

Myscheff
I kan choppe yt of and make yt agayn.

New Gyse
I hade a shreude recumbentibus but I fele no peyn.

Nowadays
Ande my hede ys all save and holl agayn. (434–46)

The speech of the characters has much of the nonsensical, gnomic quality of the folk-play idiom, the action it accompanies is similarly a 'ritual' that is patently absurd.

Yet, for all this, the play is clerkly. Most of the stage directions are Latin. The theme is homiletic and the preaching and exposition of Mankind and his confessor Mercy are ornately rhetorical, mellifluous 'eloquence', and are parodied in the mock-scholasticism of the vices. The exuberance of verbal parody, the delight in 'Englysch Laten' and the delight in *reductio ad fundamentum* implicit in the rhyme of 'wurdys' and 'turdys' and in the obscene pun on holy ('holyk' = hole-lick) all smack of youth and education. If it was *for* the folk the play was certainly not *by* the folk, and one is tempted to see it as the Shrovetide *jeu d'esprit* of a group of Cambridge clerks.

The structural function of these 'folk' elements and of the inventive improvising of the vicious characters is to offset and parody the sermoniousness of the moral theme, giving an embodiment to the evil world in which Mankind finds himself. The cast is in effect two 'teams', whose behaviour is governed by entirely different rules and who speak different languages. Mercy and Mankind are conceived as expository characters, whose characteristic is preaching or prayer. Their language is that of the soul, ornate, Latinate, abstract:

All naturall nutriment to me as caren ys odybull. (739)

---

and I may if I can help it   *recumbentibus* knock-down blow   *odybull* hateful
caren carrion

On the other hand Mischief, Nought, New Guise, Nowadays and Tityvillus are entertainers: they run in and out of the audience, clowning, mimicking Mankind, delighting in obscene words and gestures, playing games. At its most elementary level the conflict of good and evil in the play is a struggle between the two teams for possession of the acting place. Each team must shoo the other off in order to command the audience's attention. Mercy scolds the vices; they in turn jostle and trip him.

The texts preached by Mercy and Mankind have no plan of action. In fact, the only physical action that Mercy gives to Mankind is digging—the role of Adam in the old play referred to by Nowadays. In Mankind's digging and sowing the metaphorical meaning of the 'corn and chaff' of mankind, expounded by Mercy in his introductory premonition of the Last Judgment, is realized. Upon this theme the vices 'improvise' entertainment: they pretend to admire Mankind's spade-work, but point out that the play garden is much too small to provide a year's grain; they suggest that he water and manure it with his own excrement. Taunted beyond endurance, Mankind uses his spade as a sword to attack them, and New Guise claims to have been castrated. Mankind's digging is finally thwarted by a board placed under his plot by the 'invisible' Tityvillus. In the oldest trick of mimic tradition (cf. *Le Garçon et l'Aveugle*, *Le Mystère d'Adam*) an 'invisible' character plays stage tricks on another in full view of the audience. A further gambit from the same stock is Tityvillus's distracting Mankind from his prayers by prompting him, 'Aryse and avent þe! nature compellys!'.

The vices make much of the advantage they enjoy over the less active team in 'making game' with the audience. Nowadays tells Mercy,

> Men have lytyll deynté of yowre pley
> Because ȝe make no sporte. (267–8)

Again, Tityvillus, the invisible shape-shifter, shown commercially to the audience as a folk-play devil, takes his leave of them with:

> Farewell, everychon! for I have don my game,
> For I have brought Mankynde to myscheff and to schame. (605–6)

Tityvillus's farewell underlines the pejorative meaning of 'game-playing' in clerical drama generally, how often it is opposed to the dull earnest of the framing sermon. The scurrying stage-hand demons of the *Adam* and the sophisticated parodists of *Mankind* belong in a continuous tradition. In the Corpus Christi plays, though game-playing is the indulgence of some of the 'good' characters (the Towneley Noah and the shepherds of the *Prima Pastorum*) the only true counterpart to these popular mimic entertainers is Mak.

Mankind may be seen, then, as belonging in the tradition of early pre-cycle plays in England, a tradition propagated by worldly clerks and friars of preaching orders, whose method was the conversion of popular 'game' by joining it to sermons. The use of a collection signposts the continuity from folk to clerical popular drama. This drama flourished side by side with the community drama of the cycle plays, which shared some of its motifs and its sense that drama consisted of a mixture of pious exposition and vigorous, often pantomimic, conflict between actors and audience.

Almost all the surviving English drama before the sixteenth century was 'popular', reaching a wide audience of all classes. What was invented 'by the people' is as hard to judge as to decide who 'the people' were. Written records will not take us close to the thing itself and we have to rely on those literate playwrights and scribes who adapted or alluded to dramatic practices which normally would have been unrecorded gestures, words in the wind of oral tradition. I have argued for the existence of many and diverse dramatic traditions in the Middle Ages, emphasizing four major streams, trying to locate the specially fertile places where the streams come together. The mainstream is by definition clerical. But, because the dramatist must, through his actors, meet and collaborate with an audience, this clerical drama in its vernacular manifestations is often remarkably responsive to the pressures of popular expectation. I have chosen to end my brief exploration of the later medieval drama with the Croxton play and *Mankind* because both seem to me excellent examples of plays that are undeniably both clerical and popular. Typically clerical in their respective dependence on play cycle and sermon, each of them finds a place and thematic use for dramatic activity that is, so far as one can tell, purely 'folk'.

In the course of the sixteenth century, as a result of religious, social and economic changes in England and in France, the ecclesiastical drama ceased. The liturgical drama, which depended upon the offices and fabric of the Roman Church, was swept away in England by the acts of Reformation, while the community cycle drama, weakened by social and doctrinal changes, but still the seasonal occasion of politically dangerous tides of religious emotion, was suppressed by Parliament.[8] In England and France there was no practical possibility or incentive for the professional troupes of actors which proliferated during these years to duplicate the dramatic experience which the great cycles had given audiences for two centuries. The new 'popular' drama was, like *Mankind* and the Croxton play, professional or semi-professional, it was compact and portable. These plays, which depend so much upon the forms and energies of popular medieval traditions, hint also at the shape of things to come.

NOTES

Chapter 1. Mimicry

1. Text: *Anthologia Latina*, Ed. A. Riese, I:2 (Leipzig 1906), no. 487a. For this interpretation of the lines, see G. Gougenheim, 'Le mime Vitalis', *Mélanges Gustave Cohen* (Paris 1950), 29.

2. See especially E. K. Chambers, *Medieval Stage* (2 vols, Oxford 1903), I, 23ff., and J. D. A. Ogilvy, '*Mimi, Scurrae, Histriones*: entertainers in the Middle Ages', *Speculum* XXXVIII (1973), 603.

3. Edmond Faral, *Les jongleurs en France au moyen-âge* (Paris 1909, 2nd ed. 1964), Appendix III, no. 15.

4. Ogilvy, 611. See also Mary Marshall, 'Theatre in the Middle Ages: evidence from dictionaries and glosses', *Symposium* IV (1950), 1–39, 366–89.

5. Allardyce Nicoll, *Masks, Mimes and Miracles* (London 1931), 138.

6. Chambers, I, 32n.

7. Ogilvy, 608, 612.

8. *Ruodlieb*, Ed. Edwin H. Zeydel (Chapel Hill, N. C., 1960). See introduction, 10–11.

9. Chambers, I, 59ff, II, 262. He gives a scene from the manuscript (Bodleian MS 264) as his frontispiece.

10. The earliest English usage I know is Robert of Brunne's condemnation (*c.* 1303) of 'entyrludës, or syngynge, / Or tabur bete, or oþer pypunge' in church or churchyard 'whyle þe prest stondeþ at messe' (*Handlyng Synne*, 8991ff.). In *Sir Gawain and the Green Knight*, King Arthur's mention of 'layking of enterludez' as appropriate to Christmas, and the Green Knight's appearance between the first and second courses of the feast at Camelot, suggest a play at mealtime.

11. *Interludium* text: *Early Middle English Verse and Prose*, Ed. J. A. W. Bennett and G. V. Smithers (2nd ed., Oxford 1968), no. XV.

12. 'W.S.', 'The fragments of a drama', *Revue Celtique* IV (1880), 258.

13. *Dame Sirith* text: *Early Middle English Verse and Prose*, no. VI.

14. *Ruodlieb*, Fragment X, 92ff.

15. Text: *Le Garçon et l'Aveugle*, Ed. M. Roques (Classiques Français du Moyen Age, 2nd ed., Paris 1921). Trans. R. Axton and J. Stevens, *Medieval French Plays* (Oxford 1971).

16. Text: Chambers, II, 326.

17. See Rosemary Woolf, *The English Mystery Plays* (London 1972), 27. The *Terence des Ducs* picture is reproduced by Richard Southern, *Medieval Theatre in the Round* (London 1957). See also L. W. Jones and C. R. Morey, *The Miniatures of the MSS of Terence Prior to the Thirteenth Century* (2 vols, Princeton 1931).

18. Translated from a quotation in Dino Bigongiari, 'Were there theaters in the twelfth and thirteenth centuries ?', *Romanic Review* XXXVII (1946), 201 (211).

19. *Troy Book*, Ed. H. Bergsen (EETS, Oxford 1906), I:2, 900ff.

20. Roswitha. Quotations translated from *Hrotsvithae Opera*, Ed. H. Homeyer (rev. ed., Paderborn 1970).

21. See E. H. Zeydel, 'Were Hrotsvitha's dramas performed during her lifetime ?', *Speculum* XX (1945), 443; Sister Mary M. Butler, *Hrotsvitha: The Theatricality of her Plays* (New York 1960). Around the end of the tenth century the MS illuminations of Terence's plays undergo a marked change which may reflect performance. But Jones and Morey (I, 203ff.) are sceptical.

22. *Hrotsvithae Opera*, 367.

23. Texts and French translations in Gustave Cohen, *La comédie latine en France au XIIe siècle* (Paris 1931).

24. See *Babio*, trans. M. M. Brennan (Charleston, S. C., 1968), 26ff. and also G. Vinay, 'La commedia latina del secolo XII', *Studi Medievali* n.s. XVIII (1952), 209.

25. On clerical condemnations of all sorts, see Chambers, I, 11ff; on the Feast of Fools, ibid., II, 274.

26. Ailred cited by Karl Young, *The Drama of the Medieval Church* (2 vols, Oxford 1933), I, 548.

27. Young, II, 524–5.

Chapter 2. Combat

1. Faral, *Les jongleurs*, 275, no. 20 a, b, c.

2. See W. O. Hassall, 'Plays at Clerkenwell', *Modern Language Review* XXXIII (1939), 564.

3. Chambers, I, 191n, II, 270.

4. Text printed by C. Kraus, 'Das gotische Weihnachtspiel', *Beiträge zur Geschichte der Deutschen Sprache und Literatur* XX (1895), 224.

5. See Bertha Phillpotts, *The Elder Edda and Ancient Scandinavian Drama* (Cambridge 1920).

6. See C. R. Baskervill, 'Dramatic aspects of medieval folk festivals in England', *Studies in Philology* XVII (1920), 19–87 (43).

7. J. Harrison, *Epilegomena* (Cambridge 1921), 23; cf. A. P. Rossiter, *English Drama from Earliest Times to the Elizabethans* (London 1950), 22.

8. An excellent account of the English plays is given by Alan Brody, *The English Mummers and Their Plays* (Stony Brook/London 1971).

9. *The Return of the Native*, bk II, ch. 4. Hardy edited a Dorsetshire *Play of Saint George*, printed by F. E. Hardy (Cambridge 1921).

10. Netley Abbey text: Brody, 131. Leicestershire text: J. Q. Adams, *Chief Pre-Shakespearean Dramas* (Cambridge, Mass., 1924), 355.

11. Chambers, II, 270. In another form described by Olaus, bows and bells are substituted for swords.

12. Text: Brody, 137, reprints the text of Norman Peacock in *Journal of the English Folk Dance and Song Society* VIII (1956), 29.

13. Texts: C. R. Baskervill, 'The mummers' wooing plays in England', *Modern Philology* XXI (1924), 241.

14. Here I am pursuing suggestions made by J. F. Szwed, 'The mask of friendship' in *Christmas Mummings in Newfoundland*, Ed. H. Halpert and G. M. Story.

15. Baskervill, 'Dramatic aspects of medieval folk festivals', 78ff.

16. Text: *Musica Britannica* XV (Music of Scotland), no. 30. See the discussion by H. M. Shire and K. Elliott, 'Pleugh song and plough play', *Saltire Review* II:6 (1955), 39.

17. J. Harrison, *Themis* (2nd ed., London 1963), 143.

18. The relevant part of 'Laneham's Letter' is printed by Chambers, II, 264.

19. Chambers, I, 155.

20. Lübeck text: K. von Müllenhof, 'Schwerttanzspiel aus Lübek', *Zeitschrift für Deutsches Alterthum* XX (n.s. VIII), (1876), 10.

21. The Latin text of Meinhard's letter is given in *Briefsammlungen der Zeit Heinrichs IV*, Ed. Carl Erdmann and Norbert Fickermann (MGH, Weimar 1950), 120.

22. Gerhoh is quoted by Young, II, 411.

23. Latin text: Young, II, 412.

24. Latin text: Young, II, 542.

25. Young, II, 524–5.

26. *Antichristus* text: Young, II, 371.

27. The relation between Passion play and pagan rites of the dead is suggested in an important article by Walther Lipphardt, 'Studien zu der Marienklagen, Marienklage und der Germanische Totenklage', *Beiträge zur Geschichte der Deutschen Sprache und Literatur* LVIII (1934), 390.

28. Honorius' *Gemma Animae*, quoted in Young, I, 83.

29. Muri text: Ed. K. Bartsch, *Germania* VIII (1863), 273. 'Strif of Jesu and of Satan' text: *English Miracle Plays, Moralities and Interludes*, Ed. A. W. Pollard (8th ed., Oxford 1927), 166.

Chapter 3. Dancing-game

1. See J. Huizinga, *Homo Ludens* (London 1949) and the illuminating discussion of medieval meanings of *game* and *play* by V. A. Kolve, *The Play Called Corpus Christi* (Stanford 1966), ch. 2.

2. Chambers, I, 189n; Baskervill, 65.

3. J. Bédier, 'Les plus anciennes danses françaises', *Revue des Deux Mondes* XXXI (1901) i, 398–424. The texts cited in this chapter are printed by Bédier, unless stated otherwise.

4. P. Dronke, *The Medieval Lyric* (London 1969), 189, 194.

5. *Carmina Burana*, Ed. A. Hilke and O. Schumann, I:2, Die Liebeslieder (Heidelberg 1941), no. 167a.

6. *Le Tournois de Chauvency*: see the discussion by Dronke, 197ff.

7. Lecoy de la Marche, *La chaire française au moyen âge* (Paris 1886), 447.

8. R. L. Greene, *Early English Carols* (Oxford 1935), xci.

9. See Chambers, I, 166.

10. Baskervill, 58n.

11. J. Huizinga, *The Waning of the Middle Ages* (Harmondsworth 1955), 136.

12. Text: *Le Jeu de Robin et Marion*, Ed. K. Varty (London 1960). Trans., with transcription of the songs, Axton and Stevens, *Medieval French Plays*.

13. Chambers, II, 172. Ernest Langlois, 'Le jeu du roi qui ne ment et le jeu du roi et de la reine', *Mélanges Chabaneau, Romanische Forschungen* XXIII (Erlangen 1907).

14. J. Chailley, 'La nature musicale du *Jeu de Robin et Marion*', *Mélanges offerts à Gustave Cohen* (Paris, 1950), 111. On the relationship between *Robin* and traditional French folk-play, see W. Powell Jones, 'The pastourelle and French folk drama', *Harvard Studies and Notes in Philology and Literature* XIII (1931), 129.

15. Evidence for ring-dances: Chambers, I, 162ff.; H. Spanke, 'Tanzmusik in der Kirche des Mittelalters, *Neuphilologische Mitteilungen* XXXI (1930), 143-70.

16. Baskervill, 65, 66n.

17. *The Chronicle of Lanercost, 1272-1346*, trans. Sir H. Maxwell (Glasgow 1913), 29.

18. On the *vigilae*, see E. Auerbach, *Literary Language and its Public in Late Antiquity and the Middle Ages*, trans. R. Manheim (London 1965), 283-6; and A. Viscardi, *Le origini: storia letteraria d'Italia* (Milan 1939), 460-87.

19. Bibl. Escurial MS T-i-1, Cantiga no. 5, reproduced by R. Menéndez Pidal, *Poesia juglaresca y orígenes de las literaturas románicas* (6th ed., Institutio de Estudios Politicos, Madrid 1957), 72.

20. Chambers, I, 163n.

21. The text of *Mei amic* (Bibl. Nat. MS lat. 1139, f. 48r-49r) is printed by A. Roncaglia in *Cultura Neolatina* IX (1949), 67. On dating this manuscript, see J. Chailley, *Romania* LXXVI (1955), 212; and *L'Ecole musicale de Saint-Martial de Limoges jusqu'à la fin du XIe siècle* (Paris 1960), 109. A transcription of the music is given by Friedrich Gennrich, *Der Musikalische Nachlass der Troubadours* (Darmstadt 1958), no. 1.

22. Modranacht: Chambers, I, 231-2.

23. 'De l'annunciment nostre sygnor', *Predigten des H. Bernhard*, Ed. A. Schulze (Tübingen 1894), 33.

24. Bédier, 24.

25. Greene, cxiv.

26. The origins of the Dance of Death are comprehensively discussed by Hellmut Rosenfeld, *Der Mittelalterliche Totentanz* (Münster/Cologne 1954).

27. Text: Young, I, 518. I have regularized the orthography, taking account of Hartl's edition.

28. This apocryphal episode of Magdalene is treated at greater length in the St Gall *Passionsspiel* (Ed. Eduard Hartl, Halle 1952) of about 1300. There Magdalene dances in company with a girl and two youths, while her sister Martha begs her to repent. There is also a merchant, pedlar of aphrodisiacs and life-restoratives.

Chapter 4. Church ceremony

1. Text: David Dumville, 'Liturgical drama and panegyric responsory from the eighth century', *Journal of Theological Studies* n.s. XXIII (1972), 374.

2. Quoted from the translation of the Latin B text by M. R. James, *The Apocryphal New Testament* (Oxford 1924), 133-9. The Latin text is in Young, I, 149-50.

3. Young, I, 103-4.

4. Barking text: Young, I, 164.

5. See Woolf, 29, n. 21.

6. This is a complicated subject and a rough summary will only scratch the surface. According to Young's view, which has been confirmed by musicologists who have studied the melodies of the *Quem quaeritis*, the play arose from a 'spontaneous' development of the trope form, resulting in the removal of performance from the beginning of Mass to the end of Matins. This traditional view is challenged by those who think that trope and play are cousins rather than parent and child. O. B. Hardison Jr (*Christian Rite and Christian Drama*, Baltimore 1965) proposes the origins of the play in an as yet putative ceremony of the Easter night vigil. His theory is attractive, but questionable in its details on musical grounds and not well documented in early manuscript sources; see W. L. Smoldon, 'The melodies of the medieval Church dramas and their significance', *Comparative Drama* II (1968), 185. Hardison associates the play's action with the candle-bearing procession of the Blessing of New Fire and he cites St Augustine, who 'stresses the parallel between the Marys and the faithful keeping watch through Easter Eve. This anticipates the function of the Marys in the *Visitatio* as representatives of the congregation, through whom the people participate in dramatized history' (Hardison, 228–9). Most recently, Rosemary Woolf supports the traditional view by judicious discussion of examples of the non-dramatic procession to the Sepulchre (*The English Mystery Plays*, 9ff.).

7. e.g. Hardison, 35.

8. Text: Young, I, 249. Trans. in J. Q. Adams, *Chief Pre-Shakespearean Dramas*, 9.

9. On the liturgical Easter customs, see Young, I, 112ff., and N. C. Brooks, *The Sepulchre of Christ in Art and Liturgy* (University of Illinois Studies in Language and Literature VII, no. 2, Urbana 1921).

10. Origny text: Young, I, 685.

11. The phrase is Mary H. Marshall's, 'Aesthetic values of the liturgical drama' (*English Institute Essays*, 1950), reprinted in *Medieval English Drama: Essays Critical and Contextual*, Ed. J. Taylor and A. H. Nelson (Chicago 1972). See p. 33.

12. Ripoll text: Young, I, 678 and R. B. Donovan, *Liturgical Drama in Medieval Spain* (Toronto 1958), 78.

13. Neither Donovan (loc. cit) nor Hardison (239ff.) notes the Solomonic language. Magdalene, rather than the Virgin, is identified as Ecclesia in an undated *Dialogus* printed by Young, I, 683.

14. See Young, II, 4ff.

15. Text: Young, II, 85.

16. Young, II, 34.

17. Limoges text: Young, II, 34–5.

18. Young (II, 125ff.) argues for a 'logical' genesis via dramatic reading; but all such versions are later than the extant plays in which each prophet *sings* his own versified testimony. Spanish settings of the Sibyl's hexameters foretelling the end of the world survive from the ninth century. Descriptions of an impersonated Sibyl, ornately costumed and attended by minstrels and tambourine players, are sixteenth century. See S. Corbin, 'Le *Cantus Sibyllae*: origines et premiers textes', *Revue de Musicologie* XXXI (1952), 1–10; H. Anglès, *La música a Catalunya fins al segle XIII*, Instiut d'Estudis Catalans (Barcelona 1935) gives transcriptions of the chants.

19. Young, II, 150.

20. Young, II, 175ff.

21. *Le Mystère d'Adam*, Ed. P. Aebischer (TLF, Paris 1963), lines 883ff.

22. *Ordo Rachelis* text: Young, II, 109. The manuscript contains also the *Mei amic* dialogue, the *Sponsus* (discussed below pp. 101–4, a *Visitatio* and an *Ordo Prophetarum*.

23. J. Stevens, 'Music in some early medieval plays' in *Studies in the Arts*, Ed. F. Warner (Oxford 1968), 40.

24. This view is advanced by Benjamin Hunningher, *The Origins of the Theater* (Amsterdam 1955).

Chapter 5. Plays in Latin

1. Paduan texts: *Uffici Drammatici Padovani*, Ed. G. Vecchi (Florence 1954).

2. 'Fleury playbook': texts in Young, II, 96, 116. S. Corbin thinks the famous playbook may have been written at Blois, see *Romania* LXXIV (1953), 1–43. Texts and music are edited by Noah Greenberg and William L. Smoldon, *The Play of Herod* (New York 1965). The plays are recorded by the Pro Musica Antiqua of New York on Decca Gold Label Series, EL 10095.

3. Dr J. Stevens tells me that recent musicology inclines to the view that the *planctus* are not properly Gregorian in their aesthetic.

4. J. Stevens, 'Music in some early medieval plays', 40.

5. Hilarius text: Young, II, 276.

6. Beauvais text: Young, II, 290. A musical transcription is given by W. L. Smoldon, *The Play of Daniel* (Plainsong and Medieval Music Society, London 1960).

7. Chambers, I, 284.

8. Smoldon, *Daniel*, 4.

9. Young, II, 126, 147.

10. G. Wickham, 'Stage and drama till 1660' in *English Drama to 1710*, Ed. C. Ricks (Sphere History of Literature in the English Language, vol. 3, London 1971), 30.

11. Young, II, 396. *Antichristus* text: 371. Trans. J. Wright, *The Play of Antichrist* (Pontifical Institute of Medieval Studies, Toronto 1967).

12. See Wright's useful introduction.

13. Norman Cohn, *The Pursuit of the Millennium* (London 1970). P. Classen, *Gerhoh of Reichersberg* (Wiesbaden 1960), ch. 6: 'Der Antichrist'.

14. *The Two Cities: a Chronicle of Universal History to the Year A.D. 1146*, trans. C. C. Mierow (New York 1928).

15. Young, II, 388. The most recent editor prefers layout on an oval plan, with the Greeks to the north, though this is where the audience would sit, according to the manuscript rubrics. See *Der Antichristus*, Ed. G. Günther, Hamburg (1970), 158.

16. Ernst Kantorowicz, *Laudes Regiae* (University of California 1946), 79.

17. Perugia text. Vicenzo de Bartholomaeis, *Laude drammatiche e rappresentazioni sacre* (Florence 1943). *Le Jour du Jugement*, Ed. Emile Roy (Paris 1902). *Chester Plays*, Ed. H. Deimling and J. Matthews (EETS, Oxford 1892–1916).

18. *Paradiso* XXXI, 71–2.

19. P. Dronke, *Poetic Individuality in the Middle Ages* (Oxford 1970), 150–92 · The music is given in *Ordo Virtutum: Ein Singspiel*, Ed. Abtei Sankt Hildegard, Eibingen im Rheingau (Berlin 1927).

20. Dronke, *Poetic Individuality*, 170.

21. *The Apocryphal New Testament*, Ed. M. R. James (Oxford 1924), 253. The Four Daughters of God dance their reconciliation in heaven at the Harrowing of Hell in Langland's *Piers Plowman* (B XVIII, 424ff., and C XXI, 471ff.). A dance may also be indicated in the 'N-Town' 'Parliament of Heaven' (*c.* 1468) (*Ludus Coventriae*, 103).

Chapter 6. Plays in the vernaculars

1. *Sponsus* text and music: d'A. S. Avalle, *Sponsus: Dramma delle Vergini Prudenti e delle Vergini Stolte* (Documenti di Filologia IX, Milan/Naples 1965). Text only in Young, II, 362.

2. *Missale Mixtum Secundum Regula B. Isidori*, PL LXXXV, col. 441.

3. This mural is now largely destroyed, but see the reproduction in J. Puig y Cadafalch, *Les pintures murals catalans, Fasc. I: Pedret* (Institut d'Estudis Catalans, Barcelona 1909).

4. See Donovan, 26, 56.

5. *Exsultet:* the relevant passage is printed in translation by Hardison, 147–9.

6. See E. Mâle, *L'art réligieux du XIIe siècle en France* (Paris 1924), 148ff.

7. Text: 'Das Spiel von den zehn Jungfrauen', Ed. Max Rieger, *Germania* X (1865), 311.

8. *Cronica S. Petri Erfordensis Moderne*, MGH, *Scriptorum* XXX(i), 448–9.

9. Young, II, 218–9.

10. Young, II, 524.

11. Montecassino text: D. M. Inguanez, 'Un dramma della Passione del secolo XII', *Miscellanea Cassinese* XII (1936), 7–38; reprinted by S. Sticca in *Latomus* XX (1961), 568–74.

12. Origny text: Young, I, 413. The play is recorded by the Ensemble Polyphonique de Paris (direction Charles Ravier) on Valois MB 744.

13. *Auto* text and facsimile: R. Menéndez Pidal, 'Auto de los Reyes Magos', *Revista de Archivos* IV (1900), 453.

14. See the study made by W. Sturdevant, *El Misterio de los Reyes Magos: Its Position in the Development of the Medieval Legend of the Three Kings* (Baltimore 1927), 77.

15. Texts: *La Seinte Resureccion*, Ed. T. A. Jenkins *et al.* (Anglo-Norman Text Society, Oxford 1943). Trans. Axton and Stevens, *Medieval French Plays*.

16. See W. Noomen, 'Passages narratifs dans les drames médiévaux français', *Revue Belge de Philologie et d'Histoire* XXXI (1958), 716–85; and Omer Jodogne, 'Recherches sur les débuts du théâtre religieux en France', *Cahiers de Civilisation Médiévale Xe–XIIe siècles* (Université de Poitiers) VIII (1965), 1–24.

17. On the staging see Hardison, 253–83; Axton and Stevens, 49.

18. *La Seinte Resureccion*, cxi–cxiii.

19. *Le Roman de l'Estoire dou Graal*, Ed. W. A. Nitze (CFMA, Paris 1927), lines 439ff.

20. N. C. Brooks, *The Sepulchre of Christ*, 72.

21. Text: *Le Mystère d'Adam*, Ed. P. Aebischer. Trans. adapted from Axton and Stevens, *Medieval French Plays*.

22. *Platea* is discussed by R. Southern, *Medieval Theatre in the Round*, Appendix, pp. 219–36.

23. See J. Chailley and G. Cohen, *Le Jeu d'Adam et Eve* (Paris 1936); Hardison, 260.

24. An Old Testament play at Regensburg in 1194 ended with prophets (Young, II, 542).

25. Text: Pollard, *English Miracle Plays*, 166.

26. *Dialogus* text: *The Latin Poems Commonly Attributed to Walter Mapes*, Ed. T. Wright (London 1841), Appendix E.

27. E. Auerbach, *Mimesis*, trans. W. Trask (New York 1957), 138.

28. Cambridge University Library MS Gg.l.i. f.390c.

29. A. Watson, *The Early Iconography of the Tree of Jesse* (Oxford 1931).

30. Hardison, 261.

31. *De originali peccato* (*MGH*, Auctorum Antiquissium, VI.2.212): 'O felix mundique decus pulcherrima virgo' (line 145).

32. See R. Woolf, 'The Fall of Man in *Genesis B* and the *Mystère d'Adam*' in *Studies in Honor of Arthur Brodeur* (University of Oregon 1963), 187.

33. The continuation of the Peterborough Chronicle up to A.D. 1155 shows this.

34. R. E. McNally, *The Bible in the Early Middle Ages* (Westminster, Maryland 1959), 36.

35. For this suggestion I am indebted to a former pupil, Mr Andrew Jameson.

36. *Mimesis*, ch. 7.

37. *De Conflictu Corporis et Animae:* Ed. T. Wright, *The Latin Poems Commonly Attributed to Walter Mapes*, 321:

> Alme desconseillee,   mar fustes unkes nee . . .
> Que nus par ta folie   perdum durable vie . . .
> Si pensas le forfait . . .
> Tu le mal enginas . . .
> De male mulier   ço li fist cummencer;
> Ensement feis tu,   maldite seies tu!
> Mal conseil me dunastes . . .

Chapter 7. Plays of Arras

1. For my remarks on the Arras 'background' I am much indebted to Marie Ungureaunu, *La bourgeoisie naissante: société et littérature bourgeoise d'Arras aux XIIe et XIIIe siècles*, Mémoires de la Commission des Monuments Historiques du Pas-de-Calais, VII:i (Arras 1955).

2. Text: *Le Jeu de Saint-Nicolas de Jehan Bodel*, Ed. A. Henry (Paris/Brussels 1962). On the sources, see Patrick R. Vincent, *The 'Jeu de Saint-Nicolas' of Jean Bodel of Arras* (Johns Hopkins Studies in Literatures and Languages XLIX, Baltimore 1954); and Grace Frank, *The Medieval French Drama* (Oxford 1954), 95ff.

3. *Mémoires de l'Académie d'Arras*, 2e serie, XIV (Arras 1883), 335.

4. See Charles Foulon, 'La représentation et les sources du *Jeu de Saint-Nicolas*' *Mélanges offerts à G. Cohen*, 66.

5. Alexander Neckham, *De Naturis Rerum*, Ed. T. Wright (London 1863), ch. 183.

6. Printed by P. Meyer, *Romania* XI (1882), 572.

7. See my note on *hazard*, *Medieval French Plays*, 307.

8. Text: *Courtois d'Arras*, Ed. E. Faral (CFMA, Paris 1911/60).

9. See *Fabliaux*, trans. R. Hellman and R. O'Gorman (London 1965).

10. Text: *Le Jeu de Robin et Marion*, Ed. Varty.

11. See the transcriptions in Axton and Stevens, *Medieval French Plays*, and J. Stevens's notes (259). The songs are recorded by the Pro Musica Antiqua of Brussels on Archive ARC 3002.

12. The Knight's name, Sire Aubert, is another form of Robert. There is no evidence Adam's wife was a jongleuresse, but women did perform dancing-plays (see above pp. 48, 52).

13. Text: Ed. Varty.

14. *The Latin Poems Commonly Attributed to Walter Mapes*, Ed. T. Wright, 300.

15. Text: *Malone Society Collections* I, Ed. W. W. Greg (Oxford 1909); cf. Chambers, I, 176.

16. Text: *Mystères et moralités liègeois du MS 617 de Chantilly*, Ed. G. Cohen (Paris 1920).

17. *La bourgeoisie naissante*, 69ff., 181ff.

18. Text: *Le Jeu de la Feuillée*, Ed. Ernest Langlois (CFMA, Paris 1951). Trans. adapted from Axton and Stevens, *Medieval French Plays*.

19. Bigongiari, *Romanic Review* XXXVII, 211.

20. *Decretorum Liber Decimus de Poenitentia*, PL CXL, col. 971.

21. T. Wright and J. Halliwell, *Reliquiae Antiquae* (2 vols, London 1841–4), I, 285–6. Baskervill, 70.

22. *De nugis curialium*, Ed. M. R. James (Oxford 1914), 13ff.

23. *Les Congés d'Arras*, Ed. P. Ruelle (Travaux de la Faculté de Philosophie et Lettres, XXVII, Brussels 1965).

24. e.g. 'Le mariage Rutebeuf', 'La complainte Rutebeuf', *Oeuvres complètes*, Ed. E. Faral and J. Bastin (SATF, Paris 1959), I, 545ff.

25. *Ars Versificatoria*, 56, 58: E. Faral, *Les arts poétiques du XIIe et du XIIIe siècles* (Paris 1924), 129–32.

26. *Ruodlieb*, Fragment XV, 3–34.

27. See A. Adler, *Sens et composition du 'Jeu de la Feuillée'* (Ann Arbor 1956), 6.

28. The examples are from A. Långfors, *Recueil général de jeux-partis français* (2 vols, SATF, Paris 1926), nos. CIX, LXXXXVI, CXVIII, CXXXVII, CXXXVIII.

29. I disagree here with the delightfully ingenious biographical interpretation made by Alfred Adler (see n. 27).

30. Text: *Congés d'Arras*, Ed. Ruelle.

Chapter 8. The earliest English drama

1. See Catherine B. C. Thomas, 'The miracle play at Dunstable', *Modern Language Notes* XXXII (1917), 337.

2. See Otto Pächt, *The Rise of Pictorial Narrative in Twelfth-Century England* (Oxford 1962), 44; and *The St Albans Psalter*, Ed. O. Pächt, C. R. Dodwell, F. Wormald (London 1960), 144.

3. See above p. 143 and n.

4. Chambers, II, 234 n.

5. Text: Young, II, 539.

6. See Ogilvy, 613; Chambers, I, 279; Young, II, 417.

7. Young, II, 542.

8. *De Gestis Pontificum Anglorum* V, *PL* CLXXIX, col. 1679. See Lipphardt, 'Liturgische Dramen', *Die Musik in Geschichte und Gegenwart*, VIII (1960), 1019.

9. Chambers, II, 399.

10. Woolf, 19–22.

11. Text: *Non-Cycle Plays and Fragments*, Ed. N. Davis (EETS, Oxford 1970), 1–7. See my arguments against the 'transitional' nature of the Shrewsbury Fragments in *Medium Ævum* XLI (1972), 159.

12. G. R. Owst, *Literature and Pulpit in Medieval England* (2nd ed., Oxford 1961).

13. Text: Carleton Brown, 'An early mention of a St Nicholas play in England', *Studies in Philology* XXVIII (1931), 594.

14. Text: Carleton Brown, 'Caiaphas as a Palm Sunday prophet', *Anniversary Papers by Colleagues and Pupils of G. L. Kittredge* (Boston 1913), 105.

15. Chambers, I, 91.

16. Young, II, 417–18.

17. Text: *Non-Cycle Plays*, no. IX. See also no. X.

18. Text: *Non-Cycle Plays*, no. VII. On the date, see p.c.

19. Text (from Shetland, 1788): *Chief Pre-Shakespearean Dramas*, Ed. J. Q. Adams, 350.

20. Text: *Non-Cycle Plays*, no. VIII.

21. R. Southern, *Medieval Theatre in the Round*. The MS diagram is reproduced in *The Macro Plays*, Ed. Mark Eccles (EETS, Oxford 1969), frontispiece.

Chapter 9. The cycle plays

1. *The Play Called Corpus Christi*, 41.

2. A. C. Baugh has shown the dependence of the Chester plays on an early form of *Le Mystère du Viel Testament* (*Schelling Anniversary Studies*, New York 1923), 35–65.

3. See especially M. Marshall, 'The dramatic traditions established by the liturgical plays', *Publications of the Modern Language Association* LVI (1941), 962; and P. E. Kretzmann, *The Liturgical Element in the Earliest Forms of the Medieval Drama* (Minneapolis 1916).

4. *Ludus Coventriae*, Ed. K. Block (EETS, Oxford 1922), 35.

5. *Chester Plays*, 344.

6. *Ludus Coventriae*, 104.

7. Mary H. Marshall, 'Aesthetic values of the liturgical drama', 30.

8. *Ludus Coventriae*, 98.

9. ibid., 107.

10. ibid., 74.

11. ibid., 123ff.

12. Kolve, *The Play Called Corpus Christi*, 180.

13. Text: *The Wakefield Pageants in the Towneley Cycle*, Ed. A. C. Cawley (Manchester 1958).

14. Cawley, 91.

15. Towneley names: Greynhorne, Gryme, Down, Donnyng, Mall, Stott, Lanyng, Morell, Whitehorn. Scots Pleugh song names: Haken, Brandie, Broun Humly, Trowbelly, Chow-bullock, Whytehorn, Grayhorn, Cromack, Marrowgair.

16. *Chester Plays*, 194.

17. ibid., 197, lines 297–300.

18. Glynne Wickham, *Early English Stages, 1300 to 1600* (3 vols, London 1959–73), I, 138.

19. Harleian MS 2345, f.5or.

20. Harleian MS 1948, f.62v.

21. Harleian MS 1944, f.9o.

22. Harleian MS 2125, f.304/123.

23. *Chester Plays*, 329 (MS D, lines 281–2).

24. See the photograph in M. D. Anderson, *Drama and Imagery in English Medieval Churches* (Cambridge 1963), pl. 3c.

25. *Chester Plays*, 203.

26. ibid., 63.

27. ibid., 84 (MSS B, W, h, lines 485–7); 112.

28. ibid., 114.

29. ibid., 52.

30. *Carmina Burana* text: Young, II, 172 (186).

31. *York Plays*, Ed. Lucy Toulmin Smith (Oxford 1885), 118.

32. M. Carey, *The Wakefield Group in the Towneley Cycle* (Göttingen 1930). This is a most useful study of the motifs common to the Shepherds' plays.

33. Durham Halmote Rolls record an inquisition of 1364 about encroachments on a moor, mentioning that shepherds of Usseworth and Heworth had been accustomed to come with their stock to a place called the Blackletch and there 'play in turn' (*invicem ludere*). These were possibly sports or contests, rather than dramatic affairs. See Baskervill, 69.

34. *Chester Plays*, 134.

35. Kolve, 151ff.

36. *The Wakefield Pageants*, 'Prima Pastorum', 34.

37. A. C. Cawley, 'The "Grotesque" feast in the *Prima Pastorum*', *Speculum* XXVI (1955), 213.

38. *The Wakefield Pageants*, 'Secunda Pastorum', 47.

Chapter 10. Epilogue: Miracle and morality

1. The reader is referred particularly to V. A. Kolve, *The Play Called Corpus Christi*; Eleanor Prosser, *Drama and Religion in the English Mystery Plays* (Stanford 1961); Arnold Williams, *The Drama of Medieval England* (East Lansing, Michigan 1961); Rosemary Woolf, *The English Mystery Plays*; Stanley Kahrl, *Traditions of Medieval English Drama* (London 1974).

2. Text: *Non-Cycle Plays*, no. VI. See introduction, lxxiii.

3. ibid., 72ff.

4. Text: *Altenglische Sprachproben*, Ed. Eduard Mätzner, I, pt ii (Berlin 1869), 222. See Kolve's discussion of Corpus Christi, 33ff.

5. e.g. the writings of Kirchmeyer, Googe, and Gilpin, excerpted by Young, II, 531.

6. D. Bevington, *From Mankind to Marlowe* (Cambridge, Mass., 1962), 48. Text: *Macro Plays*.

7. *Macro Plays*, 168ff.

8. See the standard work of H. C. Gardiner, *Mysteries' End* (New Haven 1946).

FURTHER READING

The following select list includes most of the extant plays composed earlier than 1400 and a few later plays. Entries are by language, with volumes containing texts listed first, as far as this is possible, followed by secondary books and articles of general interest.

GENERAL

Anthologies

ADAMS, J. Q., Ed., *Chief Pre-Shakespearean Dramas* (Cambridge, Mass., 1924, repr. 1955). A good selection of Latin plays included with English translations.
GASSNER, J., Ed., *Medieval and Tudor Drama* (New York 1963).

Bibliography and reference

STRATMAN, CARL J., *Bibliography of Medieval Drama* (2nd ed., New York 1972).
HARBAGE, ALFRED, *Annals of English Drama 975–1700*, rev. by S. Schoenbaum, (London 1964).
CHAMBERS, E. K., *The Medieval Stage* (2 vols, Oxford 1903).
NICOLL, ALLARDYCE, *Masks, Mimes and Miracles: Studies in the Popular Theatre* (New York 1931).
ROSSITER, A. P., *English Drama from Early Times to the Elizabethans* (London 1950).
SCHMIDT, LÉOPOLD, *Le Théâtre Populaire Européen* (Paris 1965).
TAYLOR, J. and NELSON, A. H., Eds., *Medieval English Drama: Essays Critical and Contextual* (Chicago 1972).
WEIMANN, ROBERT, *Shakespeare und Die Tradition des Volkstheater* (Berlin 1968).

LATIN

Comedy

HROTSVITHA, *Opera*, Ed. H. Homeyer (Paderborn 1970).
—— *Plays of Roswitha*, trans. H. J. W. Tillyard (London 1923).
—— *Dulcitius, Paphnutius*, trans. M. M. Butler, in Gassner, *Medieval and Tudor Drama*.
COHEN, GUSTAVE, *La 'Comédie' latine en France au XIIe siècle* (2 vols, Paris 1931).

Liturgical music-drama

DE BOOR, HELMUT, *Die Textgeschichte der lateinischen Osterfeiern* (Tübingen 1967).

DE COUSSEMAKER, EDMOND, *Drames liturgiques du moyen âge (texte et musique)* (Paris 1861, repr. New York 1964).

DONOVAN, R. B., *The Liturgical Drama in Medieval Spain* (Toronto 1958).

HILDEGARD OF BINGEN, *Ordo Virtutum: Ein Singspiel*, Ed. Abtei Sankt Hildegard, Eibingen im Rheingau (Berlin 1927).

—— *Ordo Virtutum*, Ed. P. Dronke, *Poetic Individuality in the Middle Ages* (Oxford 1970), 180–92.

INGUANEZ, D. M., 'Un dramma della Passione del secolo XII', *Miscellanea Cassinese* XII (1936), 7–38, repr. in *Latomus* XX (1961), 568–74.

VECCHI, G., *Uffici drammatici padovani* (Florence 1954).

YOUNG, KARL, *The Drama of the Medieval Church* (2 vols, Oxford 1933). The standard introduction with the largest collection of texts and commentaries.

Acting versions (with musical transcriptions, Latin text and English translation)

SMOLDON, W. L., *Officium Pastorum* [Rouen] (Oxford n.d.).

—— *Planctus Mariae* [Cividale] (Oxford n.d.).

—— *Visitatio Sepulchri* ['Fleury'] (Oxford 1964).

—— *The Play of Daniel* (Plainsong and Medieval Text Society, London 1960).

SMOLDON, W. L., and GREENBERG, N., *The Play of Herod* (New York 1965).

Recordings

Ludus Paschalis (St-Quentin MS 86), Ensemble Polyphonique de Paris, Valois MB 744.

The Play of Daniel, New York Pro Musica Antiqua, Decca DL 9402.

The Play of Herod, New York Pro Musica Antiqua, Decca EL 10095.

COLLINS, FLETCHER, Jr, *The Production of Medieval Church Music-Drama* (Charlottesville, Virginia 1972).

HARDISON, O. B., Jr, *Christian Rite and Christian Drama in the Middle Ages* (Baltimore 1965).

LIPPHARDT, WALTHER, 'Liturgische Dramen', *Die Musik in Geschichte und Gegenwart* VIII, Ed. F. Blume (1960), cols. 1010–51.

MARSHALL, MARY H., 'Aesthetic values of the liturgical drama', *English Institute Essays*, 1951, repr. in Taylor and Nelson, *Medieval English Drama*, 28–43.

PÄCHT, OTTO, *The Rise of Pictorial Narrative in Twelfth-Century England* (Oxford 1962), 33–59.

SMOLDON, W. L., 'Liturgical drama' in *Early Medieval Music up to 1300*, Ed. Dom Anselm Hughes (*New Oxford History of Music* II, 1954), ch. 6.

STEVENS, JOHN, 'Music in some Early Medieval Plays' in *Studies in the Arts*, Ed. F. Warner (Oxford 1968), 21–40.

STICCA, SANDRO, *The Latin Passion Play: its Origins and Development* (New York 1970).

ANGLO-NORMAN

Le Jeu d'Adam (*Ordo representacionis Ade*), Ed. W. Noomen (Paris 1971).
Le Mystère d'Adam, Ed. P. Aebischer (Paris 1963).
La Seinte Resureccion, Ed. T. A. Jenkins, J. M. Manly, M. K. Pope and J. G. Wright (Anglo-Norman Text Society IV, Oxford 1943).
Medieval French Plays, trans. Richard Axton and John Stevens (Oxford 1971).

BYZANTINE GREEK

MAHR, A. G., *The Cyprus Passion Cycle* (Notre Dame University, Indiana 1947).

CORNISH

The Ancient Cornish Drama, Ed. and trans. Edwin Norris (2 vols, Oxford 1859).
The Cornish Ordinalia, trans. Markham Harris (Washington, D.C., 1969).
'W.S.', The fragments of a drama', *Revue Celtique* IV (1880), 258.

ENGLISH

Folk plays

BRODY, ALAN, *The English Mummers and Their Plays* (Stony Brook/London 1971).
CHAMBERS, E. K., *The English Folk Play* (Oxford 1933, repr. 1969).
HELM, ALEX, and CAWTE, E., and PEACOCK, N., *English Ritual Drama: a Geographical Index* (Folk-Lore Society Publications 127, London 1967).
BASKERVILL, C. R., 'Dramatic aspects of medieval folk festivals in England', *Studies in Philology* XVII (1920), 19–87.

Religious plays

The Chester Plays, Ed. H. Deimling and J. B. Matthews (EETS, 2 vols, 1892 and 1916, repr. 1959).
Ludus Coventriae or The Plaie Called Corpus Christi, Ed. K. S. Block (EETS, 1922, repr. 1960).
The Macro Plays, Ed. Mark Eccles (EETS, 1969).
Non-Cycle Plays and Fragments, Ed. Norman Davis, with an appendix on the Shrewsbury Music by F. Ll. Harrison (EETS, 1970).
The Towneley Plays, Ed. G. England and A. W. Pollard (EETS, 1897, repr. 1952).
The Wakefield Pageants in the Towneley Cycle, Ed. A. C. Cawley (Manchester 1958).
The York Plays, Ed. Lucy Toulmin Smith (Oxford 1885, repr. New York 1963).

ANDERSON, M. D., *Drama and Imagery in English Medieval Churches* (Cambridge 1963).

CRAIG, H., *English Religious Drama of the Middle Ages* (Oxford 1955).

DENNY, N., Ed., *Medieval Drama* (Stratford-upon-Avon Studies 16, London 1973).

GARDINER, H. C., *Mysteries' End* (New Haven 1946, repr. 1967).

KAHRL, S., *Traditions of Medieval English Drama* (London 1974).

KOLVE, V. A., *The Play Called Corpus Christi* (Stanford 1966).

PROSSER, E., *Drama and Religion in the English Mystery Plays* (Stanford 1961).

SALTER, F. M., *Medieval Drama in Chester* (Toronto 1955).

WICKHAM, GLYNNE, *Early English Stages* I (London 1959).

WILLIAMS, ARNOLD, *The Drama of Medieval England* (East Lansing, Michigan 1961).

WOOLF, ROSEMARY, *The English Mystery Plays* (London 1972).

FRENCH (see also Anglo-Norman and Provençal)

ADAM DE LA HALLE, *Le Jeu de la Feuillée*, Ed. E. Langlois (Classiques Français du Moyen Age, Paris 1923, repr. 1958).

—— *Le Jeu de Robin et Marion*, Ed. K. Varty (London 1960).

—— *Le Jeu de Robin et Marion* (Recording): Archive, The Central Middle Ages, ARC 3002.

Aucassin et Nicolette, Ed. M. Roques (2nd ed. rev., Paris 1929).

BODEL, JEAN, *Le Jeu de Saint Nicolas*, Ed. F. J. Warne (Oxford 1951).

—— *Le Jeu de Saint-Nicolas de Jehan Bodel*, Ed. and trans. A. Henry (Paris/Brussels 1962).

Courtois d'Arras, Ed. E. Faral (Société des Anciens Textes Français, Paris 1911, repr. 1959).

L'Estoire de Griseldis, Ed. M. Roques (Textes Littéraires Français, Paris 1959).

Le Garçon et l'Aveugle, Ed. M. Roques (CFMA, 2nd ed., Paris 1921).

Le Jour du Jugement, Ed. E. Roy (Paris 1902).

Medieval French Plays, trans. Richard Axton and John Stevens (Oxford 1971).

MERCADÉ, EUSTACHE, *Le Mystère de la Passion*, Ed. J.-M. Richard (Arras 1893).

Le Mystère du viel testament, Ed. James de Rothschild (6 vols, SATF, Paris 1878–91).

Mystères et moralités du manuscrit 617 de Chantilly, Ed. Gustave Cohen (Paris 1920).

La Passion d'Autun, Ed. Grace Frank (SATF, Paris 1934).

La Passion du Palatinus, Ed. Grace Frank (Paris 1922).

La Passion de Semur, Ed. E. Roy, *Le Mystère de la Passion en France du XIVe au XVIe siècle* (2 vols, Paris 1905).

Rutebeuf, *Le Miracle de Théophile*, Ed. Grace Frank (Paris 1925, 2nd ed. 1949).

FRANK, GRACE, *The Medieval French Drama* (Oxford 1954).

Mélanges d'histoire du théâtre du Moyen-Age et de la Renaissance offerts à Gustave Cohen (Paris 1950).

UNGUREAUNU, MARIE, *La bourgeoisie naissante: société et littérature bourgeoises d'Arras aux XIIe et XIIIe siècles* (Arras 1955).

GERMAN (including Swiss and Netherlandish)

Das Benediktbeuer Passionsspiel, Das St. Galler Passionsspiel, Ed. Eduard Hartl (Halle 1952).
Das Drama des Mittelalters, Ed. Richard Froning (Stuttgart 1891–2, repr. Darmstadt 1964.) The best anthology of texts.
Donaueschinger Passionsspiel. Das Drama des Mittelalters: Passionsspiel II, Ed. Eduard Hartl (Leipzig 1942, repr. Darmstadt 1966).
Maastrichter Paachspel. De Middelnederlandsche Dramatische Poezie, Ed. H. E. Moltzer (Groningen 1875), 496–538.
Muri Passion. Karl Bartsch, 'Das alteste Deutsche Passionsspiel', *Germania* VIII (1863), 273–97.
Ein Rheinisches Passionsspiel des XIV Jahrhunderts, Ed. Berthold von Regensburg (Halle 1909).
Das Spiel von den zehn Jungfrauen (1322), Ed. Albert Freybe (Leipzig 1870).

CREIZENACH, WILHELM, *Geschichte des neueren Dramas* I (Halle 1893).
STEINBACH, ROLF, *Die Deutschen Oster- und Passionsspiele des Mittelalters* (Cologne/Vienna 1970).

ITALIAN

D'ANCONA, ALESSANDRO, *Sacre Rappresentazioni dei secoli XIV, XV e XVI* (3 vols, Florence 1872).
—— *Origini del teatro italiano* (2 vols, Turin 1891, repr. Rome 1966).
DE BARTHOLOMAEIS, VINCENZO, *Laude drammatiche e rappresentazioni sacre* (3 vols, Florence 1943, repr. 1972).

APOLLONIO, MARIO, *Storia del teatro italiano* (Florence 1946).
AUERBACH, ERICH, *Mimesis*, trans. Willard Trask (New York 1957), 148–51.
TOSCHI, PAOLO, *L'antico teatro religiosi italiano* (Matera 1966).

PROVENÇAL

Le Jeu de Sainte Agnès, drame Provençal du XIV siècle, Ed. Alfred Jeanroy, avec la transcription des mélodies par Th. Gerold (CFMA, Paris 1931).
'*L'Esposalizi de Nostra Dona*: Drame provençal du XIIIe siècle', Ed. Susanne Kravtchenko-Dobelmann, *Romania* LXVIII (1944–5), 273–315.
La Passion Provençal du manuscrit Didot, Ed. William P. Shepard (SATF, Paris 1928).
Sponsus: Dramma delle Vergini Prudenti e delle Vergini Stolte, Ed. d'A. S. Avalle, (Documenti di Filologia IX, Milan/Naples 1965).

SPANISH

Auto de los Reyes Magos, Ed. R. Menéndez Pidal, *Revista de Archivos* IV (1900), 453–65.

Auto de los Reyes Magos: Texto Castelhano Anónimo de Século XII, Ed. Sebastião Pestana (Lisbon 1965).

Teatro medieval: textos integros, Ed. Fernando Lazerro Carreter (Valencia 1958).

ANGLÈS, HIGINI, *La música a Catalunya fins al segle XIII* (Barcelona 1935).

SHERGOLD, N. D., *A History of the Spanish Stage* (Oxford 1967).

INDEX

Main page references are italicized